WHEN PIGS FLY

WHEN PIGS FLY

How a Fast-Food CEO Used His Wits to Save His Bacon

MULTI-FRANCHISE RESTAURANT OPERATOR

DOUG AUGUSTINE

WITH JOYCE BEVERLY

WHEN PIGS FLY: How a Fast-Food CEO Used His Wits to Save His Bacon
Published by Mountain Goat Press
Newnan, Georgia

Cataloging-in-Publication Data
Names: Augustine, Doug, author. | Beverly, Joyce, author. Title: When pigs fly : how a fast-food CEO used his wits to save his bacon / multi-franchise restaurant operator Doug Augustine with Joyce Beverly.
Description: Newnan, Georgia : Mountain Goat Press, [2025]
Identifiers: ISBN: 9798992768909 (paperback) | 9798992768916 (hardback) | 9798992768923 (ebook) Subjects: LCSH: Augustine, Doug. | Businessmen--United States--Biography. | Restaurateurs--United States--Biography. | Chief executive officers--United States--Biography. | Fast food restaurants--United States. | Franchises (Retail trade)--United States. | Taco Bell (Firm) | Leadership. | LCGFT: Autobiographies. | BISAC: BIOGRAPHY & AUTOBIOGRAPHY / Memoirs. | BIOGRAPHY & AUTOBIOGRAPHY / Business. | BUSINESS & ECONOMICS / Franchises. Classification: LCC: TX945.3 .A84 2025 | DCC: 394.1/0973--dc23

Cover and interior design by Victoria Wolf, wolfdesignandmarketing.com. Copyright owned by Doug Augustine.

Author photograph by Grant Augustine

This book is a memoir. I have made a good-faith effort to convey the truth and essence of what happened. Dialogue, especially in scenes from the distant past, represents what was spoken based on my recollections.

For information on quantity purchases, interviews, or other inquiries, reach the author through the website, dougaugustine.com.

In memory of my father,
Eugene Augustine
Thank you for getting me out of my comfort zone

In honor of my mother,
Jane Augustine
Thank you for believing in me

For Andrea, Grant, and James
Thank you for loving me for who I am

In memory of
Joe Salemi, my father-in-law
Thank you for listening to me

PROLOGUE

"All of our dances will end someday ..."

— JOHN P. WEISS

OCTOBER 2000

I'm not the only guy who ever ran out of money in Vegas.

In the Paris Hotel, a sky-blue ceiling cast the perpetual optimism of a cloudless day. Ordinary cares of life were as far away as reality. In a building straddled by a replica of the Eiffel Tower, was anything real?

I was enjoying myself at a nationwide convention of Taco Bell franchisees with my mother and grandparents. Our delegation represented Georgia-Texas Enterprises, founded by my parents in 1988. We operated seven Taco Bells in the Atlanta market at the time. Business was on our minds, but we were also having a good time simply being together. I hadn't felt this happy in a long time.

Midway through the weeklong conference, we chatted over coffee with other franchisees between sessions. Easily a thousand owner/operators like us were at this annual event. It was fun reconnecting with friends we had met at meetings like these over the years. The national gatherings served triple duty as a strategic planning retreat, family reunion, and well-deserved break. These hardworking entrepreneurs, who seldom blocked out a vacation day on the calendar, enjoyed comparing metrics and challenges.

"How's sales?" "How are food costs?" "What are you doing about staffing?"

Any of these questions was a guaranteed conversation starter.

We also looked forward to the company's big reveals. The upcoming year's marketing calendar and new commercial campaigns always generated a big buzz.

My break ended abruptly when my Blackberry rang. A lump rose in my throat when I saw the number. Charles, our CFO, would not be checking in to see if we were having fun. He had a problem on his hands back home. Otherwise, he wouldn't be calling. Feeling the tension humming over two thousand miles of airwaves, I reluctantly answered.

"Hey, Charles, what's up?"

"Dude, we can't make payroll," he said.

They must pump pure oxygen into the atmosphere of Vegas hotels. The whole place is a magic act. Otherwise, how do people remain upright, even cheerfully applauding, while thousands of dollars disappear? What else prevented me from having to sit down right there on the floor of the crowded room?

"I don't know what to tell you right now," I said. "I'll call you back."

I hung up, thoughts racing through my mind, all lightheartedness forgotten. *How would we get through this?* If there's one thing I know, it's that when you don't pay people, they don't show up. We were done.

"What's wrong?" my mom asked.

Brittle from grief and years of entrepreneurial trauma, her eyes filled with fear. Shock trumped my instinct to protect her.

"We don't have money for payroll."

She began to cry. I wanted to cry too.

Huddled with my family, I spoke out loud my first thought:

"Grandpap, can I borrow some money?"

My instinct was to turn to my strongest supporters. From opening day, my mother's father had been the biggest cheerleader of this business. He and Grandmother were endlessly encouraging.

"How much do you need, son?"

"Probably somewhere around a hundred grand."

"I would be happy to loan you a hundred thousand dollars, Doug, but can you pay me back?"

The question deserved an honest answer.

"Grandpap, I can't sit here today and tell you as a man that I can pay you back. I can't guarantee you that. Right now, I don't know what I can do."

"Then I can't give you the money. I don't want to see you pour more resources into a black hole."

Oh, the irony of hearing those words in Vegas, where money falls into an endless void twenty-four hours a day. I didn't blame him, though. If I were him, I wouldn't loan me the money either.

Who gives a hundred G's to a twenty-eight-year-old who's spent three years running an exhausting race against the crisis and chaos of a group of underperforming fast-food restaurants? Finally, catastrophe had caught up with me. How the heck was I supposed to handle this? Men twice my age would fall apart over this news.

Grandpap was right. Like the guy losing borrowed money all night at the roulette table, I was in a hole. A deep one.

"God," I prayed, "please let this be the bottom."

PART ONE

Base Camp

Six-(almost seven)-year-old me with Bart Starr

CHAPTER ONE
Foundations

"If you don't ask, the answer is always no."

— JEFF TWEEDY

I WAS SIX YEARS OLD, TWO MONTHS SHY OF SEVEN, when my father, Eugene James Augustine, introduced me to one of the loves of his life.

It was 1978, and we were living in Detroit. The Green Bay Packers played the Detroit Lions at Pontiac Silverdome on Sunday, September 3. Somehow, my dad found out where the Packers were staying and made plans to put us in their path. On Friday night before the game, we headed to the hotel to stake out a position in the lobby.

Of all the facts I could tell you about my dad, none would be truer than this: he loved the Green Bay Packers. A native of Wisconsin, he had grown up barely a hundred miles from Lambeau Field, when it was still known as City Stadium. When Vince Lombardi became head coach, my father was fifteen years old.

I think he saw it as a parental and patriotic duty to convert me from my allegiance to the Dallas Cowboys. Born in Fort Worth, I cut my teeth thirty miles from Texas Stadium. While I certainly had a soft spot for the Packers, like my dad, I was loyal to my roots. So much so that I thought I should wear my Cowboys shirt for our stakeout, but he helped me see the strategic wisdom in swagging for the Packers that night.

I don't know who was more excited. Nearly thirty years separated our ages, but my dad and I were both kids on Cloud Nine. Armed with a pen and printed notepad, "From the desk of Gene Augustine," my little-kid enthusiasm was Dad's key card for accessing heroes he'd followed for years. His obvious pleasure gave me more pleasure, too.

My father knew many of our prospects by sight, but I watched in general for men who looked like football players, the giants of the day. As the team members slowly made their way down for a meeting, I approached the stream of massive men dressed in coats and ties.

"Excuse me, sir, may I have your autograph?"

Sometimes, they'd be alone. Other times, two or three emerged at once. In every case, these athletes were kind to the tow-headed boy in the lobby. Some asked my name and wrote notes, "To Doug." Players penned jersey numbers under signatures ranging from clear-as-day to barely legible.

The pint-sized kid in the Packers shirt must have been irresistible because, after a good two hours in the lobby, I came home with twenty signatures representing nearly half the team. A carefully bound home-made autograph book, fourteen pages of signatures, photos, and even a sketch by my dad, who was a pretty good amateur artist, preserved one of the most memorable highlights of my childhood.

Head coach Bart Starr anchors the first page. He also took time for a photo, the Super Bowl ring on his right hand weighing so heavy on my shoulder that my arm sagged.

Quarterbacks Lynn Dickey, #10, and David Whitehurst, #17, also posed for pictures. John Anderson, #59, who logged 146 games in his career with Green Bay, also signed the first page.

As the years went by, our shared love of football strengthened, as did my understanding of the valuable lesson I learned from my dad that night: if you show up and ask someone for something, there is a good chance you will get it.

My father grew up in Wausau, Wisconsin, where his father, a raging alcoholic, made a meager living in a paper mill. The family was dirt poor.

They bathed once a week in a washtub. My dad's first bike was a girls' model, a hand-me-down from his sister.

A pretty good athlete, Dad played baseball in high school, where his father embarrassed him by showing up for games drunk. His mother was tough, really tough, the way the wife of an alcoholic has to be. The disease and dysfunction left their mark on the family. With no real father figure or role model, my dad knew what he did not want to be. Everything else he had to figure out for himself.

Besides a fierce, lifelong loyalty to the Packers, three character traits followed my father from his Wisconsin childhood: a love of working with his hands, a gritty determination to make something of himself, and the courage to leave behind an impoverished childhood in search of a better life. That journey began in the Navy.

Dad met my mother while he was serving as a dental technician at the Naval Air Station in Key West, Florida. Jane Anne Squires, the oldest of eight, lived with her devoted Catholic family in Miami. Mutual friends introduced them on a blind date. When her father saw that the relationship was getting serious, he told my dad, "If you're going to marry my daughter, you have to go to college."

Later, when my father followed Mom's family to Texas, Grandpap helped pay Dad's way through the University of Texas at Arlington. Remarkably, my father paid him back, even though Grandpap never asked him to. It's the kind of person he was, the kind of people they both were—honest men of integrity.

My parents struggled to start a family. After six years of marriage, they adopted my older sister, Lisa. Almost immediately, Mom became pregnant, and I was born eleven months later. It was like having twins, my mother says. Four years after I came along, my sister Jennifer was another happy surprise.

After my younger sister was born, Dad's career moved our family eleven hundred miles northeast from Fort Worth to Detroit, where he worked for Olsonite, a company that made toilet seats. "Tops for bottoms," that's what my father said. "I sell tops for bottoms."

At Olsonite, Dad often traveled to one of the company's manufacturing plants, Royal Molded, located in Newnan, Georgia. He fell in love with the town, the climate, and the people.

"If you ever retire," he told the vice president there, "I want your job. I think I'd like it here."

Dad was recruited away from Olsonite by Gott Corporation, a startup company that made the ubiquitous orange coolers you see on the sidelines of athletic events. This time, we moved eight hundred miles southwest from Michigan to Arkansas City, Kansas, situated right on the border of Oklahoma, about an hour south of Wichita. We lived there from the time I was in second grade through my freshman year in high school.

Having three kids in five years, my parents' strategy for maintaining order was "divide and conquer." My father raised me. Mom, a schoolteacher, raised my sisters. It might not have been an official arrangement, but it was what they did. Dad was the disciplinarian. Mom was the caregiver, organizer, and educator, both by nature and by training. They agreed on the fundamentals of life and parenting, if not the approach.

"God, family, work," my father would say. "You've got to have these priorities, and they've got to be in that order."

Educated in Catholic schools, my mother loved teaching and thrived in the classroom. She loved being with children, and they loved her. This remained true all her life. Mom set aside her career when she and my father started a family but returned when my youngest sister went to kindergarten. Mom made sure we had the kind of education she'd been brought up with by teaching in the Catholic school we attended in Kansas.

Mom taught second grade in the morning, kindergarten in the afternoon, and catechism classes for kids who attended public schools. Her responsibilities included bringing students through first communion and reconciliation, as well as her duties in the classroom. We never missed Mass before school in the morning or on Sundays when we attended together as a family.

We were exceptionally close to our parish priest in Kansas, Father Kevin Trayers, who famously showed up most Friday nights with pizza. He was a great friend and mentor, and everyone in the family loved him.

A gifted salesman, Dad provided an excellent income for our family, but it meant he wasn't home a lot. When he was home, he stayed busy with projects around the house, always juggling several at once. I never saw him sitting still. For instance, while building a successful sales career in Michigan, he finished all the interior carpentry in our home, which he had purchased unfinished. After dinner in the evenings, until eight or nine o'clock at night, he tackled home improvements. He continued on weekends, all day long, except for when we went to church. He was always doing stuff.

Whether he was framing a room, building a table, or completing other projects or chores, he had me close by, watching. Hours and hours of my childhood were spent watching my father work. And while he worked, he talked to me.

"Measure twice, cut once, Doug," he might say. Or "If a job is worth doing, it's worth doing right."

He was meticulous, methodical, and precise but also creative—impressively so. When we moved to Kansas, he bought a house with an unfinished basement, which he completed himself, putting my bedroom down there. I saw him build it from scratch. I didn't have a lot of say in what he was doing. Sometimes, he would ask me for a tool or to bring him some other item, but other than that, my role was to observe and learn. While he worked, he would tell me what he was thinking.

"Hey, I'm going to build some shelves over here for your books and stuff." "I'm placing your closet here." "I'm putting insulation over these concrete walls to keep your room warmer in the winter." Comments like that were more informational than up for discussion.

He must have consulted me on the décor, however, because my dad, the die-hard Packers fan, decorated my room in Dallas Cowboys colors. I'll never forget it. One wall was navy blue. The other three were finished with gray and blue striped wallpaper. There was no HGTV. He didn't look at a picture in a magazine. He just had a vision for what it could be, and he did it.

A perfectionist, he taught me that details matter and to take pride in my work. He talked to me all the time about working hard. His expectations were high. He wanted things done right. Every project was like a puzzle, and I loved watching him put it together. I loved seeing him create something out of nothing.

Gradually, my father taught me to take care of stuff around our home, too. He was a hands-on teacher, demonstrating more than he explained. He showed me how to do a chore—one lesson was usually all he ever gave—and then I became responsible for that task. For example, he kept his vehicle spotlessly clean and taught me his section-by-section system for washing a car. I learned to focus on one area, like the front driver's side door, cleaning just that part of the car really well, then washing it off and moving on to the next section. One by one. Until it was done.

After a careful tutorial, he said, "All right, Doug, you're going to wash our cars. This is your job."

He taught me to mow the lawn by breaking it down in sections, too. I learned to focus on bite-sized chunks of a task rather than getting overwhelmed by the whole job. Once he showed me how to cut the grass, from then on, he expected it to be done without any nagging.

He showed me how to clean the pool, giving careful instructions about water chemistry, then said, "Okay, Doug, you're going to clean the pool every week. And you can't mess this up because you've got to keep the chemicals and stuff balanced."

By the time I was ten years old, I was expected to complete these and other chores before my father came home for dinner. Dad wasn't the kind of guy who would say, "Great job, Doug! You did an excellent job washing the cars." He wasn't big on praise or compliments, but he didn't have to be. I knew when my work was good because he had shown me what excellence looked like.

I took my time and mimicked his processes. I wanted to please him. More than anything, I wanted his approval. I wanted to make him proud. My biggest fear was letting him down.

Dad worked his way up to vice president of sales at Gott. Because it was a startup, the leadership team was offered stock instead of high salaries. As a result, my father accumulated a tremendous amount of stock in the company.

In 1987, Gott Corporation sold itself to Rubbermaid. The new ownership team gave Dad a choice—he could continue to work for the company but not as a vice president, or he could leave with two shares of Rubbermaid stock for every one share of Gott stock that he owned. Dad took the stock and returned to work for Olsonite, which deployed him to the one-hundred-fifty-year-old Southern town he'd fallen in love with years earlier. This time, we relocated nine hundred miles east to a town thirty miles south of Atlanta.

I was fifteen years old when we unloaded the U-Haul in Newnan, and I was not happy about the move. This was before I discovered what it meant to live in the Southeastern Conference. When I learned this, I was mad as hell.

I had grown into my love of football in Kansas, where, as a freshman, I was my high school's starting quarterback. It never occurred to me that star status would not follow me to the quarterback position at Newnan High School. It turns out football is as serious as business gets in the South, and Newnan was an incubator for the National Football League.

No fewer than six NFL players hail from Newnan or one of the other small towns in Coweta County. People like Karsten Mario Bailey, wide receiver for the Seattle Seahawks; Keith Brooking, linebacker for the Atlanta Falcons, Dallas Cowboys, and Denver Broncos; Calvin Johnson Jr., a.k.a. Megatron, wide receiver for the Detroit Lions; John Martin Keith, safety for the San Francisco 49ers; William Lutz, placekicker for the New Orleans Saints and the Denver Broncos; Alec Ogletree, linebacker for the St. Louis Rams and the New York Giants; Michael Cheever, center for the Jacksonville Jaguars; and Vernon Strickland, a linebacker who walked on at Georgia Tech and went on to the NFL. Some of these guys are younger than me, but the wheels of the program that carried them to success were rolling fast by the time I arrived in Newnan.

For that matter, baseball was a major sport in my new hometown too. An equal number of Major League Baseball players are also from this new and strange place. Far from being a star, I wasn't big enough, fast enough, or strong enough to stand out anymore. I was literally out of my league.

Having grown up in Catholic schools, the education system itself was another huge adjustment for me. There were no parochial schools in Coweta County. Furthermore, five hundred kids were in my class, which, to me, felt enormous.

In Kansas, I was the cat's meow—super popular, a great athlete, the clichéd big fish in a small pond. When we moved to Newnan, I lost all my friends and connections. I was a fish out of water and a very small one in a huge ocean. For a couple of years after our move, I was seriously depressed.

"Boys, we've got to get bigger. We've got to get faster. We've got to get stronger."

The booming voice and Southern accent of Newnan High School Coach Max Bass are vivid memories of my first experiences in our new hometown. Coach Bass was a big guy in a land of big guys, and I was the scrawny new kid. "Bigger. Faster. Stronger." Coach Bass had these words on repeat.

"Doug, you can accomplish anything you set your mind to if you're willing to work hard," Dad always told me. "Never take no for an answer."

I'm an optimist. I believe in everyone's ability to improve, but I'm also a realist, and looking around, it was clear to me that I was never going to be big enough, fast enough, or strong enough to play on this field. Despite the odds, I headed to the weight room to gain some strength and be as competitive as I could be in this new world.

I couldn't afford a gym membership, and my parents would not pay for one for me, so I pestered the owner of the Newnan Racquetball and Health Club to give me a job cleaning bathrooms and wiping down equipment. Eventually, my persistence paid off. I became a gym rat, working on Sunday afternoons and a couple of times during the school week for $2.85 an hour and a membership.

On Sundays, the owner assigned me to work upstairs to make sure no one on the second floor was dropping weights, which he was petrified would crash through the floor. This is where I met Bobby Burgess, the guy who introduced me to a whole new world.

It was his shirt that first got my attention. The front read "Coffee's Gym" with a picture of a bodybuilder and a squat bar. The back said, "Grow or Die."

"That's the coolest shirt in the world," I said. "Where'd you get that?"

He grunted.

Bobby, I learned, was a man of very few words. It was never easy to get information from him.

"Olympic weightlifting gym," he said.

"Tell me more about Olympic weightlifting."

He side-eyed my 150-pound build.

"It's hard," Bobby said. "Not for sissies."

Challenge accepted. For six months straight, I drove that guy crazy, accosting him as soon as he came into the gym.

"I want to know more," I would say to him. "I want to know what you're doing."

Gradually, Bobby started showing me some of the Olympic lifts, and I began trying to do them. Often described as gymnastics with weights, Olympic weightlifting requires you to be fast, agile, flexible, and

11

absolutely fearless. Once you get the bar in the air, you literally throw it down. The problem was that not only was dropping weights prohibited where I worked, but it was also my job to make sure people didn't do this. If you wanted to see the owner of the gym come flying up the stairs with his hair on fire, just drop a weight. He'd come running, ready to beat the you-know-what out of whoever was responsible. So there I was, trying to execute lifts without getting in trouble or fired.

Finally, Bobby agreed to take me to meet Ben Green.

"Before we both get kicked out of this place," he said.

From the exterior, the single-car-garage-turned-gym behind Ben's house gave up few secrets, but when I stepped inside, I knew I had found my place in this new world. Ben had been lifting weights since he was a teenager. In the mid-'80s, he won the World Masters title in the 40–44 age group. He also coached several lifters who represented the USA in the Olympics, including Michael Jacques (1988) and Bryan Jacob (1992 and 1996).

Ben and I hit it off immediately. He demonstrated a few Olympic lifts, and I fell in love with the sport. From then on, I was either working at the gym or lifting weights. I thrived on seeing how much more I could lift, doing the same thing every day and improving incrementally, a theme that stuck with me.

John Coffee, a pioneer coach of female Olympic weightlifters, drove down from his gym in Marietta once a week to work with Robin Byrd, who lived in Newnan. Robin competed in the Olympics in 2000.

Ben's gym turned out to be a fraternity of misfits, a Wild West of weightlifting. Everyone there was eccentric and, in some cases, flat-out weird, but no one judged you. As different as we all were, we got along well and were respected all over the country for how we competed. It was all about encouraging each other to lift a shit-ton of weight overhead. We lifted on a platform flanked by park benches where others observed and cheered. A squat rack hugged the back wall. If one of us got hurt, we wrapped the affected body part in an Ace bandage and kept lifting.

"Wrap the dog shit out of it and come on," Ben would say.

I thrived in this no-wimp zone.

As often as possible, I went to Ben's hidden world, where I lifted as much as two hundred and seventy-five pounds overhead and then threw the weights down on the ground as hard as I could. I felt like such a badass.

My efforts weren't enough to land me on the football team, but the sport helped me find my way out of the darkness. I was furious with my parents, who had no idea how depressed I was. I was mad about moving. I didn't have many friends, and I had completely lost my identity. Instead of losing myself in drugs and alcohol, or who knows what, weightlifting became my coping mechanism, my escape. Weights were an outlet for my anger, which, after thousands of slams to the ground, I was finally able to release.

Through Ben and the training, I progressed to the point that I could squat over four hundred pounds, more than twice my body weight. Ultimately, I ranked in the top ten nationally among high school athletes in my weight division—165 pounds—for the Clean and Jerk, one of two Olympic lifts.

Ben Green remains one of the greatest influences in my life. The discipline he taught gave me a structure, routine, and process. More importantly, I learned how to deal with change and discomfort. It shaped who I am in ways I couldn't understand at the time.

While I was busy mastering a new sport and my new environs, my parents took their entrepreneurial pursuits to another level. The gig economy has nothing on my father. He always looked for opportunities outside of his primary job.

In Kansas, when Dad traveled extensively for Gott, he was frustrated by the lack of dry cleaning facilities in the town where we lived. He was very particular about his appearance. Looking successful was important to him. Therefore, he took his clothes to be cleaned professionally, which meant driving an hour each way to dry cleaners in Wichita, where the fastest turnaround time was three days. This ridiculous inconvenience drove him crazy, so he talked a friend into building a shopping center, where he rented space and fixed his problem by becoming a franchisee of Comet Cleaners, which specialized in one-hour service. He went from making two round trips to Wichita, spending four hours on the road, and waiting three days for his dry cleaning to having his clothes cleaned nearly instantly.

Mom, to be fair, was along for the ride and not necessarily all that happy about it. When the dry cleaners opened, managing day-to-day operations fell to her. She'd open the cleaners before going to school in the mornings. In the afternoons, after teaching all day, she was back at the cleaners to close. Eventually, she gave up teaching second grade in the mornings.

When we left Kansas in 1987, Mom was adamant.

"We're not taking the dry cleaners with us."

Once he had a taste of owning his own business, though, my father was ready for more. Not long after we moved to Newnan, Dad saw an ad in the Atlanta newspaper about Taco Bell franchising. He had never heard of Taco Bell, had never eaten an item on the menu—my father was a meat and potatoes guy—but he was intrigued.

"Have you lost your mind?" my mother said when he told her about it. "We don't know anything about the food business! Absolutely no way. We're not doing it."

The dry cleaners had taught her more than she wanted to know about running a business. The next week, though, he saw the ad again and asked Mom if she wanted to go along to the meeting. She refused.

"No. I'm getting back into teaching. That's what I want to do."

My sister, Jennifer, said she'd go, and the two of them met the Taco Bell corporate team at a hotel in Atlanta. Dad was impressed with their professionalism as they rolled out the red carpet to explain their vision and plan.

"There's just something about this brand that I love," he told my mother that night. "I'm in. We're building a store."

"If you have the dream and determination," the ad in The Atlanta Constitution said. Having plenty of both, Dad was all in.

The doors opened at Taco Bell #3846 in Newnan, Georgia, October 24, 1988.

CHAPTER TWO
A Moment of Weakness

*"Nobody plays this life with marked cards, so
sometimes we win and sometimes we lose."*

— PAULO COELHO

ALL MY MOTHER'S SIBLINGS, but especially her five brothers, loved my
father. As the oldest, Mom was frequently at home watching younger
siblings for her parents. Dad came along to keep her company. Driving
up from Naval Air Station Key West, he'd arrive at my grandparents'
home in Miami to take the brothers to ball games, movies, or the beach. A
talented baseball player, he often played catch with them in the front yard or
good-naturedly submitted to their ganged-up efforts to wrestle the sailor to
the ground. I don't think my father spent much time with his own brother
and sisters, but he loved hanging out with my uncles. He was everyone's pal.

Over the years, when I'd ask my uncles for stories about my dad, they would unanimously disavow having any dirt on him at all.

"Did you ever see him drunk?" "Did you ever see him do this or that?"

"We have no stories," they'd always say.

When his commitment to the Navy was up, Dad followed Grandpap's edict that he earn a college degree before getting married, so he went back to Wisconsin to study biology at the University of Wisconsin at Madison. At the same time, my mother's family moved to San Antonio, where Mom attended Southwest Texas State University to become a teacher.

Long-distance dating was no fun, though, and soon my dad came to San Antonio to join my mom at Southwest Texas State. He pooled some GI funds, earnings from a part-time job at a department store, and money borrowed from my grandfather to pay expenses. After graduating and marrying my mother, he went to work in sales for a pharmaceutical company.

When I was eleven years old, I phoned my Uncle Bill one evening about interviewing him for an essay contest about great Americans. Uncle Bill, who may have been the closest to my parents among all the brothers, responded to me with a letter about a great American he knew, my father.

"People become what they end up being because of the influences of other people," he wrote me. "I was greatly influenced to do what I am now doing as a scientist by your father."

Turns out my dad told him once that, of all the people he knew, Bill had the most potential to do good scientific work. Uncle Bill pursued a career in science, which led him to become a professor at Baylor College of Medicine and later to work for NASA. He gives my dad the credit for encouraging him to live up to his potential.

It was Uncle Bill who made up the difference when my parents, after cashing in their Rubbermaid stock and scraping up all their savings— including retirement and our college funds—still fell a little short of the upfront investment needed to open a Taco Bell. Uncle Bill and his wife, Elaine, joined my parents as partners to form Georgia-Texas Enterprises. The name was born from our twin geographies. My parents lived in Georgia. Uncle Bill and all my mom's family lived in Texas, where my sisters and I were born. Taco Bell approved the family company for a franchise in May of 1988.

A lot had changed since Glen Bell introduced the first Taco Bell in Downey, California, in 1962. A retired Los Angeles policeman, Bell opened the first franchised location in Torrance, California, in 1965. In 1977, PepsiCo Inc. acquired Pizza Hut. A year later, more than 868 Taco Bells became part of PepsiCo, too. Kentucky Fried Chicken became part of Pepsi's fast-food trifecta the same year my parents opened a Taco Bell in Newnan.

At that time, the franchise agreement required an owner to complete restaurant management training and work at the store. Dad knew he needed to continue working full time to keep the family's bills paid. Mom, on the other hand, had been working part time as a substitute teacher. By default, Dad decided, she was the best choice to attend the training and work in the restaurant.

Mom would be the first to tell you that my father never took "no" for an answer. I've often seen him deploy a God-given talent for wearing people down.

"It's good for you to know what's going on in the business world," Dad said when she protested. "You're not going to be doing this forever. You're just going to get us started."

She had heard that story before.

Dad wasn't above using fear as a sales technique.

"If something happened to me, you'd be living on a teacher's salary."

The legendary Charles "Chuck" Kuehl

I was sixteen years old and a rising junior in high school the first time I met Charles Kuehl. Fresh out of college, only six or seven years older than me, he was drinking a glass of wine in the hot tub at a hotel in Atlanta. My sisters and I had come up to visit our mother, who, once again, had given in and drawn the short straw to become the manager of the family business.

Mom and Charles were going through Professional Restaurant Operations training at the time, staying at the same hotel. Charles helped her get through the program, which she says was harder than completing her master's degree. The class involved a ton of memorizing recipes and food safety procedures. Charles had already spent 20 percent of his life with Taco Bell, starting while still in high school and working all through college in Huntsville, Alabama. In the midst of a recession, he was headed for an assistant manager's position at a corporate store in his hometown and glad to have a job. The training was easy for him. In his version of this story, he helped Mom because she was slowing down the class.

"We need somebody like Charles," Mom told my father. "We have no idea what we're doing."

She was apprehensive about opening a restaurant by herself. She knew the only way they were going to get that store open was to have somebody with experience, and Charles would be perfect.

"See if he'll come to work with you," Dad said.

It was against corporate policy for Charles to leave the parent company to work for a franchisee, but when Mom approached him with an offer, he liked the idea of living near Atlanta. After training, he quit working for Taco Bell and went to work for a grocery store for ninety days, the minimum amount of time required to keep us all out of trouble with the franchise. He joined us in Newnan on October 1, 1988.

At the time, nobody in the area had even heard of Taco Bell. A Del Taco was operating in Newnan, but Atlanta was a new market for Taco Bell. There may have been twenty Taco Bells spread around the metro area, but the company was not doing a lot of advertising.

Corporate helped my father get a site that people in the local community laughed at. At that time, the retail center of the city was in its downtown.

"It's too far out of town to do any business," they said.

Few imagined what it would mean to us to be positioned in front of the town's brand-new Walmart or what downtown would look like in a few years.

Even though Taco Bell was an unknown, people were still excited about us. Our debut generated a lot of energy and buzz. Many of my friends and members at the gym were looking forward to having a new restaurant in town. At our private opening, the parking lot and the house were packed. My parents hired a mariachi band, and it was a fun event.

Charles's parents made the trip from Alabama for the grand opening on October 24, 1988.

My parents, Gene and Jane Augustine, at the grand opening of Georgia-Texas Enterprises' first Taco Bell.

Mom and Charles had to run the store for the first five years. Mom, who wasn't drawing a paycheck, was working to replenish the college funds that had been poured into the business. Charles was establishing himself in his career.

They worked well together if you don't count that time when he knocked her out in the restaurant. She was standing behind him when he turned quickly, catching her in the jaw with his elbow. It laid her flat-out and she was unconscious for several minutes.

Terrified, he called my father.

"Mr. Augustine, I've got some bad news. I think I killed your wife."

"Is the store open?" Dad asked.

"Yes."

"You run the store. I'll worry about my wife."

When he wasn't working, you could often find Charles at the Red Barrel Pub, where everyone knew him as "Chuck." Apparently, people knew him as Chuck before he moved to Georgia. At Georgia-Texas, he became Charles, except on his birthday, which was always noted on the calendar as "Buy Chuck A Beer Day."

The Red Barrel Pub was like a second office for him. Sitting at the bar in his Taco Bell uniform, he worked over food costs, running numbers, ordering supplies, and creating staffing schedules. He'd be smoking a cigarette, drinking a draft beer, working, and chatting with the many friends he made there, especially the owner, who loved him.

"Chuck!" was a common greeting heard in the establishment.

Cheers had Norm. The Red Barrel Pub had Chuck.

My parents were unaware that my sisters and I had listed Charles on school documents as one of our legal guardians. With Dad's traveling and Mom's work at the restaurant, they weren't aware of many of our misdeeds. To be fair, my generation was not blessed (or cursed) with helicopter parents. Even with school, weightlifting, and work, I found the time and energy to be a typical teenage hellion. When we felt like hanging out at the mall rather than going to class, we'd complain at school about not feeling well, and Charles would say it was okay for us to leave when the school called. Mom and Dad were, for the most part, oblivious. Years later, my mother still doesn't believe we did this, but skipping school with Charles's permission was a thing.

I won't say for sure that when we left beer money in the office, we would find a six-pack in the walk-in cooler later. It could have happened. We were all just growing up together.

Dad did fire Charles once, though, for a few hours. By the early '90s, my father had left his day job to run the restaurant. When Royal Molded asked him to relocate to Michigan, effectively making him choose between Taco Bell and his job, he quit. He maintained several side hustles, selling sticky tabs for Velcro, grills heated with newspaper, and other odds and ends, but the budgets still weren't balancing.

One day, he asked Charles to come by the house for a chat. It was an unusual request. Charles, who knew what the financial situation looked like, gave his wife a heads-up.

"If I come back and ask for a drink, it means I got fired," he said.

At their meeting, Dad explained that there wasn't enough money for everyone.

"We'll give you great references and free Taco Bell for the rest of your life," he said.

Charles went home and made daiquiris.

"Have you lost your mind?"

This was my mother's only question when she heard the news.

A few hours later, Charles ran out of ice. His wife drove him to the Newnan store, where we had the best crushed ice in town. When he arrived, he found my father in a state. People were calling off. The fryer was out. It was chaos. From Charles's perspective, it was business as usual, but Dad had no idea what to do.

"We need to talk," he said to Charles. "I don't know if I can always pay you, but please come back to work."

"Sir, I'm pretty drunk right now. I can't work today, but I'll be there tomorrow."

My father required me to work at the restaurant during summer breaks in high school. That's when Charles taught me nearly all there was to learn about running a quick-service restaurant. How to keep it clean, how to make the food, how to ring up orders, and a lot about the business—these lessons were sprinkled in with just enough foolishness to make it fun.

It was fast-paced, hard work. I vividly remember being on my feet all day, standing in the walk-in cooler during breaks because the air conditioner could never keep up with Georgia's heat, serving demanding customers who waited impatiently with their arms crossed.

From the time I clocked in at eight in the morning until the shift ended at three, the pressure was intense. There was lettuce to chop, cheese to shred, beef to cook, beans to cook and drill. (Just like it sounds—beans were cooked and then mashed in an enormous pot with an instrument that looked like a supersized version of everyone's favorite power tool.) And if you had the fry job? That was the worst. You literally stood over a fryer for six hours, from eight until two.

Charles gave nicknames to the people he liked. I don't remember having one, but then I don't know how much he liked me. I still don't. I was the boss's kid, after all. It's hard to overcome. If I had a nickname, it was "The Boss's Kid."

One morning, before the store opened, I lost a bet to "Kip," Charles's shortened version of "Ken Idiot Parks." A great athlete, already on the scouts' radar, Kip could throw a 90-mph fastball, even in high school. When he made a mistake in the restaurant, Charles would say, "You know what you are? You're a KIP—Ken Idiot Parks." The nickname stuck, and of course, he hated it.

"Kip" was usually our fryer. For some reason—I have no idea what provoked it—we decided to wrestle over the fry job that week. Surrounded by coworkers, we wrestled on the grass outside the store that morning. Although I had been a decent wrestler in Kansas, I was no match for his strength.

Coming outside for a smoke break, Charles discovered the ruckus. "Get back to work, you idiots!" he yelled. And I went to the fry station for the rest of the week.

Fond memories aside, restaurant work wasn't fun enough for me to want more. It's hard. You're on your feet for ten or more hours a day.

Your back hurts. It's hot. I did not enjoy it. Anyone who knew me as a teenager and college student would attest to this. No one was expecting me to return home to help with the family business. It held no attraction for me.

Also, in the back of my mind, I knew the store couldn't support all of us. I didn't see any opportunity for the company to grow, and I didn't see a future there for me.

My first memories of our new home in Georgia are all about the geography and the weather. In Kansas, the wind blew all the time across miles and miles of flat land with few, if any, trees. Even on a calm day, winds were 15 mph. It gave me a headache. I hated those winds. In our new home, the trees were almost suffocating. And nothing prepared me for the Georgia summer. It wasn't just hot; the humidity kicked my ass. I could barely move outside. It made me miss the wind in Kansas.

Besides the grueling heat and cluttered terrain, the next scene I remember when we moved to Georgia is meeting the kid next door, Ryan Brooks, who came to visit me within a day or so of our arrival. I had been setting up my room, and Ryan noticed my beer can collection. What followed was a typical peer-to-peer chat between fifteen-year-olds.

"Do you like to drink beer?" he asked.

"Well yeah, sure," I said.

"Well, let's go drink some beer!"

"Okay!"

Ryan and I procured a couple of 40 oz. cans of Schlitz Malt Liquor and became best friends that evening. Ryan is the reason I went to Auburn University. *(War damn Eagle!)* Somehow, we survived living together during college and remain friends to this day.

Initially, I was a pre-med major at Auburn. I planned to move into exercise science to train and rehabilitate athletes. Chemistry showed me I needed to reconsider those plans. Dad helped me with that decision.

"I'm thinking about changing my major," I told him after that first year. "Do you have any thoughts on what I should be looking at?"

"Doug, I think you ought to look at business," he said. "In fact, consider accounting. It's the life of business. If you can understand accounting, you can get a job anywhere, and it will really help you later on in life."

"All right, I'll check it out."

I changed my major to accounting, and the next quarter, I made a 4.0.

Accounting was easy for me. I liked how you could put a business together on a piece of paper and quickly analyze whether or not it was viable. I appreciated the objective reality that numbers convey. I enjoyed seeing on a single sheet of paper where you really were and how to improve. Category by category, whether income or expense, it was easy to see where tweaks could be made. It made perfect sense.

Accounting reminded me of weightlifting. I loved how in both endeavors, a number always told you where you were.

I also loved that I could have a life outside of school and still make really good grades.

When I graduated from Auburn, I moved to Nashville to work for a small accounting firm and began a career in the field I had chosen to study. I had already passed the law portion of the CPA exam and was on my way to reaching my goal of becoming a certified public accountant.

I liked the company's family atmosphere and that it was local, Tennessee-based, not one of the enormous firms many of my peers aspired to work for. We audited local banks. My job was to drive around the entire state, checking petty cash and loans from regional financial institutions.

While I was in Nashville, my father expanded the business.

Within months of my parents becoming a part of Taco Bell, the company embarked on a huge growth trajectory. Rather than seeking franchisees, they began opening company-owned stores across the country. The brand grew from about three thousand stores in 1989 to 5,800 restaurants in 1995. Unit growth was all they cared about. By the mid-'90s, three-fourths of all stores were corporately owned and operated. One day, the leadership team woke up and realized they had a big footprint of units they couldn't run. So, Taco Bell began offering corporate stores for sale to franchisees.

The fancy term for this was asset optimization. It worked well for the company because a pent-up demand for growth festered among franchisees, who had not been allowed to open or purchase new stores for several years. Taco Bell gave nearly every franchisee who applied for the opportunity—as many as 93 percent—a green light during the financial approval process. In a short time, they reversed the ratio of corporate to franchised units.

My parents were among the first to buy company stores in the Southeast. Eight years after opening the first Taco Bell in Newnan, Georgia-Texas Enterprises grew from a single store that was finally running fairly smoothly and profitably to seven stores. In the spring of 1996, two restaurants in Atlanta and four south of the city were added to their territory.

On a warm spring weekend in March, I came home from Nashville for the acquisition party. While the expansion surprised me, I was happy to have a reason to visit my parents. Honestly, I don't remember much about the celebration, but what happened as I was leaving is seared into my memory.

I wasn't looking forward to the four-hour drive back to Nashville. As I loaded my car for the return trip, Dad joined me in the driveway. A two-pack-a-day smoker, he had a cigarette in his hand. I could tell he was deep in thought. I had the sense that he didn't want me to go.

"Doug, what would it take for you to come to work for me?"

In a moment of weakness, I said, "Make me an offer."

"How much are you making at the CPA firm?"

"Twenty-six thousand dollars."

"I'll pay you that if you come to work for me."

"Okay."

"When can you start?"

"I'll give my two-week notice."

This photo of my father appeared on the cover of
Franchise Times magazine in 1996.

CHAPTER THREE

Crazy Train

"I accept chaos; I'm not sure whether it accepts me."

— BOB DYLAN

LEAVING NASHVILLE DIDN'T TAKE LONG. My employer released me without requiring notice. The relationship with the girl I followed to Tennessee had been fizzling for a while. It wasn't hard for either of us to say goodbye. Mom came up to help me pack, and in a matter of days, I was living in Newnan again.

Looking back, I see that I was ready for a change, but joining my dad scared the hell out of me. Although I never could have anticipated the challenges ahead, I knew that working with my father would not be easy. Growing up, I had a healthy mixture of admiration and fear for him. Mostly, he intimidated me. Our relationship was respectful, but I never understood what made him tick. We had little in common, or so I thought. My father was unconcerned about being popular or fitting in. People liked him, but I don't know that he had any close friends. He wasn't cool like my friends' fathers. He wasn't interested in playing golf or having a beer with the guys. Conversely, those things mattered to me.

He was a scientist, a unique nerd, and very set in his ways. And this I knew for sure: It would be his way or the highway. Always.

I drove away from a safe, solid position in the career I had chosen onto a long road of uncertainty. In the rearview was a cushy job, a place I probably could have stayed as long as I liked. Ahead was a homecoming with no small measure of anxiety.

I'm a shoot-ready-aim decision-maker. I've never been one for back-pedaling or second-guessing, which is good, because it was too late for any of that. I was terrified and out of my comfort zone, but by the end of March 1996, my career with Georgia-Texas Enterprises was underway. It didn't take long for me to see how much work we had to do.

Taco Bell repeatedly promised that they weren't unloading poor performers as they sold package after package of stores to eager franchisees like my father. Typically, though, a few high-volume stores, affectionately known as "cash cows," were grouped with three or four low-volume, hard-as-hell-to-run units, sadly known as "dogs." We ended up with two great stores that generated profits pretty quickly and four stores we struggled with for years.

In addition to the original Newnan store, Georgia-Texas Enterprises now owned Taco Bells in McDonough, LaGrange, Forsyth, East Point, Union City, and Atlanta. Overnight, we went from having thirty employees to more than two hundred. Well, for a few days, anyway.

Dad's plan for operating the additional restaurants was simple. Charles and my mom would run the store in Newnan. Charles had divorced his wife since the early days with Mom and Dad. Now his girl-friend, Carla, was a shift manager. Overnight, Dad made Carla, Carla's mom, Carla's sister, Carla's sister's kid—basically all of Carla's family—plus his brother (my Uncle Ben) and Ben's wife, Sonya, general managers of restaurants. It was kind of like one of the lucky days on Oprah. "You get a store," and "You get a store," and "Hey, you can have a store, too."

Dad assumed that all the new stores would run like Newnan. Unfortunately, none of them did. The first of his flawed premises was that he thought everybody could run a store the way Charles ran Newnan, with one hand tied behind his back. But Charles was uber-talented, a complete anomaly. I don't think any of us appreciated just how special he was at the time. Nobody in this newly minted group of restaurant managers was even remotely like Charles. Most had worked in our store, but they'd never been trained for restaurant management. They had no idea what they were doing.

Dad's second flawed premise is that he assumed we had teams in place in each of the stores. Unfortunately, just before we bought the corporate stores, Taco Bell had given dramatic raises, well above industry standards, to all hourly employees. When Dad took over, he refused to honor the raises, bumping everyone back to minimum wage. You can imagine how that went over. Everybody left, of course, and consequently, we had virtually no employees.

Problems with inventory were rampant. The people who remained were constantly calling off work, or worse, simply failing to show up. We were running around just trying to keep the stores open. No two days were ever the same. You couldn't work enough hours in the week to keep your head above water. It was absolute, total chaos. There was no culture, no honesty, and no shortage of horror stories. One day, a store manager and all of the employees left the restaurant and went down the street to see a popular musician performing. You can imagine what happened while they were gone.

Like I said. It was nonstop crazy.

My primary responsibility was to keep track of the money. The most important concept I learned in accounting is that cash is king. You must protect it. Therefore, my number one fiduciary responsibility was to make sure money was in the bank, but it was not easy to do. The simplest part of this job—making sure deposits made it to the bank every day—was far from simple. The first task I did every morning was confirm that fourteen deposits, two per store—one for the day shift and one for the evening—had been made.

To do so, I called every manager to verify the deposits. I had them fax me the details, then made sure the correct amount of money was in the bank. It wasn't like it is today. I couldn't log onto the bank's website and see a record of transactions. Instead, I spent half a day, every day, on the phone making sure our managers were doing their jobs. The process stretched my sanity, but at least it was familiar.

What wasn't as familiar was tracking down missing money. It seemed like all I did was chase stolen deposits. The night manager was responsible for taking the closing deposit to the bank's night deposit drop, but many of these never made it to the bank. Robberies were such a frequent problem for us that I was on a first-name basis with detectives in all the police departments in towns where we had a restaurant.

I also became our resident expert on safes. I had everyone's PINs as well as a master key for the safes in every store. When deposits disappeared, I needed to be able to determine who had accessed the safe. The data could be read by scrolling a small display panel, but I carried around a printer that allowed me to print a list that was much easier to review.

My experience in auditing served us well as I built my case against people who were stealing from us. It was nonstop and endless. I felt like the weatherman trapped in the time loop in *Groundhog Day*, but I wasn't Bill Murray, and it wasn't funny. It was maddening.

Wednesdays were the worst. All it takes to stop me from cursing technology is this little trip down memory lane. I couldn't get all the information I needed via fax or computer, so this was the day when I went to every location to pick up payroll records and each store's weekly business summary, reports I used to compile income statements.

I rolled out of my driveway at six thirty in the morning in my Honda Accord, heading straight south to LaGrange. From there, the route continued seventy miles east to Forsyth. I spent about an hour in each location, chatting with managers, looking at the cleanliness of the store, and generally putting eyes on the operation. The next stop took me thirty-three miles straight up the interstate to McDonough, which was usually in the midst of lunch rush by the time I arrived. At that hour, the drive-thru and dining room were overflowing, so it wasn't uncommon to spend more than an hour there.

Next was the trek to the Atlanta store, north then west, covering thirty-five miles of the city's busiest freeways. This was a forty-five-minute trip on a good day, but when timing or bad luck dumped me into traffic, this leg of the trip could take an hour and a half or more.

From the Atlanta store, I backtracked eleven miles east and south to East Point, then southwest eleven miles to Union City before the twenty-mile path took me back to Newnan. By the time I arrived home late in the evening, I'd put more than two hundred miles on my vehicle and clocked at least a sixteen-hour day.

As chaotic as business was, I settled into a stable life in Newnan. About six months after coming to work with my dad, I bought my first house in a new subdivision about a mile from my parents. Mom, who for decades had served dinner at 5:30, set a place for me each evening.

At a card game with friends not long after I became a homeowner, one of my buddies told us about a litter of Labradors he was raising. On a whim, I went to see these puppies, and the runt of the litter approached me. Noticing a tick above her eye, I reached down to remove it, and from that moment on, she followed every step I made. I had no choice but to bring her home with me.

Barkley became my loyal buddy and an important part of my predictable evenings. Except for Wednesdays, I left the office around five every day and headed to my parents for dinner. I picked Barkley up on the way unless Mom had picked her up earlier. Often, Mom would go over to my house, let Barkley out of her crate, and take her back to her house for a walk. On the long list of kindnesses my mother has done for me, this is one of the nicest.

During college, I gave up Olympic lifting and working out entirely. Beer was a food group for my buddies and me. Aggressively cheering on the Auburn Tigers was about as close to exercise as I got during those years. Consequently, by the time I graduated, I found myself with a pretty good-sized gut on my five-foot, eight-inch frame. My pants waist ballooned to thirty-six inches, and I was over a hundred and seventy pounds.

After graduating, I fluctuated up and down and struggled to keep the weight off. A grueling travel and work schedule at the accounting firm made it hard for me to turn the situation around. I was tired and inflamed most of the time and knew subconsciously that I needed to get into shape. When I began working for my dad, I was determined to take better care of myself. I started a consistent running schedule in the evenings to relieve the stress from the day and lose weight.

Between work and heading to my parents' house for dinner, I'd go for a run. It became my release, my escape, my therapy. Sometimes, my dad, on his way home from work, would see me and roll down the window, cigarette in hand.

"How far you goin'?"

"I don't know. Three or four miles."

"Doug, if you ever see me running, call the police because something's wrong," he'd say, laughing as he drove off.

Over dinner, Dad and I usually talked business. Afterward, I'd stick around for a while before leaving to go home or hang out with friends. I have fond memories of these pleasant evenings with my parents. The nurturing ritual of family dinner steadied the disarray of the day. I probably never said a proper thank you to my mother for providing an unwavering sanctuary for all of us, including Barkley. *Thanks, Mom.*

I could always count on Barkley's enthusiastic greeting any time of the day. Barkley was named after my favorite Auburn athlete, Charles Barkley, who played sixteen seasons in the NBA.

My grandfather, a district sales manager for a pharmaceutical company, loved to tell this story about my father. After marrying my mom, Dad went to work for one of her father's competitors. They lived in the same area, and Dad sold seven days a week. While my grandfather's salespeople were out on Fridays drinking beer and playing golf, my father worked. In Grandpap's sales meetings, he'd relay with a mixture of pride and rebuke, "My son-in-law is selling more than all of you guys combined. What's going on here?"

Maybe it was his childhood. Maybe it was just his nature. I don't know, but Dad thrived on a challenge. All grit and determination, he loved obstacles. Constantly thinking, his mind never turned off. Invariably, he found a way to figure out how to get a job done.

Making connections was his specialty. He always had time for people and had great relationships with the managers. He loved to talk to them on the phone, even at nine or ten o'clock at night.

He was an amazing leader who could sell an idea as easily as he had sold toilet seats. Confident, persistent, tough, scrappy—he loved the "art of the deal." For the first time in my life, I was getting to know my father, really learning who he was as a person. He was smart, well-respected, and honest. He believed your word was as good as a contract, and he kept his word.

He treated me like a partner. We talked about business all the time. I learned a lot from him about being resourceful, unrelenting, and determined. We spent every single day together, driving to stores, going over numbers, and working with vendors and the team. We called ourselves *The Problem Solvers.*

My father and I both understood the value of relationships, the hedge on all bets in the gamble of business. I learned this as an auditor investigating the integrity of Tennessee's community banks, where I observed how important good connections were to small-town economies. Collateral, I discovered, is less important than how well you got along with the president of the bank.

For instance, I would see people get loans that were secured by hunting dogs. As an auditor, my job was to make sure this hunting dog existed to verify that the borrower can pay back the loan. If the dog ran away or got hit by a car, we had to write these off as bad debt.

"You can't loan this guy $10,000 with no collateral because you like him," we'd tell the bankers.

But scenarios like this were repeated over and over again. Should the president have given these people money or not? Who knows? I think the loans were usually repaid. What I do know is that most of the time, people just want to help each other out. Relationships matter more than anything.

This may be why Dad was great about always including me in important meetings. I had little to say but paid attention. The proverbial seat at the table was a priceless education that also made me much more comfortable with many people I dealt with later.

Ironically, one of the first people I sat down with in a setting like this was Bob Lore, the president of our local bank. Bob mentioned in passing that he was hiking the Appalachian Trail. Each spring and fall, he would spend several weeks hiking a part of the trail he had not done before. His objective was to walk the entire 2,193-mile trail from Georgia to Maine over time.

This strategy is known as section hiking, and I was instantly intrigued. My father and I both were excited when he invited me along. Not only did hiking fit in well with my health and fitness goals, but it never hurts to keep a good relationship with your banker. Dad, who was no fan of taking time off, happily approved these vacation days.

Bob taught me how to hike over the course of several years. Together, we covered all of Georgia, Virginia, and Maryland and sections of Pennsylvania and North Carolina, about a third of the total trail length.

You learn a lot from a man when you walk more than seven hundred miles with him. For starters, I learned that hiking the Appalachian is no joke. Bob was twice my age, but I still worked hard to keep up. Rising with the sun and quickly on our way, we walked up and down over roots and rocks until five or six at night. It's an intense workout, really hard.

A very successful businessman, Bob was brilliant when it came to finances. In fact, he retired in his early fifties, just a couple of years after we met. We were two guys who understood the power of a decimal point, but in the wilderness, he schooled me to another level. On the Appalachian Trail, I began to truly appreciate the power of the details.

I quickly learned that the weight of my clothing and supplies made all the difference between making seven or eight miles in a day and putting fifteen miles behind us before setting up camp each night. The idea became a challenge and an obsession for me.

I weighed all my hiking supplies and every gram of food in order to cover as much distance on the trail as I could. Wearing lightweight tennis shoes was better than boots. When making tens of thousands of steps in a day, reducing even eight ounces transferred to a big overall difference in energy consumption.

Everyone hiking the AT has a trail name. Mine was "Travelin' Lite." Author Bill Bryson hiked the trails about the same time we did, publishing *A Walk in the Woods* in 1998. In Bryson's travelogue, his buddy famously flings supplies off the side of the mountain, even coffee filters, to reduce the weight of his pack. This is a scene I understand.

Bob Lore and I set off toward the Appalachian Trail.

Weightlifting, hiking, and running all taught me that small things are not really small. In fact, they can be hugely important. You can work and train consistently but miss one seemingly little detail, and a project falls apart. Paying attention to the particulars impacts how much you can lift, how far you can go, and whether you can make it to the finish line. Minutiae matters.

In the same way that I looked for methods to get stronger and faster as an athlete, from the beginning, I looked for ways our company could operate better. It was my job to make sense of the numbers—from inventory to schedules to profits. Early on, the biggest opportunity I saw for us to improve was in food cost management.

At one point, we were running labor at around 24 percent compared to an industry average of 28 to 30 percent. Aside from Charles, our managers had no idea how to manage food costs. Our inventory reports, for example, were inaccurate, made up by employees who didn't care about the truth, didn't care about the job, or didn't have the proper training—or all of the above. Our managers produced fantasy schedules that often changed hourly, causing us to have too many people on one shift or another. Or worse, they didn't create a schedule at all.

I estimated that these and many other overlooked or disregarded details were costing us as much as eight hundred dollars a week at each store. The first change I suggested to my father was to increase labor costs to 30 percent and make up the money by saving on food costs, which, at the time, were running around 34 percent.

"Let's get people in the stores who can run them like they should be run and pay them a couple hundred dollars more per week," I proposed. "In the long run, this will save us tons of money. We'll have better employees, which will increase sales and reduce food costs to 30 percent."

Dad was convinced we could not afford to pay people more. He steadfastly refused to increase salaries as a strategy for cutting food costs. I didn't think about money in terms of not being able to spend it, though. Instead, I focused on the best way to leverage our resources.

"If you pay someone $30,000 instead of $20,000, but they're stealing $10,000 from you, you're not getting anywhere," I argued. "You're a great salesman, but you're not buying a car. You may be able to hire someone for $20,000, but you're not going to get the results you need."

I was sure if we paid people more, we'd reap a tenfold return on food costs. No matter how many times I suggested it, he refused. Dad countered most of my ideas with one of two responses. "You're going to bankrupt the company," he'd say, or "We'll take that out of your salary."

In every great story, conflict is essential. Ours was no different. I loved working with my father. Most of the time. Some of the time. Maybe.

Dad's "my way or the highway" statute was frustrating for me.

Sure, I was twenty-four years old. Somebody needed to tell me what to do and what direction we were headed, but I had ideas, too. Lots of them. My father rejected most of them simply because he couldn't see another way to do things. He believed in himself so much that he didn't want help from anybody.

"I got us in this situation, and I can get us out of it," he would say. "I can fix any problem we have."

Oh, how I wish that had been true.

See that smile? Young and dumb. That's me at my desk in the office shared with my father, Carla, and Charles. All four of us were in a room no larger than 500 sq. feet.

CHAPTER FOUR

911

On Courage:
"I'm willing to act in the presence of fear."

— BRIAN JOHNSON

THE HEADQUARTERS OF GEORGIA-TEXAS ENTERPRISES was a cluster of rooms we rented in a building just down the street from the Newnan restaurant. When I came to work with my father, our five hundred square foot office held four cheap desks for my father, me, Charles, and Carla. It was modest, but Dad loved to paint, so it was always freshly painted. He'd spend hours going over the walls with a brush. I've wondered if this was something he carried over from his days in the Navy, if it was a stress reliever, or if it was both.

"If you let me have a roller, I'll help you," I'd offer.

"I don't roll. I paint," Dad said.

"Well, then I can't help you."

As we grew, we rented a kitchen down the hall. Dad and I turned it into an office for the two of us, him on one end and me on the other. He was on the phone all the time. In fact, I don't think he ever wasn't on the phone. Unless, maybe, when he was painting. He'd stand in the door smoking a cigarette, one every fifteen minutes, talking on the phone.

Early in 1998, Dad took a call from a company asking to talk to the person who handled our payroll. He passed the message along to me. Our previous accounting firm had told the rep that we loved saving money, and if the company could do that for us, we'd be a great candidate as a new client.

I was happy doing payroll with our CPA firm, so I didn't return the call.

The rep called again. Dad took the message and passed it on to me, and I didn't call back. This cycle repeated itself regularly for six or seven months. Finally, in August, I returned the call.

"I'll meet with you," I said, "but I'm not interested in a payroll solution. I want nothing to do with your company, but if you want to come in so we can close this chapter, come on."

When Andrea Salemi walked into my life on a Friday afternoon, I reconsidered. I could feel the energy radiating from her petite frame.

"I'm just letting you know, Dad," I whispered, "I'm buying whatever she's selling."

He thought that was the funniest thing in the world.

Andrea had a trainee with her. They sat down in my office, she made her pitch, and I started asking her questions. Relevant questions. Crazy questions. Whatever I could think of because I didn't want her to leave. Andrea loved it because this provided a great learning opportunity for her protégé.

Cell phones were still pretty new then, so it thrilled me when she gave me her cell phone number before she left.

"If you have any additional questions this weekend, call me. I'd be happy to answer them."

I had a lot more questions.

"I may have some questions, so I may call you," I said.

As she left the building, Dad gave me a thumbs-up.

"I think he was into you," the trainee told Andrea in the car, I later learned.

"Oh, I don't think so. He's got a picture of his girlfriend on his desk."

"You never know. It could be his sister."

It was my sister.

I called her on Sunday evening. We talked for five minutes about payroll and then for hours about everything else.

Few of Dad's calls were as pleasant as Andrea's. His favorite tool, a pager he wore like a badge, precipitated most of them. It constantly beeped with digital messages from stores with "911" behind the phone number.

"We don't have enough people. We have to close the dining room." "No one showed up today." "The freezer is out." "We don't have water." Pick a problem. He received a page about it.

Disasters blew up all over the place, sparking nonstop insanity every day. Like firefighters, we constantly responded to what seemed like never-ending alarms. Everyone's role was reactive. The biggest fire received the attention, and we never knew when that call would come in.

Leading the emergency response brigade, Charles and Carla usually deployed to stores in crisis. They might run lunch in McDonough and then drive back to Newnan to close. Or they'd close up after the night shift in Forsyth, and we'd put them up in a hotel so they could open McDonough, which was going to be short-staffed the next morning. We had to turn on a dime and couldn't plan any day because every day was different.

Dad rotated 911 duty, handing off his badge to me, Charles, or Carla on the weekends. We all loathed that pager. Nothing pissed me off more than being controlled by a device that exploded all the time. Our company was running us. We weren't running it.

Some of the biggest battles between my father and me were about work styles. Balance was important to me. It didn't have to be perfect or rigidly proportioned, but I believed everyone needed an escape from the job. The big appeal for me in accounting in college was that I could have a career and still have a life. Dad, on the other hand, was a workaholic. He had no interests outside of work. He was on the job twenty-four hours a day, seven days a week, and he wanted me to operate like that, too. He expected me, along with all his managers, to report at 8 a.m. on Saturdays.

"I don't need to be in the office on Saturday," I argued. "I've got all my work done."

A couple of times a month, I relented and put away a truck. Food was delivered via truck twice weekly. "Putting away the truck" meant dating every item, then rotating the existing product to make sure we used it first. It took two or three hours to do the job that I believed we could trust managers and assistant managers to do.

Dad spoiled the Newnan store, putting the truck away on Wednesdays and Sundays. We had seven restaurants and three express units, essentially ten restaurants, and the owner of the company handled the Newnan store himself. I refused to do tasks other people should do, and it drove my dad crazy.

My father was reluctant to embrace Taco Bell's corporate systems, tools, and training. In my opinion, they had become one of the most successful quick-service restaurant chains in the country by optimizing workflows and processes. I always looked for the most efficient way to operate. I advocated for following their guidelines, but my lobbying campaigns changed nothing.

Dad was more determined than efficient. He loved being part of Taco Bell. One of his favorite checks to write was for the franchise royalty every week.

"Doug, if we named this restaurant Gene's Tacos, we'd be out of business the day we opened."

He knew our success was because of the brand, but he wanted to do it his way. He liked to make it up as he went along, preferring to blaze a trail rather than follow other people.

"These are my stores," he'd say. "I'm going to run them the way I want to run them."

Sharing information was another point of conflict. Dad was pretty transparent with me, but it didn't matter because he was going to do things the way he wanted to do them. I was convinced that people needed to know where we were in order to help us get better. He was quick to answer when I'd say, "I want to share this with this person."

"You can't do that."

"Why not?"

"Because that's on a need-to-know basis, and they just don't need to know that."

We were night and day as far as how we prioritized tasks and information. I don't sweat the small stuff, and my dad didn't sweat the big stuff, but small things drove him berserk. He'd fire people over a small infraction, but he was level-headed, cool as a cucumber, when it came to the big problems.

"We'll get through it," he'd say. "We can figure this out."

One of his favorite ways to get through it was to say, "Doug, just fix it!" He thought if we worked harder, particularly if I worked harder, we could fix just about anything.

"Dad, it takes resources to fix things!" I said. Repeatedly.

Many of our disagreements were rooted in his rationale that you can overcome any obstacle by working harder. I think his philosophy came from having to work as hard as he could for every single thing he ever had. His strategy in any situation was to outwork everybody else.

His upbringing had taught him that the only person he could rely on was himself. As a kid, it was all up to him. Every problem that arose, he had to resolve. It made him resilient, but it also made it hard for him to trust others. No matter how far away he moved from his childhood, he couldn't outgrow the feeling that no one would help him.

Ironically, Dad's work ethic, plus many wise decisions, provided a much different backdrop for me. My life had given me an opposing perspective. I believed long-term solutions require planning and investment. I knew from experience that you can't lift more weight by merely putting in more reps. You have to think about what you want to do, map out a plan, and follow it.

One of these quarrels escalated into harsh words and a heated exchange of letters.

"I don't like you taking weekends off," headed the list of issues he yelled at me about, and he rattled off a string of stuff I was doing that he didn't like. I took it personally.

"You know what? It has nothing to do with how I'm working and everything to do with the handcuffs, the parameters, and the rules you're making me follow!"

As great as my father was at building good relationships, he was famous for leaving scathing notes and letters when he was upset or disappointed. Rather than dealing with people face-to-face, he dropped memos like bombs on your desk when he was unhappy about how things were going. I received my share of these notes, including one letter that drove me to counter with a thousand-word letter of my own.

> *Dad,*
>
> *Since you wrote a letter, I feel as though I should respond to it via a letter. Before I respond, however, I would like to vent some of my frustrations about this company to you.*
>
> *First of all, I want this company to be a first-class organization. I want our stores to shine well above the rest of the competition. To do so, we must have good people to depend on to run the stores. I feel as though we accept mediocrity in this area, and I don't know why. I go into the stores, and for the most part, I am extremely disappointed in us. No one is accountable for anything, and they should be.*
>
> *I do not want a $100,000 payroll, but let's get someone in the stores who can run them like they should be run and pay them $100 to $200 more a week. To tell me I need to get in there and fix it is a cop-out on your part. I cannot solve all the problems myself. I NEED HELP!!!*
>
> *When I say that, I mean someone strong, either in the office or out in the field, who is willing to do what it takes to make our company a fun place to work and excel.*
>
> *I cannot run this office, which includes making sure deposits hit the bank, paying bills, doing payroll, reconciling bank statements, filling out Georgia New Hire reporting sheets, sweeping money, transferring money, gathering information to give to the accountant, filling out Georgia Department of Labor claims for unemployment information, being a detective on lost deposits, auditing daily control sheets, answering the telephone, putting the truck away, making sure employees are paying for uniforms, fixing safe problems, putting in user codes for the alarm system, talking to vendors about erroneous billings, helping*

managers with *TACO* system problems, and every other thing I do around here.

I am not happy with what I am doing in this company. I am not making a difference because I am too busy. I know the stores need attention, but I have not been able to allocate my time effectively in doing both because there are not enough hours in a day to do everything I need to do.

I do not, however, want to work like you do. I do not find it enjoyable to work fifteen hours a day, seven days a week. I want to do things in my life other than work. I do not want to be fifty-three years old and hate golf and never fish and not have time to run or go hiking. I want a balanced life, which means work hard as hell and play hard as hell.

You give me a guilt trip if I am not working all the time. I don't know. Maybe I give you a guilt trip for not enjoying life more? Anyway, I am not happy about our current situation because we are understaffed.

I feel that you do not think I am doing everything that I can be doing to help this company prosper, and that is not true. I want nothing more than this company to be a world-class operation. To have Taco Bell recognize us for our outstanding efforts, to have customers lined up outside our doors waiting to be served because the food is good, fast, and the service is outstanding.

I cannot do it by myself and you cannot do it by yourself, but we can do it together, but we need good help in the stores to achieve our desired goals.

I am not going to read over this letter, so if it sounds like I am rambling, it is because I probably am. Anyway, I feel better now that I typed all this on paper. Let's sit down and talk about it.

Your son and business partner,

Doug

I have no idea what happened to his letter to me that precipitated my tirade—I may have burned it—but my frustrated response has survived the decades. This was by far our biggest disagreement. We were 180 degrees different in how we thought the business should run. He didn't understand how relying on other people was essential for success. Maybe it was pride. Maybe it was his ego, but his "I can do it" mantra prevented him from hearing alternative solutions. I wasted a lot of time trying to convince him to work smarter, not harder.

One tenet we agreed on, though, was paying bills. Dad didn't believe in solving any of our problems with money, but he taught me early on how to treat vendors. Even as a kid, I remember him saying, "Doug, you always pay your bills. If you owe somebody, you pay them, and you pay them on time, no matter what."

Dad might squeeze a price until it hurt, but when the deal was struck, he paid his bills. He took pride in paying people on time.

"You do the right thing, Doug. That's just what you do."

Meanwhile, I wrestled with the financials. When I was in college, I wrote a Lotus spreadsheet to help Charles manage inventory. I doubled down on that solution after coming to work for my father. It took us two months to get a profit and loss (P&L) statement from our CPA firm. By the time these reports arrived, the numbers weren't even relevant anymore. So, in the back of the house, I designed spreadsheets to track inventory and cash.

This is the store my father built in East Point, Georgia, in October 1998.

In the fall of 1998, Dad built a new store in East Point to replace the twenty-five-year-old original unit, Store #1160, which was the first Taco Bell in Atlanta. He borrowed money from Bob Lore's bank for the project to reopen a brand-new restaurant nearby. He closed the original store just before we scheduled the new one to open on October 1.

Unfortunately, we hit a snag with the health department. The inspector required us to replace the three-compartment sink in the kitchen with a four-compartment sink. Equipment like this was not available from a distributor. It had to be custom-made, a process that delayed the opening for a month. We took an enormous hit to cash flow when the East Point location ended up being closed for about six weeks.

Consequently, Dad was under a lot of stress. We all were. We shuffled from problem to problem with no plan, never fixing what was broken, just plugging holes. Challenges stacked up like a house of cards, and I was beginning to wonder if we could avoid a collapse.

Cash flow was nightmarish. The situation at East Point was fright-ful; the express units were nearly as gloomy. Over the summer, Walmart relocated from behind our Newnan restaurant to a superstore across the interstate, two miles away. Dad told people it actually helped our business, and maybe he believed that, but in truth, it hurt us badly. Not only did the store move, but the trade area also moved with it.

Dad was also dreading a difficult personnel issue. He had hired a nice guy he'd enjoyed working with at Royal Molded to be a district manager. It wasn't working. Dad had fired plenty of people in the past, including his own brother, but he never enjoyed it. Soon, he would have to fire a good friend.

Finally, the new East Point store opened the first weekend of November. Andrea and I had been together as much as possible since we met, and the two of us had planned to go to a football game with my sister and her husband in South Bend, Indiana. Charles and Carla went to Minneapolis for a Vikings game, so Dad handled the opening alone. Unfortunately, it didn't go well.

The following Saturday was more routine. Andrea and I went to a NASCAR race, and Mom and Dad had an unusually relaxing weekend. Dad complained of being tired and having pain in his arm on Sunday, but against Mom's protests, he unloaded the truck at the Newnan store anyway.

By six in the morning on Monday, November 9, he was up sending memos and leaving a company-wide voicemail rant about food and labor costs. He was in a foul mood when I got to the office around 7:45.

"Labor costs are going to bankrupt this company," he told me.

Accustomed to his "freak-out moments," I took it with a grain of salt. "We're going to be bankrupt" was a constant refrain. "You're overreacting," was my line. I hoped I was right.

He stormed out of the office while I pored over deposits from Friday, Saturday, and Sunday. Thirty minutes later, the Newnan store manager called.

"Holy shit, Doug, you need to get over here ASAP. Your dad has collapsed in the parking lot!"

"I'm on my way!" I said. "Be there in a second!"

Flying out the door, I called Mom.

"Dad collapsed," I told her. "He's in the parking lot at the Newnan store. I don't know what's going on, but I'm heading over there now."

The day was mild but overcast. I felt the gray clouds settling all around us. The first person I saw on the scene was an EMT I went to high school with.

"What's going on?" I asked.

"I don't know yet," he said, "but we're taking your dad to the hospital."

He didn't have time to tell me more.

Andrea was at the grocery store when I reached her.

"Hey, I'm at the Newnan store. They're taking my dad to the hospital," I told her. "I'm not sure what happened to him, but he fell over at the store."

As they were loading him into the ambulance, they gave me his wallet, car keys, cigarettes, and a few other items. At that moment, I hated those cigarettes more than anything in the world. I followed the ambulance to the hospital, but before I went through the door, I emptied the pack and destroyed every one of them. Mom and Andrea arrived soon after. We spent a very long day together in the ICU waiting room.

Until that morning, I had never imagined life without my father. He was only fifty-four years old. He had no health issues that we were aware of. Yes, he smoked like a chimney in a cold winter. His diet consisted mainly of greasy burgers, meat, and potatoes, but he was in decent shape. I knew he wasn't sleeping well, but then he drank Diet Dr. Pepper in the middle of the night, so what could you expect?

"Mom, whatever happens here," I told her, "I've got you. Don't worry about anything. I'm going to take care of you."

My sister, Jennifer, her husband, Josh, and Father Trayers flew into Atlanta. They were with us when the doctors told us that he had suffered a heart attack. During the incident, he lost oxygen for a long time. Tests revealed that his brain was no longer functioning.

"He's not going to make it," they told us. "We can leave him on the ventilator and keep him alive as long as you want, but he's gone."

My mother knew he would not want that.

"No," she said. "Turn it off."

They pronounced him dead early in the morning on Tuesday, November 10, 1998.

The rest of the week was, and still is, a blur. Andrea never left my side. Family from around the country swarmed us with support. Employees and many people in the community came to pay their respects Wednesday evening at his wake and Thursday morning at the funeral. His brother and my mother's brothers were pallbearers. Father Trayers delivered the funeral Mass. The obituary summed up a lifetime in two sentences.

"Born Oct. 27, 1944, in Schofield, Wisconsin, Mr. Augustine was the son of the late Adam John Augustine. He was owner-manager of Taco Bell in Newnan and a U.S. Navy veteran."

Sometime during that week, my Uncle Bill gave me some advice I have never forgotten.

"Doug, 'When in command, command,'" he said.

At the time, those words sounded ridiculous to me. I didn't know they were famously spoken by Admiral Nimitz during the Battle of Midway. I had no idea what Uncle Bill was telling me, but I did feel like I was in a war zone. I understood that I was twenty-six years old, at the helm of a company with seven stores and more than two hundred employees, and that, somehow, I had to keep the ship afloat.

Charles sat with the family at the funeral, changed clothes afterward, and headed back to work. The show had to go on.

He was nervous. We both were, but he nailed the situation with one statement:

"Who put us idiots in charge?"

Two years after my dad's death, while pacing the halls at the Paris Hotel in Las Vegas, I asked myself this question again. *What did Charles and I know about fixing a problem like this? Where would we get the money to pay our people?*

There was only one solution. It was one of the hardest decisions I've ever had to make, but "When in command, command."

Gene Augustine always—*always*—paid creditors on time. I held my breath, temporarily shelved this fundamental policy, and called Charles back.

"Defer paying the vendors. We'll catch it up later. Make sure we get payroll out."

I knew this would buy us some time. More than ever, this was "game on."

"Got it. I'm on it," he said.

God help us, I thought at the end of the call. *What would my father think?*

PART TWO
TRAINING

You never know what's ahead.

CHAPTER FIVE

Day by Day

"As you start to walk on the way, the way appears."

— RUMI

THERE'S A FINE LINE BETWEEN making progress and getting yourself in trouble. A very fine line.

The Appalachian Trail spans 2,200 miles across fourteen states, beginning in Georgia and ending in Maine. Forty-one of those miles are in Maryland, where the southern end of the path begins on the banks of the Potomac River at Harpers Ferry. From there, it heads nearly straight north to Pen Mar, Pennsylvania. In a feat known as the Maryland Challenge, fierce trailblazers travel this section from beginning to end in twenty-four hours. The spring before my father died, Bob Lore and I decided to join their ranks.

A lot of planning goes into hiking the AT. Fortunately for me, Bob did all of that for us. He outlined our itinerary, chose where we stayed, and determined where we should drop off the car and supplies. The day before our Maryland Challenge, we met in West Virginia, drove to Pen Mar, dropped off our car, and caught a ride back to Harpers Ferry, where our hotel was conveniently located a couple of blocks from the trail. As soon as we arrived at our room, we set our alarms for 3:30 in the morning and went to bed. The next morning, we were up and out the door as soon as those alarms went off. We started the hike with headlamps. It would be another hour and a half, around 5:30, before first light. We had to cover a lot of distance if we were going to make it to Blue Ridge Summit, just over the Pennsylvania line, by 9:30 that evening. There was no time to waste.

On previous hikes, I carried around thirty pounds in my pack and covered 2.5 to 2.8 miles an hour. On this trip, I was really living up to my trail name, *Travelin' Lite*. Slack-packing, hiking with as little weight as possible, allows you to move farther and quicker. Bob and I both were slack-packing. I had weighed my food and water down to the gram and was ready for an adventure. Maryland is one of the flattest sections on the entire AT. With less than six pounds on my back, I figured I could cover three and a half miles an hour. Even taking breaks, I should make it to Pennsylvania by dark. The goal was to move fast and keep moving.

Soon after we hit the trail, Bob and I got separated. This is not uncommon. Hikers start out together, but usually, one is faster than the other, so they spread out and catch up with each other at the end of the day. Toward the end of the afternoon, I realized I didn't know where I was or how I had gotten there. The Appalachian Trail is well-marked with blazes of white paint. Side trails, which may lead to scenic views, are marked with blue blazes. At some point, I took one of those side trails by mistake. Tired and dehydrated, I looked at my watch and began to consider the possibility that I might have to spend the night off the trail. With no tent, no food, and only a light jacket to protect me from the cold, my trail name teetered on the brink of *Travelin' Too Lite.*

Cold and scared out of my mind, the only idea I had was to start backtracking. When you're diverted, getting back on course is the most important step you can take. Every time I turned a corner, I hoped to see a blaze of white. All the way, I was thinking about what to do if I failed to find the main trail.

Hypothermia is entirely possible in the woods in the spring in Maryland, when temperatures can fall into the thirties at night. My what-if plans included making a shelter of sticks and logs covered with leaves to keep me warm. At best, I was going to be uncomfortable. At worst? Well, it could be bad. Fortunately, I rounded a bend and saw a white blaze beckoning me back to the trail. I was late meeting Bob but slept in a warm and dry hotel room that night.

Six months after completing the Maryland Challenge, I found myself lost and alone again. Dad's death uprooted me. He had been my compass, and then he was gone. The entire environment around me felt unfamiliar and dangerous, and I had to figure it out on my own.

I never really had a good cry over my dad dying. A week after his death, I turned twenty-seven years old. I can't tell you a single detail about that birthday or the rest of November or December. Those two months are a blur. Part of me was in denial about the magnitude of what had happened. Survival was the number one priority, and this meant two things: keeping the company going and taking care of my mom. Everything else, including time to grieve, took a back seat to staying afloat.

Mom was catatonic, in shock, I think. After Dad's death, I reiterated the promise I had made at my father's deathbed.

"I've got you. Don't worry. I'm going to take care of you."

I had no idea how I would do that, but I didn't want her to know how bad the situation was. She had just lost her husband. The last thing she needed was to hear about our dicey reality. The truth was that even before he died, the business was a war zone. It was attacked from so many directions that it was hard to know where the front line was.

I didn't want my mother to worry. She'd been fighting long enough.

"You go get yourself right," I told her.

Mom spent a lot of time with her parents and close-knit siblings the year after Dad died.

Thank God for Andrea, who was there for me the entire time, because I was in shock, too. For about six weeks, I was just hanging on. I remember being so tired, so mentally exhausted, and just going through the motions at work. All I knew for sure was that we had to make it. I had to find my way out of the woods and to a path forward.

By the New Year, I was more focused, and just in time, too, because from the corporate bosses to lenders, it seemed everyone had their sights zoomed in on us.

"Look, you need to find something else to do."

Those were the harsh words delivered by the emissaries Taco Bell sent to meet with me and Mom shortly after my father's death.

The Atlanta market as a whole was not performing well, but unfortunately, Georgia-Texas was the boat anchor, dead last in their metrics. Uncomfortable with my age, our debt load, and our performance, they basically read us the riot act.

"You're not cut out for this. You're not going to make it."

They wanted us out of the system as soon as possible.

"You've got your whole life ahead of you. This isn't for you."

They asked us to sell, but Mom and I had already considered our options. She could go back to teaching, and I could go back to accounting, or we could fight to save the life savings and a decade of brute energy she and my father had poured into the company. If we quit, not only would all that equity be lost, but she would also be upside down by at least two million dollars. But if we kept going, we had a chance to recover the investment and preserve my father's legacy.

We both wanted to keep going.

"Give us five years," Mom told them. "Five years is what it takes to break even with a new business. You did that before, and by five years, we were making money. I really think with my son we can do it in five years."

She had 100 percent faith in me, but I'm sure she said a few prayers every night.

After Dad died, everyone moved up a slot. Barely twenty-seven years old, I was suddenly in charge of a company with several hundred employees. Although I had been handling our accounting for two years, I didn't have a clear grasp of the big picture. It's easy to feel like all is well when you have money in the bank, even when it's not. I gave my father updated daily cash balances, but he held onto the bank records.

As Charles and I dug into the books, we discovered that Taco Bell was right to be concerned. We knew we were still reeling from having closed East Point for a month, but there were a lot of vital facts we didn't know.

For instance, as Dad expanded into Taco Bell Express units, he borrowed money from local banks. These loans paid for the projects and gave the company a little bit of cushion, too.

"We've got to build, build, build," I remember my father saying.

Now, I understand that he was chasing cash flow by opening stores and generating a wave of cash before the bills were due. Dad operated like other serial acquirers in those days. He knew that as long as he was opening stores, he'd generate cash. The piper didn't have to be paid until the growth stopped.

We also received an unexpected bump from a savings and rebate program from Pepsi. In addition to annual refunds for up to 70 percent of purchases, Pepsi gave us $17,000 per store at the beginning of a ten-year contract agreement. One of the first stark truths we uncovered was that the residuals from these two funding sources were all that was keeping us in business.

My hiking buddy Bob offered to review my financial statements. He barely began turning pages before he saw it.

"You've got a cash flow problem, Doug."

The roof over our heads was the wobbly top of a precarious house of cards. And the house was built on sand. A shelter of branches and leaves in the woods would have been more secure. We had a lot of work to do.

Our accountant at the time wasn't much help. By the time she sent us financial statements, they were so far behind they were irrelevant. You don't know what you don't know, and you can't know if you can't get information.

She did do me a favor, though, a big one. She gave me a copy of Michael Gerber's book *The E-Myth*.

"Read this, Doug."

Gerber gave words to what I knew in my gut. Somehow, I had to stop working in the business and start working on it. I had to run it like the president and CEO.

Before my father died, Charles was bouncing between being our district manager and running the Newnan store, which he dubbed the "Bucking Bronco" from opening day. He wrangled that bull every time it threw off a manager, which was often. He had always been able to run that restaurant better than anyone. Besides being a supremely efficient operator, Charles had a degree in finance. With Dad gone, I moved Charles to the office and had him take over my previous duties of keeping up with the accounting.

Amazingly, he still tamed Newnan. He took responsibility for closing the hometown restaurant sixty-eight nights in a row after my father's death. Closing involves an extensive checklist of cleaning and prepping for the next day and rarely ends before three in the morning. A streak of sixty-eight consecutive closings may be unheard of. Unbelievable. Nobody can do that. Even after closing, he'd come to the office the next morning, check all the deposits, pay all the bills, and head back to the Bucking Bronco in the afternoon.

I let Charles worry about the day-to-day finances while I focused on improving cash flow and operations. For two years, I lived in the restaurants. My three goals were to improve cash flow, grow sales, and clean up the stores.

On my hit list of ways to improve our bottom line, eliminating three express units was number one. Toward the end of the year that I came to work with my father, we succumbed to a big push from Taco Bell to open express stores, which were essentially mini restaurants. By the end of 1997, we added three within a two-hour drive from Newnan. Two were attached to gas stations. The third was near a college campus in Carrollton.

Unfortunately, the express stores were unwieldy and unprofitable. These locations enlarged the geographic territory we managed. Although two were conveniently along the corridor roads and interstates connecting our restaurants, the college store was twenty-six miles northwest of Newnan. Adding these units complicated operations and moved our bottom line into negative territory. It wasn't just our company that struggled to make this work. They didn't work for Taco Bell. The concept flopped nationwide.

On January 11, 1999, I wrote the first letter to our landlord in Barnesville, explaining that this location had never produced the sales we had expected. I told him we would remove our equipment from the store by January 20. A week later, I wrote to our landlord in Carrollton and Hogansville—the company we leased these spaces from owned both locations—informing him that we would cease operations and leave our equipment in exchange for terminating the lease agreement. By the end of January, all three units were closed. Recouping the money from these losing operations freed up thousands of dollars for us every month, a big step in the right direction.

The next move in the strategy to improve cash flow was to inform our leadership team about the obstacles we were facing. Like most large restaurant groups, Taco Bell follows thirteen four-week accounting periods per year. In the first quarter of 1999, I initiated meetings with store managers to review the financials following each period. This was a new approach for our company, a practice we had never done when my father was alive. That kind of information definitely came under the category he deemed "none ya," as in, "none of your business."

I believed that our managers needed a clear picture of our situation. Why? Because when people don't know what's going on, they tend to think all is well. It's human nature to believe "no news is good news." The truth was that our situation was challenging, and I didn't think we should candy-coat it.

At the initial meeting, which took place in the basement of my parents' home, I gave a "State of the Business" update. One of the first facts I had to address was the elephant who wasn't in the room.

"Just because my dad died, that doesn't mean this company is going to die with him," I said. "We're all replaceable. Me included. It's a brutal reality, but this is bigger than any one person. We can't let my father be bigger than the company. We're going to figure this out, and we're going to move on. That's what he would want us to do."

From this sobering reality, we moved to the stark truth of profits and losses. Newnan was the only restaurant that was profitable at that time, which is why Charles hunkered down at that location and kept operations on track. Other than Charles and me, I don't think anyone in the room had ever seen a P&L statement. I was amazed at how many of our people thought that sales equaled how much money we had. We covered the very basics of accounting in that first candid conversation.

When a dollar comes in, that doesn't mean that we made a dollar, I explained. Food costs, labor, utilities, etc., take a bite out of every taco we sell.

Another one of the first layers Charles and I peeled back was what we were making on each taco. It wasn't pretty. We needed to make three cents more on each of those tacos we sold, nearly double what we were clearing at the time.

"After all the bills are paid, if we can keep six to eight cents of that taco, then we've done well," I told them.

Stunned, one of our managers asked, "You mean, on one taco, we only make one or two pennies?"

"That's if we're lucky," I said. "Our food costs are out of line. Instead of us spending thirty-two cents on food, we're spending thirty-six cents. That may not sound like a lot, but those four pennies were our profit."

I asked the group for ideas on how we could improve. One manager suggested a dance contest.

"Tell me more about this," I said. "What are you thinking?"

"Well, I think if we can have this dance contest in the store, we can get more customers."

In today's marketing environment, social media might make that idea viable. But in 1999, I was mentally shaking my head.

"Let's start with cutting food costs," I countered. "We've got to get really good at what we're doing, and I need your help doing it. Let's come back to this thought when we've improved our costs."

We progressed from teaching managers fundamental financial concepts to implementing Taco Bell's systems and tools. Dad's MO was doing it his own way. Period. He preferred the "make it up as I go" approach over following a plan, especially one laid out by a corporate entity he believed knew less about how to run a restaurant than he did. He wasn't the only franchisee who operated this way. In fact, a dividing line, of sorts, separated franchisees who were sure they knew more than corporate and those who followed the party line. Dad was definitely on the side of the resistance.

On the other hand, my MO is to focus on doing the same thing every day and getting a little better at it over time. I love copying people. I come up with a good idea now and then, but I specialize in finding somebody who does something really well and emulating their formula. I believed Taco Bell had succeeded for nearly forty years by then because they knew at least as much about efficiency and operations as they did about tacos. They had tremendous systems, tools, and training in place. It wasn't a matter of not trusting or even wanting to tweak their plan. I was pre-sold on doing it their way, all the way. I was sure we could do a better job by following their formula. There was no need to reinvent that wheel.

Working closely with trusted advisors was another important component of getting back on track. While I inherited some problems from my father, he also left me several treasures. One of those was an honest lawyer who became a good friend. I first met Brian Wooldridge in a meeting with my dad. Like with Bob Lore, this was another one of those situations where my role was to pay attention. Even then, I appreciated that Brian was definitely a guy you want by your side when you have a big problem.

When reviewing our loan agreement with our primary lender, the two of us made a terrifying discovery. Closing the East Point restaurant while preparing to open the new location technically put us in default on our major loan with Atherton Capital. Offsetting—relocating a store within three miles of its original location—is a legitimate and common business move, but Dad had built a brand-new building that our lender had no idea about and no security interest in. And he had closed a store they held as collateral, and they had no idea it was closed. I think he planned to sell the original store and saw no problem with the action. It's unlikely he considered the loan agreement when he made what seemed like a good business decision.

On the other hand, Brian and I could see in the loan covenants that we weren't allowed to close a restaurant or open a new one without the lender's approval. Chances were better than good that, sooner or later, Atherton would pick up the phone to tell me it was time to scrape up all of the four million dollars we owed them.

Brian, an eternal pessimist, was nevertheless reassuring. By the time I worked with him, he'd been practicing law, representing many businesses with their lenders, and even working for banks for more than twenty years. He had represented my parents since the early '90s, back when closing a deal meant a full day of signing documents. In those days, several people were on hand just to seal, notarize, and witness all that paperwork. He'd been with my parents during several times like that. He was at my father's funeral. He'd seen a lot.

"If it comes to it, we'll reorganize," he said.

But I knew that would take time we didn't have. All I could do at that point was hope that dreaded call from Atherton happened later rather than sooner. We tiptoed around that sleeping dog as quietly as possible. It's one thing to slow down payments to a vendor. The due date that we could not miss, even more important than payroll, was for the loan payment to the company that held the keys, somewhat literally, to our business.

Getting through one day at a time was its own strategy. Staying active and keeping in touch with encouraging voices kept me going.

When so many people depend on you, taking care of yourself is nonnegotiable. Otherwise, how can you take care of them? I became more committed to my health and fitness. I played golf on Saturdays as often as possible. As the demands of my job intensified and I worked more and more weekends, running became my preferred way to relieve stress. I'd throw on my shoes, jump out the door, and run a quick three miles in the neighborhood before work. It was efficient and easy, and helped me prepare for tough days.

Father Trayers remained a great friend and mentor to me. He continued to visit and call often, and we played golf together when he was in town. I'd tell him stories about what we were going through. He kept us in his prayers.

I could always count on Grandpap for a boost. He and my grandmother were probably my number one fans. Over numerous phone calls, his general message was the same.

"Hang in there. You got this! You can do it!"

Scott Tocci, a dear friend of my parents who helped them secure financing when the company expanded, called regularly to check on me.

"Hey kid, how are you doing?" he would say, closing our calls with "Don't give up!"

The continued support and the belief that we could get a little bit better every day kept me moving forward. I didn't waste time worrying about tomorrow. I focused on the present, on what we could control today.

As intense as the year was, it was also full of promise. My grandmother had always advised me, "Never ask a lady to marry you until you spend four seasons with her. You've got to make it four seasons." I knew the moment I met Andrea that I was going to marry her, but I honored my grandmother's counsel.

We celebrated the one-year anniversary of the day we met with dinner at a nice Russian restaurant in Atlanta. They served vodka shots between courses, which was good because I was nervous as hell. Her father had given me his blessing a few weeks before. I arranged with the maître d' ahead of time to bring the ring out with dessert. In a weirdly unnatural moment, I left my chair and got down on one knee. Anyone nearby knew what was coming, but surprisingly, Andrea wasn't expecting the question.

"What are you doing? What is going on?" she asked, laughing.

Before she said yes, she said, "I can't marry you until I pay off all my student debt."

To my accountant's heart, those are the most loving words ever spoken. Well, I thought they were. But then, before we were even married, when the company couldn't pay my salary, she took our love language to another level.

"Don't worry," she said. "I'm making good money. You do what you've got to do."

On the Appalachian side trail, I knew I was lost. But for a long time after my father died, I had no idea how bad things were. I didn't notice that the color of the blazes had changed. Maybe that's what kept me going. It's certainly part of it.

"Get through this day," I told myself. "Don't even worry about what's next."

Charles had another version of the one-day-at-a-time strategy. He appealed for help from above.

"Dear God," I often heard him pray, "please, please make tomorrow suck a little bit less than today."

Back in The Day: Lifting at Ben Green's Southern Open

CHAPTER SIX
Making Progress

"If you get one percent better each day for one year, you'll end up thirty-seven times better by the time you're done."

— JAMES CLEAR

I LOVE ROUTINE. I get lost in repetition.

My father drilled a strong work ethic into me. "Doug, the harder you work, the luckier you get," he always said. My weightlifting coach, Ben Green, brought it home by teaching me about progression.

Add weight. Reduce repetitions. Maintain additional weight. Increase repetitions. Repeat.

Lifting a heavy weight over your head is scary. It's hard and maybe even a little crazy. Sometimes, Ben would load the bar and tell me to lift it without my knowing the weight. I never cared about how heavy it was, often doing better when I had no idea what was on the bar. He taught me to trust the process.

I learned that the demons of doubt and distraction bow to stick-to-it-ness. Just pick up the bar. Choose steady advances over a full-scale campaign. When I focused every day on the here and now—thinking only, *This is what I'm going to do today*—results added up. Even when it was hard to measure, nearly intangible, knowing I could improve energized me.

That's what I set my hands to do as the ball dropped on a new millennium. Every day, we tweaked a system, reduced a cost, or made some other incremental adjustment in our operation. Whether or not we were getting it right, I couldn't know. How heavy was the bar? I had no idea. But doing something took my thoughts off the serious possibility of going bankrupt, which was always in the back of my mind.

I was like the guy at the penny poker table, making small gains. Steady wins moved us forward. Two dollars on every hand isn't as sexy as a five-hundred-dollar pot, but it proved to be the better bet in the long run.

"Doug, I want you to answer this question as honestly as possible."

These were the first words out of Scott Curson's mouth. Scott was the new franchise business coach deployed for the Atlanta region, and he was tired of my results being near the bottom of the market.

His question was one I will never forget.

"Are you getting better, or are you getting worse? Or do you even know?"

Scott specialized in turning around tough markets. A no-bullshit guy whose previous assignment was New Orleans, one of Taco Bell's most challenging regions, Scott was mobilized to fix Atlanta. He first signaled his arrival in a blistering email to me deploring my CHAMPS scores.

CHAMPS, an acronym for cleanliness, hospitality, accuracy, maintenance, product quality, and speed, includes a systemized package of checklists, training, and tools to help stores meet the company's standards.

"Your stores are dirty," he said. "You're on the bottom of the ranker, in last place. What the heck is going on?"

Scott's observation wasn't exactly breaking news. I picked up the phone in response.

"Hey, smart guy, I know my scores are bad. Why don't you tell me how to fix them? I need your help."

Fortunately for me, Scott defines problems as opportunities, and he loves to support people who are willing to change.

"You know what? I'm going to teach you how to run restaurants," he said.

Scott became the new Ben Green in my life, but in place of Olympic weightlifting, he taught me how to lift scores and morale at our stores. Scott was my Jedi master. "*Do or do not.*" There was no try.

His mentoring would be critical to our success in more ways than I initially understood. It turned out that Scott answered to the guys who tried to strong-arm Mom and me into selling the restaurants. They hadn't changed their minds about us. As far as they were concerned, we were sinking and sinking fast. Scott was willing to help me bail water and fix leaks while also holding back the corporate whirlpool that threatened to pull us under.

We built a relationship on honesty. I had no idea how to run a restaurant, and I told him so.

"Whatever you know, teach me," I pleaded. "Let's work on this together."

In hindsight, I see that this scenario was perfect. In addition to being a turnaround expert, Scott was a training leader for Taco Bell. He knew the fundamentals of good operations, and he was a great teacher. Thankfully, he was willing, arms wide open, to take me under his wing. Together, we worked on the fundamentals and basic building blocks of what Taco Bell calls running A+ operations.

We took detailed tours of each restaurant so he could become as knowledgeable as possible about our operation. He went to stores with and without me, scouting for reality rather than the dog-and-pony show people tend to give the boss.

"Your store's got to be clean, and you've got to have friendly people," he told me. "All of your equipment has to be working, and you have to deliver fast service. I'm going to show you how to do all this stuff."

He was a straight shooter who told me what we needed to do. He didn't sugarcoat the facts. I always knew where I stood with him and appreciated his frank critiques. If he said, "Hey look, buddy, I was in your store and saw you have this opportunity to improve," I'd thank him and address it.

In Scott's playbook, running a clean store has its own chapter. Why? Because guests don't want to return to neglected establishments.

We implemented a clean-up strategy first before addressing any other challenges. Scott developed a wish list for each restaurant, a series of small steps that would perk them up, making us a little bit better with each improvement. Taco Bell's Clean Sweep was a literal form that, task by task, broke down the six areas of the store to concentrate on for cleanliness. The form included a checklist of fifty items from the exterior, dining room, bathrooms, kitchen, walk-in, and office. Each area included anywhere from three to seventeen items that needed to be clean or tidy, with each item on the checklist awarded up to two points for a total of one hundred. The dining room and kitchen accounted for 60 percent of the list. From baseboards to ceilings and all the surfaces and equipment in between, these daily to-dos, when executed properly, kept us in good shape.

"If we make sure these items are clean all the time, then your store will be clean," Scott said.

Pressure washing gets its own paragraph. Why? Because it's not only looks that people judge from the outside. A tired, dingy restaurant is not inviting, especially when the Chick-fil-A down the street is gleaming. So, I bought a pickup truck and put a standard pressure washer, the kind you'd have at home, in the back. At least two Sundays a month, I showed up at five in the morning to wash the grime off our buildings. Sunday mornings were usually the slowest day of the week, so I scoured walls and sidewalks until the drive-thru opened. I never found a fast or easy way to do it, and I never got particularly good at it. You'd need commercial equipment for that.

I'm not handy, but I kept paint cans and tools in the truck for touch-ups and quick fixes. Sometimes, I made things worse rather than better, but I was showing up. You'd be surprised, even today, how many restaurants are open with lights that don't work, broken bathroom doors and mirrors, and other visible signs of neglect. Scott taught me that you can't overlook that stuff.

"You've got to be proud of your store," Scott told me. "If you're proud of it, then your employees will be proud, and they'll respect it."

Customers notice and feel good about coming to see you, he explained, even if they don't know why.

My father's exacting standards for lawn care served me well during this time. For a while, I cut the grass at the restaurants with a push mower. You think cutting grass is easy, but what if you sling a rock into a car in the parking lot? Trust me. That's not fun. Eventually, I scouted out the landscaping at the best-maintained competitors in the market and hired the same vendor whenever possible.

Painting was immensely important. A restaurant loves a new coat of paint as much as my dad and the US Navy. Ideally, you want fresh paint on your stores at least every two years, especially back then when they weren't brick like they are today. Thankfully, I found a contractor who gave us a good deal on this service. Similarly, striping and sealing parking lots made a big difference, too.

Whenever there was any free cash flow, I reinvested it in the stores. If we made an extra thousand bucks, I'd get a store painted. If we made an extra two thousand dollars, we painted two stores. We never stopped looking for ways to make physical improvements to our restaurants.

Next, Scott pulled a variety of reports out of his toolbox to help us take a hard look at sales. These reports were also tailored to the performance at individual locations. Scott's tools told us not only where sales could be improved but also which part of the day presented those opportunities he loved so much. Compared to same-store sales growth, was it lunch or dinner that was off-peak? We discovered that during some periods in the day, we were extremely limiting our potential. Once we had this information, we dove in deep to understand why this particular time frame was declining or not growing. In most cases, we learned, not surprisingly, that the primary problem was staffing.

To address this issue, we covered another fundamental to make sure we had enough trained team members to cover us when we lost people. Having a pipeline of people ready to move into shift management or store leadership was our first goal. If someone quit or was fired, we needed someone ready to step into the gap.

Scott taught me that too many franchisees staff their stores based on today's sales or what they expect those sales to be. When they don't reach these projections, they cut employees. But proper staffing improves speed and service, which improves sales by allowing more transactions per hour and bringing customers back, he explained. To that end, we took a hard look at staffing and hiring practices.

Scott conducted our restaurant manager meetings, spending two or three hours having candid conversations with our general managers. Having the best person in each position, he taught us, is the master key to success. It sounds simple, but it is far from easy.

Scott helped me realize that some of the people we had in place weren't getting the job done. We weren't holding them accountable. The best way to turn this around, he suggested, was for me to spend more time in the restaurants. He was right. Being present and conquering the day-to-day obstacles side by side with the managers and teams changed the culture, which is easier to say than it is to do.

Nothing was too basic. Coaching opportunities included teaching people what a proper uniform looked like, how to put on a name tag, and how to keep your hat on straight. My dad never cared about uniforms, partly because he didn't want to pay for them. As a result, people were accustomed to coming to work dressed however they wanted. I kept a stack of uniforms in every size in my car. When I asked people to put on a uniform, and they said they didn't have one, I was ready.

"Guess what? I've got a whole stack of them. What size do you wear?"

I got to know the people on the front line. We talked about their kids, grandkids, husbands, and wives. We cared about family and, therefore, became one. The more they saw me investing in the stores, the more they trusted me and had my back. We worked on the basics and began to get good at them.

It was a motley crew, me included, but the trust level meant that when things went wrong, they'd tell me the truth. I'll never forget this one manager who decided to prop open the walk-in cooler to cool down the kitchen. Of course, the compressor blew up. When I asked why "Why would you deliberately leave the cooler door open?"—he explained, "Well, the air conditioner was out in the kitchen, and we were hot."

Ultimately, some of our people had to be replaced. Most of the original team, either by my choice or their own, didn't make the cut. They weren't willing to do what it takes to get better. Seeing the problems regularly, in person, reinforced those decisions. I was empathetic but firm.

"You've got to get with the program, or you've got to go because we can't tolerate mediocrity anymore."

I was ripping off Band-Aids, letting managers go who weren't pulling their weight, creating huge holes in the operation. To get better, though, I had to shake off the doubts and press on. We needed managers who knew how to run restaurants with challenges because maintaining a smooth operation and wrangling a fixer-upper are two different skill sets.

It was tough love, and it was scary. Coming home at night, I'd second guess myself.

What am I doing? I'm running more people off than we're getting. Am I being too hard? Maybe we should just settle on some of this stuff.

Charles and Carla came behind me to pick up the slack. Charles would come in and do paperwork in the mornings and then head to a restaurant to train people and maintain stability in the store. He and Carla covered lunch wherever we had the most problems while I scouted for new talent.

Charles and I used football analogies to help us articulate what we were looking for. The manager of a corporate store who was commuting nearly two hours a day from Newnan to another Taco Bell in the metro area came to work for us. We called her our Barry Sanders. We needed a running back, somebody who could actually run the operation. We brought her home to Newnan, and she did exactly that. She stabilized the restaurant, got it clean, and freed us up to focus on other stores.

I looked for people who could do this and who at least knew the basics of a P&L. When I had an extra five hundred bucks a month, I'd invest it in people like this. And then, when they were on board and performing, I would ask, "How can we make this job a little bit better for you?" Sometimes, it took a little more money. Sometimes, it was about quality of life.

"I want some time off to be with my family," our running back said. "You got it. Sunday's off."

The final piece of the operations puzzle involved a training tool I didn't know about before I worked with Scott. Taco Bell has a million acronyms. In a Taco Bell glossary, TRED stands for Target Setting–Rush Ready–Equipment Working–Deployment. TRED was developed in the early '90s to improve the speed of service at the drive-thru, where two-thirds or more of all orders were being placed, most of them during the hour-and-a-half lunch period. The strategy married kitchen design, equipment, and processes to solve the problem of bottlenecks and staffing.

"Is your headset working?" Questions like this provided operational assessments. It worked so well that the time between when a customer placed, paid for, and received an order was usually under the company-wide target of three and a half minutes. Scott taught me how to execute TRED at a high level in the Newnan store. I took this training to our remaining locations and did my best to emulate what I had learned.

This may be the best example of the difference between my father's way of running the business and my approach. TRED had been in place for years by the time I first heard of it. My father surely knew about it, but his mindset was that corporate people cause problems. When people in Scott's position came through with new ideas or company mandates, he'd send them out the door as fast as possible. But then he'd come to me internally and say, "We've got to fix this and get Taco Bell off our ass."

Dad wasn't the only one who slammed the door behind the corporate guy. Many franchisees had a similar mindset. I was the opposite. When Scott stated the obvious, "Hey, your stores are dirty, and you're on the bottom of the ranker," I said, "How do we fix it?"

In a way, I think I may have been a gift to Scott. My responsiveness was refreshing compared to what he usually experienced. And he was a priceless gift to me, one I will never be able to repay.

Scott became an invaluable mentor and a lifelong friend. He gave us the plays, the tools, and the training we needed to execute the standards that corporate and, more importantly, the customer demanded. Conquering the seemingly small, everyday opportunities to improve was our mission. The basics, the easiest and yet hardest things to do, were our daily reps. For the first time since I came to work for my father, we had a plan, and that plan gave me hope that we could get better.

Looking back on this, I am reminded of this ancient wisdom of Sun Tzu's *The Art of War*:

> *"Strategy without tactics is the slowest route to victory. Tactics without strategy is the noise before defeat."*

Scott schooled me in this battlefield principle. CHAMPS was strategy. TRED was tactics. I soaked up what he taught like a sponge, and we put the concepts to work. For two years, maybe more, we spent hours together in the stores, fixing one problem at a time, one day at a time. Scott helped us establish the importance of training. Newnan became the school where our new managers and staff learned the procedures and guidelines that led to better operations. We continued to maintain a training center in Newnan as a result of his guidance.

His fundamental strategies set in motion the flywheel concept Jim Collins describes in *Good to Great*. As Collins explains, it takes a lot of energy and time to begin to move a huge flywheel, but once it's turning, it takes less and less energy and time to sustain the movement.

Transformation didn't happen overnight, but relentless improvement created momentum that generated victories over time.

Those wins kept us alive. On Friday mornings, when his bosses teleconferenced to rack and stack franchise performances for the week, Scott defended us.

"He has the mindset and willingness to do what it takes," he told them. "We can make this a great organization. I know we can."

When corporate analysts leaned on him to push us out of business, he held our position. Between those calls, he was a powerful ally. An antidote to fear, he moved us from disaster to hope to real, measurable improvement.

Our Big Adventure

CHAPTER SEVEN

Owed to Andrea

"Alone we can do so little. Together we can do so much."

— HELEN KELLER

THE SUNDAY EVENING PHONE CALL that led to my first date with Andrea marked the beginning of our Big Adventure.

Cell phones were new at that time. People weren't in the habit of handing out their numbers. However, Andrea broke her protocol and gave me her number two days before when we met to discuss how her company could help us with payroll.

"Call me if you have any questions," she said.

I had questions, the kind that can't wait until normal business hours.

For three hours, we yakked about topics ranging from music to books to travel to outdoor adventures. She was interested in skydiving. Hiking the Appalachian Trail fueled my interest in other nature conquests. At the time, I was reading *Into Thin Air*, Jon Krakauer's personal account of the 1996 Mt. Everest disaster that killed eight climbers and stranded several more in a storm. One thing led to another, and our first date was to see the documentary film *Everest* at the IMAX theater in Atlanta.

We went to an afternoon movie. Unbeknownst to Andrea, I had made dinner reservations in case we still liked each other after the movie. Since we were having a good time, I said, "Hey, do you want to get something to eat?"

"Yeah, sure."

We made it to dinner at South City Kitchen at six o'clock. The conversation never stopped as appetizers led to entrées, which led to desserts, and another dessert, and then coffee. At ten o'clock, the waitstaff was encouraging us to wrap it up.

"You guys need to go," they said, more or less.

The next morning, I told my dad, "I've met the girl I'm going to marry." That same day, Andrea told her father, "I went out with the guy I'm going to marry."

Steve Jobs said you can't connect the dots looking forward. You can only see how a story comes together after the fact. Our Big Adventure began with talks of big adventures. And the party just kinda never stopped.

Phase one of falling in love with Andrea wasn't just exciting; it was therapeutic. I thought about her all the time. Really, I was obsessed. She was the center of all that I looked forward to, proof that life was more than work. We were yin and yang. She gave me a balance I didn't even know I needed. Andrea accepted me for who I was and became my best friend.

Weekends were nonstop. When we weren't at concerts or football games, we were on our way for beer and wings at Moe's and Joe's Tavern in Atlanta. Initially, what we had most in common was a love of music. We loved many of the same bands and expanded each other's tastes, too.

Much of the background music for our life came from new releases from REM, the Dave Matthews Band, and Lucinda Williams, whose album *Car Wheels on a Gravel Road* gave us our theme song, "Right In Time." Andrea was right in time with me.

The escapades started early.

The first time I met Andrea's father wasn't the kind of occasion that guaranteed a parental stamp of approval. We hadn't been dating long when Joe Salemi came up from Tampa to visit his daughter. On the one hand, we looked forward to a fun weekend. No pressure. Let's do the ATL.

On the other hand, this was a man who had two daughters he would walk to the end of the earth and back for. Andrea told me that even while her dad worked long hours building a successful corporate career, he still found time to make breakfast and pack lunches for his girls. And they returned his love in full measure. Here was a guy who set a high bar for what it means to be a good man. I tried not to think about his expectations or his daughter's.

A friend of my dad gave us tickets to an Atlanta Falcons game, and we took her father, also a huge football fan, along for a front-row seat on the sideline experience. Seeing and interacting with the players is always fun, so I think it's safe to say our getting-to-know-you weekend started well.

After the game, we came back to Newnan, where my plan was to take them for an evening boat ride at my parents' lakeside home. Andrea and her dad got into the boat, and from the dock, I proceeded to lower it into the water. Suddenly, the lift broke and flipped the boat over on top of both of them. Her dad's glasses, camera, and wallet ended up at the bottom of the lake.

Rather than jumping in the water in my nice clothes, I stripped down to my boxers and dove in to retrieve his belongings. I'm sure he was thinking, *What's this idiot doing, taking off all his clothes in front of me and jumping in the lake?*

So much for first impressions. Soaking wet, I fetched towels and some of my parents' clothes for us to wear, and the sun went down on a weekend the three of us never forgot.

Strangely, the memorable evening fulfilled one of my future father-in-law's lifelong dreams. He told me that for years, as long as he could remember, he had a recurring dream about his wallet getting wet. I guess it was my destiny to make his dream come true.

On his birthday, nearly a year later, I nervously asked for his blessing to marry his daughter. Thankfully, he didn't hold our initial meeting against me. Instead, the table turned, and he told me how proud he was of us and how grateful he was to have me in their lives. On that emotional day, he paved the way for my dreams to come true, too.

Joe passed down his work ethic to his girls. Andrea was phenomenal at her job. Driven and disciplined, she was a top sales rep for a payroll processing company and determined to maintain that ranking. Thank goodness because it meant she was compensated well enough to take care of us when Georgia-Texas could not afford to pay me.

Her office was in Smyrna, forty-seven miles from Newnan. Her territory was another thirty miles north of there. Both commutes put her in some of the city's worst traffic and meant hours in the car every day. Neither of us could see how to find time for a life together at the end of those long days and weeks. She resigned from her position at the end of 1999, a few months after we became engaged, with plans to come to work with me.

Unfortunately, we didn't realize the extent of the company's financial trouble when this decision was made. Shortly after the first of the year, she asked for her job back. Her company was thrilled, promoting her to a district sales manager in Birmingham, their worst market at the time.

She traded a bad commute for an impossible one, which meant she spent part of the week in Alabama and part of the week in Newnan. It wasn't what we wanted, but it was a problem we had to solve later.

Andrea wanted a fall wedding, but that was a nonstarter for me.

"In the middle of football season? No way!"

We compromised and married in May. Since home base for both of us was the Atlanta area, we opted to have the ceremony in Newnan. After a miserably hot rehearsal dinner, we woke up to a beautiful day, the kind the South delivers when she really wants to please you.

Andrea's mom, dad, stepmom, sister, and other family members came up from Florida for the celebration. My family poured in from all over the country. When your mother has seven siblings and everyone is close, the guest list swells. My aunts, uncles, and cousins easily accounted for half or more of the 175 people who came to our wedding.

Father Trayers officiated the ceremony at St. George Catholic Church. Grandpap was my best man. Andrea's sister was the maid of honor.

What we both remember most about the day was that it was a hell of a party. The band played an hour and a half longer than scheduled. When our guests pleaded with them to stay longer, offering to pay for more, they begged off in exhaustion.

"Our fingers hurt. We. Cannot. Play. Guitar. Anymore."

One of my aunts hauled out bottles of wine for everyone. A friend of Andrea's was on the dance floor with an enormous turkey leg. Even Andrea's mom, who was sober, danced on a table.

After Andrea and I left, people took up donations to reopen the bar. We heard they raided the kitchen before the night was done. It was just a crazy, fun time.

The video from the reception consists of stationary footage, disappointingly from only a single angle. Reviewing it, we were puzzled.

"Who's the guy drinking beer and dancing with all the girls?"

It was the videographer, who had put the camera on a tripod and proceeded to party along with everyone else.

My father was missed, especially by me, but I still see that thumbs-up he gave me on the day Andrea and I met. He met Andrea only briefly one other time before he died, but I know he would have loved the day and the way our families came together.

My mom had taken care of most of the wedding plans and arrangements. On our home turf, she knew all the vendors and possibilities. From venues to flowers, she was excited about every detail.

Meanwhile, both Andrea and I were drowning in work. It was year-end for her, the last month to reach sales quotas. And, of course, I was going from restaurant to restaurant, doing my best to keep the company afloat. The week leading up to the wedding was anxiety-ridden. Even with Mom's help, so many decisions and people had to be dealt with.

By the time we landed in Bermuda for our honeymoon, we were both overdue a break. It had been a while since either of us had been on any kind of vacation. I was wound tight. A breathtaking change of scenery a thousand miles away from home was the perfect antidote for too many long-ass days.

The love of travel and exploration that brought us together officially launched in Bermuda. We set the pattern for many future adventures by renting a moped and getting inside the local culture. We rode all over the island, leaving the typical tourist's beaten path to find the places where the locals lived and ate. It was a great week, with the exception of one memorably bad decision.

Just across the causeway from the airport is The Swizzle Inn Pub, a rustic local icon and favorite first or last stop for many thirsty visitors. The island's oldest pub, it is home to Bermuda's "national drink," the Rum Swizzle. Served by the jug since 1932, the fruity drink is responsible for the tagline, "Swizzle In, Swagger Out." It's officially labeled "infamous" on the menu, and I am a personal witness to this well-deserved adjective.

A couple of days before we were scheduled to return home, Andrea and I slipped into The Swizzle Inn, where we met another couple on their honeymoon. The husband's name was also Doug, and that was all it took to make us drinking buddies. The two of us downed a few jugs of the pub's potent libation before the night was over. He was probably three times my size and held his own, but by the time we left, I was drunker than Cooter Brown. And not just drunk but belligerent. Loud. Obnoxious. Absolutely out of control. Andrea was in shock.

I spent the next day in the hotel room, green as Bermuda grass. When I wasn't in bed, I was throwing up. Meanwhile, she was hanging out on the beach by herself, thinking, *Oh my God, who did I just marry?*

It wasn't pretty. And Andrea wasn't happy. But it was a great opportunity to learn a few valuable lessons.

First, a guy named Doug may drink you under the table. Beware.

Second, be sure to marry someone who doesn't hold grudges. You always know where you stand with Andrea. She will tell you like it is, but she doesn't let conflicts fester. It's one of her most admirable traits.

"I don't like how you acted, and I don't know who you are," she said, but once she got it off her chest, she was fine.

Third, never miss an opportunity to apologize.

"I have no idea what happened. I'm so sorry."

The worst hangover—*ever*—was behind us, but neither of us had any idea what was ahead. The coolest thing about Andrea is that she has always had this underlying trust that everything was going to work out.

I hadn't drawn a salary in months. We were living on her income. Neither the dire predictions of naysayers nor the concerns of well-meaning family members mattered to her. I was the man she wanted to be with. This was the life we chose. Whatever happened, it would be all right.

She was the living, breathing trifecta of faith, hope, and love. How did I ever get so lucky?

Andrea believed in me, which made me even more determined to succeed. Now I had somebody else, someone who cared about me, supported me, and helped me. From day one, even when my father died, she was there. She showed up. She was present.

Andrea was my sounding board. When I came home absolutely smoked, she heard my tales of woe. Someone stole a deposit. Someone else did something outrageous. Food costs were out of control. We'd get phone calls from managers at two in the morning. It was guerrilla warfare every day.

I am cautious with bad news. I don't go around advertising it. It doesn't do any good to worry other people about something they can't control. So when I was out in the field, I was onstage, working the plan. I couldn't show weakness. When I said, "This is what we're doing, and this is the direction we're headed," I had to be positive and upbeat.

But with Andrea, I was able to be vulnerable. I could have some humility, a chance to cry and to shake my head and say, "What in the world are we going to do?"

Level-headed and street-smart, she gave me a much-needed outside perspective and plenty of encouragement, too. She didn't try to fix things. She listened, nurtured, and consoled.

She was my balance, my coach, my cheerleader, and the voice of reason that talked me off the ledge. When I was beat down, she was the battery that charged me up and moved me back out the door the next morning.

Thank God. Because plenty of beatdowns took place that year.

Letters flew back and forth from me to lenders, vendors, corporate reps, employees, and more. The overarching goal was to free up cash flow. Running operations in the black was my first priority in the steps to reaching this goal. Our other options for stabilizing the situation were to sell stores we couldn't turn around and refinance debt whenever possible. Simultaneously pursuing all these objectives generated plenty of opportunities for disappointments and discord.

In September, the StarLink Crisis crash-landed on the scene when *The New York Times* broke the news about Kraft Foods' nationwide recall of taco shells. The shells contained genetically engineered corn that had been approved for animal feed but not for consumption by humans. It was the first recall of its kind in the country. The crisis got its name from the StarLink corn at the center of the debacle.

It was a public relations disaster. StarLink sent a tidal wave through the company and many associated industries. From big businesses to mom-and-pop franchises, people who were in business at the beginning of this story disappeared because of StarLink.

Although restaurants weren't affected as much as they could have been, particularly in the Southeast, Taco Bell's same-store sales were already down for the year. A decade of cost-cutting decisions the company had made affected quality. Even the brand's most loyal customer base noticed. They let us know how they felt about it by taking their munchies elsewhere. As far as I was concerned, external factors beyond my control stacked even more bad hands onto the house of cards we lived in.

Five months after we married, when we didn't have the cash to cover payroll and my worst fears flirted dangerously with the facts, Andrea held fast. When I wondered what more could possibly go wrong with the company, she never wavered.

"We'll get through it," she'd say. "We'll be all right."

I can never express how grateful I am to her.

CHAPTER EIGHT

Making a Run for It

"It's hard to beat somebody when they don't give up."

— BABE RUTH

UNLIKE TODAY, WHEN PAYMENTS for most expenses are automatically debited from our accounts, at the turn of the century, we were still paying invoices by check. Typical terms were Net 15, which meant the bill was due in fifteen days. If we were late sending in a payment, a penalty might be 1.5 percent. So if an invoice was for a thousand dollars, the cost of a late payment might be fifteen dollars.

The vendor we wrote the biggest and most frequent checks to was the company that supplied our food. We ran restaurants, after all. Food costs were our single biggest expense. Without food, we didn't have a product to sell. But without people, we can't deliver the product, so when we needed to find twenty thousand dollars to meet payroll, I faced a difficult decision. Initiating a slow pay strategy was dicey, but fifteen dollars was a low price to pay for staying in business another week.

It was never my intention to not pay our food vendor. You can't stay in business operating like that. I would deal with it when they called to say, "When are you going to pay your bills?"

Which is what happened. Kinda.

Our food distributor, AmeriServe, filed for Chapter 11 bankruptcy protection in the first quarter of 2000. Taco Bell and our parent company, Tricon Global Restaurants, represented nearly half of AmeriServe's business. No other company could easily and quickly handle the volume or intricate supply chain of the thirty thousand restaurants under the Tricon umbrella. From taco fixings to napkins, those weekly shipments were essential to our operations. We could not afford for them to go out of business, so Tricon loaned AmeriServe money to continue operating. This short-term financing bought time to find another solution.

A couple of months after we slowed our payments for food and supplies, a new distributor, McLane Company, took AmeriServ's place. In January of 2001, Taco Bell called and said they were cleaning up AmeriServe's books.

"It looks like you owe some money from last year," they said.

"Yeah, you're right, but I have no idea how much," I said.

"Well, we have no idea how much you owe either."

This went on for two or three months. Finally, they threw out a number.

"We have no idea how much you owe. We really don't. We think it might be around a hundred thousand, but we just don't know."

"Tell you what. I'll pay you sixty thousand dollars. I'll send you twenty thousand today and then pay ten thousand a month until it's paid off."

"Okay."

Poof! We were able to float the money we originally owed for about six months and even reduced the bill. I am sorry the situation turned out the way it did for AmeriServe, but this unexpected turn of events got us through some turbulent days. When you're living in a house of cards, a little luck never hurts anything.

McLane put all of us on an automatic draft payment system and gave us a discount for prepaying. Maybe this was already their process, or perhaps they learned from our previous vendor's demise. Either way, it was a great idea. Learning from other people's mistakes is always cheaper than making them yourself.

We were gaining momentum just by cleaning up the stores and upgrading our manager talent. It was slow, but I sensed we were getting better. We weren't making any money, but we weren't losing money anymore, either. That was a huge win.

By February of 2001, Emil Brolick, the new president of Taco Bell, was getting national press for his efforts to improve quality. Emil had been at the helm of the brand for six months, coming to Taco Bell after leading the strategy that drove Wendy's sales success for twelve years. He told the *Wall Street Journal* he planned to fix sales by keeping low-priced customer faves on the menu while adding new items at higher prices. It worked for him at Wendy's, and he believed it would help Taco Bell.

Emil had a fight on his hands, not only with the consumer but also with franchisees. Falling sales compounded by the AmeriServe and StarLink disasters did not help restaurants or the relationship between store owners and the corporate office. Although the company had created a loan program to bail out struggling owners, some large groups had filed for bankruptcy protection.

Emil entered an arena where plenty of blood had already been spilled. He brought the two sides together by being brutally honest about the facts. First, he identified our five biggest problems: slow service, dirty restaurants, unfriendly employees, poorly maintained facilities, and product quality. His team ranked all restaurants in the system with a grade level, A through F, based on CHAMPS scores and secret shopper visits, then deployed strategic forces to intervene in stores ranking D or below.

At the same time, he launched a campaign to defend the taco, which easily made up a quarter of restaurant sales. The brand was under assault for skimping on the quality and quantity of ingredients. Dissatisfied customers who grew up in the era of Air Jordans had taken to calling our signature menu item "air tacos," a moniker our new leader could not abide. Emil was on a mission to restore the reputation of our bread and butter.

"Our name is Taco Bell, and we're going to live up to it," Emil told us all. "We're going to sell a full taco. That's what we're going to do."

To that end, he pushed through a mandate to weigh every taco before it left the kitchen. Any item that came in under three ounces was sent back down the line.

He also rolled out an operating system known as Growth Cube. In another lucky break, we were one of the first franchisees asked to test these new tools, which initiated a specific set of routines as well as a process for accountability and follow-up. By now, you probably know that's my kind of plan. I'm never happier than in a den of discipline.

Emil ushered in a new era at Taco Bell. He was not afraid of problems. In fact, he went after them like they were gold. I loved that about him. Emil taught me the value of problems and mistakes. It wasn't always fun, but eventually, I learned that we don't learn much when we're getting things right. We learn from our mistakes. The more we make, the smarter we get.

This slow but steady stream of luck and progress gave Andrea and me the courage to make a change in the spring. The two of us were at a crossroads, both running on a deficit of sleep, energy, and just about everything else.

For nearly eighteen months, Andrea left Newnan on Sunday nights to drive 133 miles to Birmingham, Alabama, where she continued to dominate nationwide sales in what was once a poor-performing market for her company. Her weeks were long and challenging. My number one cheerleader, she never faltered, but there were never enough hours in the day, and none left for time together.

Meanwhile, I was in the restaurants from dawn to dark. On Saturdays, I sought sanity on the golf course. I can't toss you the cliché about ships passing in the night because we weren't even seeing each other go by. We were headed in different directions. Not only did we miss each other, but we both knew it wasn't good for us. Separation and fatigue take a toll on a marriage.

Finally, we took a leap of faith. Andrea quit her job and came to work with me. There was no plan. We'd been living on her salary since before we married, and Georgia-Texas was perpetually sixty days away from bankruptcy, but we agreed to just figure it out. Personally, our financial overhead was low. We had a small house and a small mortgage. Our bills were manageable, and Andrea cashed in some of her 401(k) to tide us over.

"Your 401(k) is there for a reason," her father warned. "You need to leave that alone."

But she was resolute.

"Look, we've got to be all in," she told him. "It's the only way it's going to work."

Andrea became an employee of Georgia-Texas Enterprises on June 7, 2001. We flipped the equation from hardly ever seeing each other to being together twenty-four hours a day. For the next eighteen months, she was my shadow.

We usually started the day in the car and headed to one of our restaurants, where she worked on the line like every other employee. She was convinced the best way for her to learn the operation was to do the work. We often covered more than one location in a day. She made tacos and burritos while I helped managers with whatever they needed.

At her former job, Andrea learned a lot about interviewing, hiring, and firing from some amazing mentors. She was excellent at reading people and honest about situations where employees weren't doing the job. Her experience as a manager was especially helpful on the people side of operations. It wasn't always easy to hear, but when she said we needed to weed some people out and start over, I knew she was right.

Andrea taught me the importance of following up with people. As they say in the military, "Don't expect what you don't inspect."

Those long days seem far away, but memories of working alongside Andrea are vivid. Early mornings in the car, going over the day's schedule, brainstorming, strategizing. Afternoons between locations, talking about personnel, problem-solving. Evenings at home, tired, but together. It's impossible to exaggerate the importance of her support to the company's survival. To my survival. I would not have made it without her. No way. Having her in my corner every day was even more important when we faced one of the biggest brawls of my life.

Atherton Capital loved my dad. They absolutely loved him. A commercial finance company, Atherton provided financing to experienced franchisors of quick-service restaurants, convenience stores, and other similarly positioned businesses. They funded my father's expansion from one to seven restaurants in what may have been the first deal they made for a Taco Bell franchisee.

Dad's story was featured on the cover of *Franchise Times* magazine, and it highlighted Atherton's huge role in the expansion of our business. They threw a party for him at the first convention I attended as an employee of Georgia-Texas Enterprises. No expense was spared for the five-star occasion at The Broadmoor in Colorado Springs.

They loved his resourcefulness, his "never take no for an answer," and his creativity. Their whole relationship was built on finding a way to get to the finish line. Unfortunately, their affection for my father did not transfer to me when he died. In fact, it seemed like they hated me with a murderous passion.

This part of my story brings to mind Mike Tyson's famous words: "Everybody has a plan until they get punched in the face."

We had a plan. We were improving operations one day at a time, finding ways to improve sales, recruiting and training our team, and reducing costs where we could. We made our payments on time, continuing to tiptoe around the sleeping dog in the Atherton situation. We could not afford for them to discover that we were in violation of our loan covenants.

The loan agreement was clear. Georgia-Texas was not allowed to close or open a new store without Atherton's permission. Yet, without their knowledge, Dad had built a new store in East Point with a new lender to replace the store they held as collateral. I'm sure he planned to continue making payments while looking for a buyer for the existing building, but he didn't live long enough to do that.

I don't remember who punched who in the face, but when they discovered we were in default because of my dad's creative financing, that dog woke up in a horrible mood. We were in trouble. Huge trouble. Atherton suited up the legal team and brought the fight.

I think they were mad at the situation and, maybe in some ways, even took my dad's death out on me. They needed somebody to pin it on. They couldn't blame my dad because he wasn't there anymore. With zero empathy, they pulled no punches. Of course, they expected their payments to continue being made on time, but they also wanted to know my detailed plan for pulling the company back from the brink of bankruptcy.

Legally, they had the right to call the loan. If they did, we would be down for the count. Game over. My mom would owe four million dollars immediately. That's a lot of tacos. It would be impossible for us to scrape that much money up. In fact, when we had the stores valued, they were worth about half of what we owed. Not that it made any difference. We didn't have two million dollars, either, nor did we have a plan for refinancing. I needed to duck and weave their jabs, deflecting their attention to protect my mom while looking for alternate solutions.

For months, Brian Wooldridge and I were in the ring together on hour-long weekly conference calls with Atherton's portfolio manager and their attorney. I gave updates on our progress, our sales reports, and what we were doing to improve our situation.

We tag-teamed them in a good-cop, bad-cop way. I was the good guy.

"I hope to sell one of our underperforming stores back to corporate," I told them. "I'll give you all the proceeds."

Atherton never let up. They were really nasty to me. Every call was brutal.

"What's going on with Tricon?" they'd ask. "Are they going to buy the store? You're still in default. What are you going to do about that?"

"Look, we're working on it, but this stuff takes time," I'd say. "I'm not arguing. There's nothing that you're saying that I don't agree with."

"Yeah? Well, we're calling back next week for an update. We better hear something new."

Whatever they threw at me, Brian always had my back.

"Don't you talk to him like that," he'd say. "Doug didn't do this. This was his dad. You've got the wrong guy. He's trying to work with you."

After these calls, I desperately looked for remedies to relieve the tension. I'm not a smoker, but I tried taking up cigars. I would pace and puff and, usually, cough. It didn't help. Sometimes, I would lie on the floor and try to catch my breath. Charles, finding me in this position more than once, was always amused by it.

"What'cha doing down there, Doug?"

"Oh my gosh, this is real," I answered from the carpet. "They're coming after us. I've got to do something."

In July, I started a sixteen-week training program for my first marathon. Because my life wasn't punishing enough? Because I needed to be able to outrun Atherton's bad guys? Because I couldn't say no to a challenge? Probably all of those statements are true.

My Uncle Steve was turning forty that year, and I was turning thirty. We both wanted to run a marathon before our respective milestone birthdays, so we agreed to run it together. We registered for the 26th Marine Corps Marathon without a clue of what that meant.

I had no idea what I was doing. I had been running since I went to work with my father, but I knew zilch about heart rate, hydration, electrolytes, or any of that stuff. The longest run I'd ever been on was a six-mile road race. I had four months to learn how to go eighteen more miles.

Jeff Galloway's *Marathon: You Can Do It!* was my textbook. His regimen gave me a plan. A lot like the CHAMPS program, it provided me with an assessment of where I was and a road map to the finish line. I had the same goal for the race that I had for the business at that time. We had to endure.

Andrea and I were in our Taco Bell uniforms on our way to work together when we heard the news on the radio about the attacks on the World Trade Center. As reports poured in all morning, the only thing that was clear was that nothing was clear anymore. Any problems we had, any plans we had, any problems or plans anyone had, were on pause.

The 2001 Marine Corps Marathon was on-again, off-again after 9/11. Canceling the race was under discussion, as was changing the route, which went right by the Pentagon. For a few weeks, we didn't know whether or not the event would take place. At the last minute, organizers decided not to let the terrorists win. Instead, they dedicated the race held on October 28 to the memory of Americans who had died on September 11, the survivors of the tragic event, and the heroes who saved so many lives that day.

It was the most patriotic event of my life. Some people ran the entire marathon wrapped in American flags. Spectators chanted U-S-A, U-S-A, U-S-A. We passed within fifty yards of the Pentagon, where nearly two hundred people had died when terrorists flew American Airlines Flight 77 into the headquarters of the Department of Defense. The crash site was a bleeding wound that made me nauseated.

Andrea had been there until that morning when she flew back to Tampa because of the death of her grandmother, so I was by myself for the race. Between miles twenty and twenty-six, I hated myself. It was freezing cold, and the dark voice of doubt told me my feet hurt, I wasn't good enough, my country was wounded, and my business was failing.

"Just start walking," I heard.

If you ever start walking in a race, it's nearly impossible to run again. The voice in your head can be a terrorist, too.

On behalf of all Americans, a guy from Hawaii came in first in two hours and twenty-eight minutes. A twenty-four-year-old guy from my part of the world, Atlanta, Georgia, came in at two hours and fifty-six minutes. I finished in four hours, twenty minutes, and forty-seven seconds. Uncle Steve was eight seconds behind me. The average finisher took four hours and thirty-eight minutes. We were eighteen minutes ahead of most other runners. As far as I'm concerned, that was a win.

Back at the hotel room, I cranked up the heat and ordered a large pizza and a six-pack. One beer and half a pizza later, I was asleep. The next day, I couldn't walk. The last thing I ever wanted to do was run another marathon.

All I could think about was, *Man, this sucked.*

Uncle Steve and I finished the Marine Corps Marathon together six weeks after 9/11.

CHAPTER NINE
Stormy Weather

"Not all storms come to disrupt your life.
Some come to clear your path."

— PAULO COELHO

IT RAINS ALL THE TIME on the Appalachian Trail. If you're not walking in the rain, then you're keeping an eye on the clouds because you'll be walking in the rain again soon. It didn't take me long to learn to put my supplies in a trash bag before loading my pack.

It's hard to walk in the rain. It beats you down mentally. Sometimes, rain turns into storms. And sometimes those storms are dangerous.

One spring, Bob Lore and I were hiking a section of the AT named after the mountain peak it scales, The Priest. The mountain towers over the Tye River Valley, about halfway across the 551 miles of trail that pass through the state of Virginia. From the starting point to the mountaintop, a 13 percent grade takes hikers up three thousand feet. It's not the steepest part of the trek, but it's a steady uphill walk.

Bob and I had separated earlier in the day. I don't know whether I was ahead or behind him, but about halfway up the mountain, a storm came out of nowhere. Lightning was popping all around me. I didn't know what to do. It's a six-hour hike for most people. Backtracking seemed like losing ground, and what would it help anyway? Finally, I sat and waited it out. For thirty minutes, maybe more, I crouched on the forest floor amid towering trees in pouring rain and lightning. I could not hide or escape from it.

The AT taught me a lot about being prepared. Shit happens out there. You better be creative, and you better be ready for it.

Charles and I were always thinking of imaginative ways to weather the business storms that came our way after my father died. One of Charles's ideas helped us climb out of a sales slump when other franchisees were sliding down the mountain. Coupons on the back of grocery store receipts had worked well for the company in the early '90s. When corporate marketing wasn't helping us, Charles took a derivative of the grocery store receipt idea and started printing coupons of our own.

He found a deal on construction paper from a company that was going out of business, used a word processing document for graphic design, and began printing stacks and stacks of coupons for the stores to distribute at the drive-thru. We alternated buy-one-get-one deals on the Nacho Bell Grande, the Mexican Pizza, and the most successful—*we called it our nuclear bomb BOGO*—the Taco Salad. Charles spent whole afternoons producing thousands of these coupons because taking them to a printer down the street cost more than doing it himself. The result was double-digit sales growth in some of our weakest markets.

We didn't make a lot of money on these promotions, but our loyal customer base grew. When corporate asked what was driving sales up so dramatically, we told them we were basically running our own marketing program.

Long before Emil came on the scene, Charles cared a lot about quality, too. Another idea he had was to be sure our team members knew exactly how much product to put in a taco.

"Before we give anybody a raise," he said, "they've got to pass a portion test."

He created a test on a single sheet of paper that included every menu item. His "students" had to write the weights out next to each one. The results, besides people cramming for his exams, were better products.

One of my ideas, while not nearly as successful, might have been the most creative. Back in the day, I took the Becker CPA exam review, a professional education program that's been around for decades. Most accountants will know of it. One of the instructors told us that if you microwave a check, machines won't process it, causing a three- or four-day delay before clearing the bank.

I'm not saying it works, but I am saying people might have tried it. Once or twice.

By the spring of 2002, problems still popped up like summer storms around us, but usually, we at least saw them coming. We still had a long journey ahead of us, but we were making progress. One thing I didn't see coming was some surprise attention from corporate. Bob Nilsen, chief operating officer of Taco Bell, recognized Georgia-Texas for improving our CHAMPS scores and delivering 100 percent Food Safety Audit results for 1999, 2000, and 2001. In March, on a national stage in front of thousands of our peers, Bob presented me with the "Flying PIG" award. PIG, in this case, is an acronym for Progress, Innovation, and Growth. At the time, the accolade was given annually to franchisees who made the most noticeable improvements in their operations.

In a letter to me, Bob called us "a tremendous asset to the Taco Bell family."

"You accomplished what others might have described as 'sure ... when pigs fly!'"

Two years after they practically wrestled us for the keys, we surprised everyone by not just surviving but achieving our personal best. It didn't save us from Atherton, but it cheered us up and renewed our determination to succeed. We'd come too far to head back down the mountain.

Flying Pig Award #97   March 20, 2002
Doug Augustine

Bob Nilsen presented the "Flying PIG" award to Georgia-Texas in recognition of the dramatic improvement in our CHAMPS scores and food safety audits in from 1999 to 2001. In the title of the award, PIG is an acronym for Progress, Innovation, and Growth.

Meanwhile, a storm was brewing on Wall Street. Investors were getting antsy about their bets on a wave of financial products similar to the ones that toppled the home mortgage market in 2008. Lenders, investors, and borrowers could see the wheels wobbling on the securitized lending wagon, a financing strategy created specifically for franchise operators.

Securitized debt allowed people like my parents to buy packages of stores with no money down. In exchange, the lender owned all the franchisee's assets and protected their investment by prohibiting operators from borrowing money against this collateral. Loans, based on the cash flow and value of the business, came with fifteen-year fixed rates, high yearly maintenance fees, and steep prepay penalties. It was expensive and nearly impossible to unwind these transactions.

In the restaurant industry, customers expect upgrades and a refresh at least every seven years. Similar to your kitchen at home, these high-traffic areas take a lot of abuse. Maintenance and refurbishing costs are significant but necessary reinvestments.

Having to sit out two cycles, fourteen years, of improvements because all your cash is going to debt service is a business killer. Unless you had the cash flow to service an expensive loan and pay for renovations—which no one had—you were in the position my dad was in when he needed to build a new store in East Point. Securitized debt deals were crippling restaurant owners across the country.

At the same time, the Taco Bell brand was suffering, too. The StarLink Crisis hurt sales nationally. Numerous franchisees were facing bankruptcy. We found ourselves hunkered down with many other companies, large and small, looking for shelter and a way out.

When the Weather Channel sends a crew to your hometown, you find out who your friends are. Sometimes, people you've never met before show up to help, too. When our troubles were fiercest, an old friend came to our aid, bringing reinforcements with him.

In 1996, Scott Tocci was vice president of commercial finance for the restaurant sector at Atherton. He wrote the deal that helped my parents expand. Scott loved my parents and had huge respect for my father. He admired Dad's courage in exchanging a corporate career for the chance to build a legacy for his family. After my father's death, Scott encouraged me for years.

Scott moved to GE Capital in 2000. A couple of years later, I called him up and ran the idea of refinancing by him. I told him about our operational improvements and progress. We were holding our own, but restructuring our debt would bring a much-needed boost to cash flow as well as relief from many restrictions.

Scott loved our family and wanted to help me make this right. An invaluable ally, he was eager to execute a rescue operation.

"We can do a deal," he said. "I got you!"

Scott set up a meeting at GE, and I told his team much of what I had told him. I showed them what was happening and shared my vision. I needed them to believe in my plan.

"We're cleaning up the stores," I explained. "We're on the verge of breaking loose. Good things are happening."

Thankfully, they saw our momentum, culture, and commitment, and they agreed with Scott. We had a deal.

Reorganizing under a new financing roof would save us thousands a month, but a heavy cloud still threatened on the horizon. Brian and I had to negotiate our way out of the existing loan without a prepayment penalty, which could be as much as half a million dollars. Striking a bargain with Atherton wouldn't be easy, but it could really change the status quo for us.

Several events and decisions over the history of the company had put me in a better negotiating position for a showdown with Atherton. The first occurred in the early '90s, when my parents' partner, Uncle Bill, divorced. In the process, he sold his shares to my parents, which made them 100 percent owners of the company.

After I worked with my father for a year, he gave me 10 percent of the stock in lieu of a raise. Having a stake in the business not only incentivized my work, but the long-run possibility of dividends made up for a lower salary and missed opportunities. More importantly, it signaled our relationship as a partnership. He was in charge, but we were in it together. It was still his way or the highway, but I felt invested.

When he died, Mom and I became partners. I ran the company with the goal of making her life easy, shielding her from the daily challenges as much as possible but keeping her informed about our situation. The threat of bankruptcy hovered over our status updates for a long time. As a personal guarantor on the company's debt, she stood to lose everything.

When making tough decisions, Mom turned to close advisors, primarily my grandfather and Father Trayers, for help. When I let her know that we needed a contingency plan because Atherton would probably call in our loan, she relied on these trusted counselors. She also leaned on the attorney who helped her settle my father's estate. We all agreed on the number one objective of protecting Mom.

Mom's attorney recommended she get rid of her ownership in the company. On his advice, she turned her shares over to me, trusting me to take care of the business and to take care of her. She never second-guessed or asked, "Are we going to make it?" She transferred those worries to me, giving me 100 percent freedom to do what I needed to do. In hindsight, it's both remarkable and terrifying.

When you owe someone money, it can feel like they own you. But if you owe enough money, it's in everyone's best interest to make life doable. This is where we were. With full ownership of the company, I had more leverage with Atherton. As a young guy with virtually no assets, no signature on any of their loans, and a lifetime to recover if the deal went south, I was the textbook definition of judgment proof. Thank God, because four million dollars was at stake.

With Scott Tocci and GE in the wings and Mom out of harm's way, those weekly calls took a new direction.

"Look, this is all on me," I told Atherton. "You guys have nothing. I didn't sign anything. My name is not on any of this stuff!"

It's hard to call a guy's bluff when he's got nothing to lose.

"I'm working on refinancing," I told them. "I can save your loan, but you have to let me go without a penalty. I simply cannot pay it, and if I don't get out of this, you're going to lose your whole investment."

They didn't like it, but they were listening. They had no choice. As much as I needed GE to believe in my plan, I needed Atherton to know we were still in danger of sinking and if we went down, they went down with us.

The exhausting back-and-forth ordeal dragged on for at least eighteen months. Finally, the parent company of Taco Bell bought one of our stores, and we gave the money to Atherton. Soon after, Atherton conceded that our situation was dire, agreed to forgo a prepayment penalty, and in 2003, we refinanced with GE Capital.

One challenge of telling a decades-old story is remembering the details. They can be fuzzy. But I'm a numbers guy. I can recall a few of these facts like it was yesterday. With Atherton, we had two loans, one for equipment and one for real estate. The equipment loan was 9.95 percent. The real estate loan was 9.9 percent. We were able to retire these loans and refinance for somewhere around 6.5 percent, immediately saving almost 350 basis points on four million dollars.

You don't have to be an accountant to see that this was a game-changer. Our cash flow went from breakeven to scratching out a little profit. This gave us breathing room.

The skies cleared, and I knew, finally, that we were going to make it.

Mom and I survey my first remodel project at
Taco Bell #5304 in LaGrange, Georgia.

CHAPTER TEN
Life-Changing Events

"If you change the way you look at things,
the things you look at change."

— WAYNE DYER

"IS THIS THE WOMAN you want to raise your kids?"

This was the question my grandfather asked when I told him I was planning to propose to Andrea. Married for more than seventy years, he and my grandmother raised eight children and loved dozens of grandchildren. From that perspective, he wanted to be sure I was looking ahead.

The thing I remember most from my first meeting with Andrea was her palpable confidence. She had this presence, this aura, that let you know she was very sure of herself. There was no insecurity.

Who doesn't want that in a wife? A mother for their children? A friend?

"She's the complete package, Grandpap." I had no clue how complete this package was when I answered Grandpap's farsighted question.

By 2003, rivers of water had flowed under the bridge in the four years since I had asked her to marry me. We had field-tested the strength of our wedding vows in two of the most challenging terrains a couple can traverse: owning a struggling business and working together. We continued to collaborate on day-to-day operations and leaned into her strengths in interviewing and hiring.

On a cold day in March 2003, I stood with the contractor in the parking lot of our Taco Bell in LaGrange, discussing the remodeling project underway at the site. My phone rang, and I saw that it was Andrea. I stepped away to answer her call.

"Hey babe, what's up?" I said.

"Oh my gosh!" she said. "I'm pregnant!"

We had been hoping for this moment for at least two years. She was so excited. I was over the moon, and even the contractor was thrilled. I remember being ecstatic the entire drive home that afternoon.

With Atherton behind us and the company's finances stabilizing, this was a natural segue into a new division of labor. I focused on the business, and Andrea transferred her attention to our family. Our son, Grant, was born on a Thursday afternoon in October.

Andrea and I always kept the future in mind, and having a child only amplified our determination to do so. It was more important than ever to consider the implications of business and personal decisions. What would this mean to us in ten years? Twenty? Forty? How would our family be affected, even after we were gone? In hindsight, the baby steps that began in 2003 led to a generational legacy.

After Grant's birth, literally and metaphorically, Andrea and I had our hands full. Refinancing the business took us from losing several thousand dollars a month to squeaking out a profit of maybe five hundred or a thousand dollars. We were profitable, but clearing one or two hundred dollars per store is a razor-thin margin. Plenty of work remained to be done. Food costs continued to be a challenge, as did maintaining clean stores. Keeping our managers informed about the situation continued to be a high priority. I laid it out clearly in our meetings.

"Okay, we've got some breathing room because now we're not losing money," I said. "But we're not even close to where we need to be."

At home, Andrea was a new mom to a colicky baby. Between four and nine in the evenings, he tuned up like he had a checklist of his own and crying was his number one to-do. That first year of parenting, a universal rite of passage, was both exhilarating and exhausting, a new kind of roller coaster. Andrea read all the baby gurus and asked experienced parents for advice. She'd be the first to tell you those early years were not easy.

Fortunately, we had experience with ups and downs and highs and lows because it was a while before we all understood each other and settled in for a level ride. We didn't see progress every day. The milestones—his first smile, first word, and first step—were beautiful but rare. Yet the difference between a newborn and a three-year-old is tremendous and easy to see.

The same kind of incremental gains were taking place in the business. We were getting better and stronger, one day at a time, by focusing on the fundamentals. If I've learned anything on this journey, it's that fundamentals never change. Whether the goal is growth or course correction, they stand by, ready to meet a challenge. Unpack the basics, see what's missing, then craft a strategy.

I came up with a plan from the step-by-steps of running great restaurants that Scott Curson had taught me. Then, I worked the plan. Every single day. Once again, I fell in love with the process. I scheduled myself to work a shift in each store several times a month, and I followed that schedule. This gave me eyes on the situation. I didn't have to ask anybody, "Hey, what's working and what's not working?" because I saw it firsthand. I could experience what wasn't working, identify broken equipment and processes, and work with the manager to fix them.

Whenever possible, I made it fun. Remember Clean Sweep, Taco Bell's fifty-item cleaning checklist? I inspected each store once a month and then rewarded the manager who scored highest by getting the person's car detailed during one of our manager meetings. People really liked that.

When Andrea called to tell me we were having a baby, I was in LaGrange overseeing a project that would change the future of both the company and our family. Our franchise agreement was expiring, and we needed to improve the property to renew it. We had no choice about the upgrade.

When my father opened our first Taco Bell in Newnan in 1988, he purchased the land to build the store. However, when a franchisee acquires multiple stores, as Georgia-Texas did in 1996, the land underneath the restaurants is often not included. Consequently, we had what's known as a ground lease in LaGrange.

With a ground lease, you own the building but pay rent to the land-owner for the property underneath. This arrangement can be a good deal for all parties involved. Business owners can lower expansion costs, and landowners can count on a steady rental income from an improved piece of property and still receive a nice chunk of cash for it if they ever decide to sell.

The LaGrange store was my first major remodel. The building was old, and there were so many problems with it that improvements felt like putting lipstick on a pig. Studying the project, I wondered if we had more options than we were considering, so I called Brian Wooldridge.

"Brian, do you think we can buy that land?" I asked.

"I don't know," he said. "Let's see what it's worth."

A survey of comparable properties revealed that the land under the LaGrange store was worth about $350,000. That's not much today, but it was a fair price in 2003.

We were paying rent for the ground lease to a trust owned by a group of siblings in Atlanta. I sent them a letter saying I needed to remodel the building and wanted to purchase the land. The owners were open to discussion, but the negotiation process was not straightforward. Once they saw the benefits of selling, they decided to put it on the market, giving us the right of first refusal. It took time and some finesse, but in the end, with the help of Scott Tocci and GE Capital, we acquired the property.

Glen Bell believed that your building says a lot about your business. Customers notice when you care about your property. I followed his vision and went "all in." The remodel was so dramatic it was effectively a brand-new building.

One thing I've learned is that everyone loves something new. Customers responded accordingly, and sales doubled over the next year. Taco Bell loved both the beautiful store and our uptick in sales. The increase was so dramatic that for a while they called us weekly, before reports were due, to track the progress. The restaurant sat in a crazy good location on a large corner lot, which made it even more valuable. Lenders don't mind making loans secured by land–it's the safest thing out there–so GE Capital loved it. Plus, rolling the land into the project protected cash flow by converting an expensive improvement into a capital investment. This made the accountant in me very happy, too.

Many operators in this situation might have opted for a quick, cheap fix. They could have done a minor remodel, just enough to appease the franchise, but that's not the philosophy that built the brand. We played a long game with this project, longer than I knew, and everybody won—customers, the brand, the lender, the original owners, our company, and my family. It was the birth of a new era and the genesis of a strategy with far-reaching consequences.

This beautiful building paved the way for a future I never imagined.

In 2005, my sister, Jennifer, told me she was interested in running the Walt Disney World Marathon. As soon as I heard this, I immediately said, "I'll do it with you!" It had been four years since my first marathon, long enough to forget some of the pain of pounding the pavement for twenty-six miles, but not so long that I wanted to repeat the trauma. I knew I needed to do it differently this time, so I took a deep dive into the theory of running a marathon.

I read a book about effort-based training and tracked down the guy who wrote it, Roy Benson. Roy ran competitively for decades. He coached track and cross country at the University of Florida for ten years. And, lo and behold, I learned that he lived in Atlanta, where he coached cross country and track and field state champions at Marist, one of the city's most revered high schools.

So I reached out to him via email.

"Coach Benson, I read your book on effort-based training and found out you live here in Atlanta. I live in the area, too. I want to run a marathon. My goal is to finish in three hours and thirty minutes. Can you help me?"

It would be easy to wonder, *Who am I to be reaching out to this person? Why would he want to help me?* But when you don't ask, the answer is always no, right? We shortchange ourselves by focusing on a potential negative response. They may say no, but what if they say yes?

Do you know what he said?

"Sure. I'd love to."

Roy taught me heart rate training, a strategy that paces your runs according to your heart rate. You train in zones based on a percentage of your maximum heart rate. I had never understood this before. Roy gave me workout plans based on my heart rate zones, and we talked once a week. The accountability was great, and so was the feedback. Depending on the plan, I ran forty to fifty miles per week, reported how I did on our call, and then he adjusted the following week's workouts.

When you settle on an objective, whether a personal or business goal, the philosophy is the same: You need a plan. Once you have a strategy, all that's left is getting started and working that plan. When you know what needs to be done, your job is simple. Wake up in the morning and do what you need to do today. Take care of the baby. Go for a run. Work through the checklist one day at a time, then trust the process.

Easy to say, harder to do. Some days will suck. Some things will hurt. Others just won't be fun. The key is to conquer your goal—and your fear—through action. As long as you keep moving forward, you can succeed.

Shortly after the New Year in 2006, I ran the Disney marathon with my sister, finishing in three hours and thirty-seven minutes. I didn't meet my goal, but this was forty-three minutes faster than in 2001. Despite this enormous improvement, I still suffered a dark period in the race. Just because you're better doesn't mean it's comfortable; there's always a moment when you have to dig deep to reach the goal line.

I've heard marathons compared to life spans. The beginning is like your younger years. You feel great. The middle is more like midlife. You're getting tired but still feel pretty good. And then you hit that last third, where it's like old age. It's hard, and you doubt yourself. That's precisely what happened to me. I was having a tough time holding my pace. Around miles twenty-two and twenty-three, I was hurting. Bad. I reached a point where I just didn't want to continue.

During this stretch, I experienced a phenomenon I cannot explain. I know it sounds crazy, but I had this conversation with my dad. He was telling me, "You've got this! You can do it! Don't stop!"

I had visions of my dad talking to me. It was like Star Wars, where I could see him and hear him saying, "Doug, use the force!"

It was emotional, hard to describe, and unforgettable. I was crying as I heard his voice in my ear, yelling, pushing me forward.

"Don't give up now, Doug! You can do anything you set your mind to! Let's do this!"

I'd never had this kind of experience before. Since his death, I've had many dreams where he's mad at me, questioning my decisions, second-guessing everything, and demanding to know, "What are you doing?!"

This was different. I felt like the race was for him, and he was rooting for me.

It sounds like a cliché, but it was a powerful experience. My dad got me across the finish line that day, and it was one of the greatest moments of my life. When it was done, I knew I could get better at marathons. I knew that I would run more races.

"Come on, man, you gotta try this. You gotta try!"

My buddy from high school, Danny Beck, was into cycling and constantly nagged me to join him in this obsession, which is exactly why I put him off.

"Man, you're a great runner. Why don't you ride bikes?"

I know my personality well enough to know that if I liked it, I would be cycling all the time. I'd just spent months training for a marathon, an enormous time investment. I wasn't looking for a new challenge.

"I'm too old to ride a bike, Danny," I said.

In high school, Danny was the funny guy, the class clown. He was super fun to be around. Our graduating class voted him least likely to succeed, or most likely to fail, something like that. When we were deciding what to do with our lives, he told us that he planned to start a cleaning company.

"I'm going to clean toilets, ha ha ha," he joked.

A couple of decades later, that joke was a very successful multimillion-dollar company. And he was still as fun to be around as ever.

Finally, he wore me down.

"All right, already, I'll do it! I'll go out for a ride with you."

And when I put my feet on those pedals, I felt like a kid again. Being outside with the wind in my face brought so much freedom, a feeling I hadn't had in a long time. I absolutely fell in love with it. After the marathon, Danny and I rode bikes nearly every day and sometimes ran together, too.

A nagging calf pain that had hurt my pace in the marathon was still present, and it was still slowing me down. Coach Benson had told me it might be an electrolyte imbalance. I had no idea what that meant, but decided I had put up with the problem long enough. I googled "cramps," and a company called Hammer Nutrition came up. I ordered their product, Endurolytes, and began taking the supplement.

The directions said to take two capsules before you run, and then if you still have cramps, take two more. I followed the instructions, and my cramps went away immediately. It was incredible.

They put the word nutrition in their name, and as I read the company's newsletter, I could see they were serious as hell about that topic. I was impressed by the articles from their staff nutritionist, who addressed nutrients and caloric intake from a very scientific perspective. I also stumbled on an opportunity that looked like fun.

Not long after we began cycling together, while celebrating an afternoon ride with a few beers, I shared an article with Danny from page three of the 49th issue of *Endurance News*. The headline read: "2006 Highline Hammer: We Want You to Come!"

Brian Frank, the founder of Hammer Nutrition, wrote about the four-day weekend the company was hosting in August, which included a 136-mile ride through northwest Montana. He painted a picture of a long weekend of gourmet feasts and an "impossible to describe" scenic tour through Glacier National Park, featuring Going to the Sun Road, Flathead Lake, St. Mary's Lake, and Star Meadows.

"What do you think, Danny? You want to go out to Montana and ride bikes?"

"Let's do it!" he said.

We signed up that night, celebrating with another drink.

A few months later, on a Sunday in June, lightning struck the front of our store in Forsyth and caught the roof on fire. Thankfully, no one was injured, and most of the damage was from water and smoke, but the restaurant closed for repairs.

Cash flow had been looking good by this time, but every store needed to produce. Closing a location hurt us. Not knowing how long it would be before we could reopen, we immediately redeployed the Forsyth team to other restaurants to keep everyone working. That was a tough week.

Six days later, on the first day of July, Andrea and I were relaxing by the pool with our son when we got a call from Carla at the Newnan store.

"Doug, I'm sorry to bother you, but the restaurant is on fire."

"What!"

"Yeah, I'm standing out here in the parking lot with the police chief. I think you need to come down here."

"I'll be there in fifteen minutes."

My thoughts raced on the drive to the store. *How is this possible? Two fires in a week? Two stores down? What in the world will we do?*

When I pulled onto the scene, flames were shooting out of the top of the building. I counted three engines and saw firefighters coming in and out of the building. It's hot as hell in Georgia in July. Add a fire at 4:30 in the afternoon, and it's a recipe for heat exhaustion. Two stations responded to the call, but off-duty firefighters were quickly called to the scene for reinforcements.

The eighteen-year-old store had been built with plywood petitions strategically placed in the attic for fire containment. Firefighters had to break through these petitions, but as soon as they did, oxygen fed the flames and turned up the heat from hot to inferno. Rotating in and out, these tough guys were struggling, literally passing out. It was terrifying.

The fire chief and I were discussing the situation in the parking lot when a customer pulled up and asked us if the drive-thru was still open.

If a look could speak, the exchange between me and the fire chief said clearly, *Are you kidding?*

"I'm sorry, we're not making any more food today," I said. "Nobody's in the store. We're closed."

Miraculously, only two firefighters were treated for heat exhaustion. Both were released quickly from the nearby hospital. Thankfully, again, no serious injuries occurred.

But we were in a mess. In less than a week, we shifted from reasonably smooth operations with decent positive cash flow to having not one but two stores closed, at least 40 percent of our revenue gone up in smoke, and forty-eight jobs to protect. Not to mention a barrage of people knocking on our door.

As you can imagine, the insurance company launched an investigation. Two fires in a week? Of course, they were suspicious. I have never been scrutinized like that before or since. Investigators, auditors, and fire experts—they all showed up with questions.

After six weeks or so, forensic engineers determined that the fire in Newnan resulted from faulty wiring. The cause of the Forsyth fire, proven to be lightning, was determined to be an act of God. Perhaps it had been a while since Charles sent up petitions requesting that tomorrow not suck as bad as today. You can be sure we both renewed our appeals to a higher power for help.

Prayers for expedited action topped the list. Nothing happens fast enough after a fire. All our reconstruction plans had to be

Fire hits Bullsboro Taco Bell

2 firefighters treated for heat exhaustion

By ALEX McRAE
alex@newnan.com

Two City of Newnan fire-fighters were treated at Newnan Hospital for heat exhaustion after battling a Saturday afternoon fire at the Taco Bell restaurant on Bullsboro Drive, according to Newnan Fire Chief David Whitley.

Both responded quickly to treatment and were released, Whitley said. No one else was injured in the blaze.

"Our men weren't injured," Whitley said, "but the conditions were really bad and we took extra precautions to get

them treated as soon as they showed symptoms of heat exhaustion."

The fire was reported at 4:31 p.m. and the first units arrived on the scene at 4:35, according to officials at Coweta County 9-1-1. Stations 1 and 2 of the Newnan Fire department responded with a total of three fire trucks. Extra off duty personnel were also called to the scene to provide relief if necessary due to extreme heat conditions, Whitley said.

The fire was brought under control quickly, according to Whitley, although considerable damage was done to the building. The initial assessment showed the fire appeared to be electrical in nature, but that has not been officially established and the investigation into the cause of the blaze continues, Whitley said.

submitted and permitted. It was like starting over again, but with a surplus of employees, bills to pay, and a nuked bank account. I was determined to meet two goals: keep every single employee on the payroll, and reopen the Newnan store before the anniversary of my father's death in November.

Restaurant industry peers who heard we were protecting nearly fifty jobs despite not knowing when operations would resume were incredulous. "What? How can you do that?"

Business loss interruption insurance helped but was far from covering the gap. The honest answer was, "I don't know. We're just going to do it."

In August, the Highline Hammer weekend that Danny and I had signed up for in the spring was a welcome relief from the trauma of fires and investigations. Four days in Montana provided a much-needed reset. However, we were the proverbial fish out of water at the event. We had no idea what we were doing. The first clue came at the meet and greet, where people were chatting about their ultra adventures, Race Across America, for instance, when cyclists cross the country riding three thousand miles coast to coast from San Diego to Annapolis. One guy held the group spellbound, talking about doing a double at Furnace Creek, a 508-mile race from California's Death Valley to the top of Mt. Whitney. He reversed the course, starting at the top of the mountain a few days before the race, then rode the route back to the top on race day. One thousand and sixteen miles. Sixty hours. Straight. And he won it. Mic drop.

We had just started riding, and these were the athletes we found ourselves with.

"So, what's your longest ride," one guy asked me.

"Fifty," I said.

"Fifty hours?" he asked. "Fifty days?"

"No," I said quietly. "Fifty miles."

He was incredulous.

"Your longest ride is fifty miles?"

"Um, yeah?"

"You know we're riding one hundred and thirty-six miles tomorrow?"

"I do now," I said, realizing we were pretty much screwed.

Standing nearby, Brian Frank, the founder of Hammer Nutrition, was cracking up.

"What are you guys doing here," he asked between belly laughs. "You are in way over your heads. You're accidental tourists!"

"Dude, where's the beer?" That's all we wanted to know.

"Seriously?" he replied. "We're athletes. We don't drink beer."

"Well, we'll just run down to the grocery store and stock up."

"I really prefer you don't drink beer here," he said.

"No worries. We'll keep it on the down-low and pour it into cups."

So, amid this group of pro athletes and serious weekend amateurs, Danny and I were drinking beer. Like it's what we came for.

"Okay," Brian said, giving in to reality. "Don't worry about tomorrow. You're going to ride European-style. I'll pick you up when you're worn out, and we'll have some fun."

For the rest of the week, we rode until we were tired, then loaded up in the sag wagon, where the driver took us to the convenience store for more beer. We had a blast.

For reasons I will never understand, Brian Frank fell in love with us. Neither our athletic prowess nor our reputations improved—*what happens in Montana stays in Montana*—but we made a lasting friend. What sounded like a simple guys' weekend when we signed up in the spring turned into a life-changing decision with far-reaching effects. In addition to making a wonderful new friend, I learned why Glacier National Park is called the Crown of the Continent. With many travels behind me now, Glacier remains one of the most beautiful places I have ever visited. Our trip was the beginning of a lifelong relationship with Montana.

The 2006 Highline Hammer with Danny Beck was much more than just a scenic ride in the park. Lifelong relationships originated with this event.

When I arrived back home, remodeling was underway in the dining room at the Forsyth restaurant. In the meantime, team members were driving thirty-six miles to work at the McDonough store. While it wasn't easy, getting back in business was relatively simple. We were open again about two months after the fire.

The situation was more complicated in Newnan. The fire occurred just two years before we were due to renew our franchise agreement, when significant upgrades were expected. We took the opportunity to scrape and rebuild the store. While new construction was underway, most of the team worked thirty-five miles away in LaGrange. Toward the end of rebuilding, loyal customers began stopping by every day, asking, "Are you guys open?" When we would be up and running again was the topic of lots of chatter around town.

"I miss my Taco Bell," people wrote in the local newspaper's sound-off pages.

We scraped together enough to pay everyone—I'm still not sure how—and reopened like gangbusters at the original store by the end of October. The line of people at the counter was out the door. Cars wrapped the building. Unbelievably, traffic flowed beyond the parking lot onto the main thoroughfare in front of our store. Then, people complained in the newspaper that we needed to hire traffic control.

I jumped back into operations, working alongside the team, all of us making food as fast as possible. I was so grateful to work with these people because they were with us before, during, and after the fires. They saw how far we had come and were just as excited as I was about getting our store back. The hometown reception was a festival of good wishes, like a family reunion. I had so much fun talking to everyone who came to welcome us back. We sold 11,000 tacos in three days and did more than seventy thousand dollars in business the first week, which was unheard of for a Taco Bell opening back then.

Moreover, the timing allowed us to be the first store in the Southeast to integrate Taco Bell's brand-new "Grill to Order" (GTO) production line. We became the training site for this new method and equipment. People came from all over the Southeast, especially Florida, to learn the new procedures. The peer-to-peer training inspired us all.

We were back in operation shortly before the anniversary of my father's death. The wildly successful reopening, along with rolling out a welcome mat to operators from all over the region, celebrated his life in ways I could not have imagined. We overcame some biggies—fire, fear, and frustration—to emerge better than before. I felt Dad's spirit again, cheering us on.

TACO BELL REOPENS

11,000 tacos sold in 3 days

By LATINA EMERSON

latina@newnan.com

The Newnan Taco Bell restaurant has reopened on Bullsboro Drive, receiving an enthusiastic response from the community which has gone several months without the local taco franchise.

From its opening on Saturday through Wednesday, lines were almost out the door, the drive-thru traffic line wrapped around the building and extended to Bullsboro Drive, and the parking lot was filled

to capacity, requiring customers to park in adjacent lots.

Taco Bell had closed after sustaining considerable damage from a July 1 fire.

According to Doug Augustine, owner of the Newnan Taco Bell location, the restaurant opened slightly earlier than anticipated due to the eager onlookers already taking post outside the restaurant. The restaurant was scheduled to open at 5 p.m. Saturday but opened its doors to the public around 4:45 p.m. to accommodate the crowd, he said.

"When we opened the doors there was a mad rush to place their order at the new store," said Augustine. "It's been unbelievable the success and the turnout from the community. We had no idea we would have a response like this," he said.

Augustine gave a report on the unexpected sales at Newnan Taco Bell. "We have sold a little over 11,000 tacos and soft tacos in the last three days," said Augustine. This number does not include other items on the menu.

See REOPENS page 2A

Photo by John Beck

Taco Bell has reopened on Bullsboro Drive, receiving a tremendous response from the community. The restaurant reports selling slightly more than 11,000 tacos and soft tacos within the past three days.

Here we grow: My first from-the-ground-up store in Sharpsburg, Georgia

CHAPTER ELEVEN
Brotherhood

"There is nothing on this earth more to
be prized than true friendship."

— THOMAS AQUINAS

THE DIFFERENCE BETWEEN MOMENT and momentous is a grand canyon. Its vast threshold welcomes equally chance, fate, and the perfectly forgettable. In the summer of 1986, when the kid next door stepped into my room as I was unpacking and attempting to reassemble my fifteen-year-old world in Newnan, I never imagined we'd be friends for life. He strode ever so coolly into my misery, an instant oasis of companionship and a ready accomplice. As glad as I was to see a friendly face in this alien territory, how could I know that the first beer we shared within an hour of meeting would turn into decades of shenanigans and adventures?

Ryan is the reason I went to Auburn University. At Auburn, we got tricked into joining Sigma Pi because our good friend Jim Boren was legacy, and the family pressure gave him no choice. Friends stick together, so we joined with him. We never even considered rushing any other fraternity.

We weren't there long before we realized we had little in common with our fraternity brothers. We met a few renegades we could hang with, but we didn't fit in. After a year, we couldn't get out of there fast enough.

One of the rebels we met was a little sister to Sigma Pi, Alexis. One day, she changed all our lives.

"Hey, I want to introduce y'all to some guys similar to you," she said. "They were in Lambda Chi and didn't like the frat life either. They're great, and I think you would hit it off."

The trio she introduced us to became our family, forming a de facto fraternity all our own. We moved into neighboring duplexes and did all our favorite things together. Beer, music, Frisbee, golf, and mountain biking topped the list. Somehow, we went to class, too.

I became particularly close to one of our new friends, a guy named Mike Bender. We bonded over our mutual love of music and athletics. From day one, Mike and I were inseparable. We hit Auburn's nonstop music scene first. Widespread Panic was big on campus back then. We road-tripped to see bands in Atlanta and elsewhere. Weekends were spent on concerts and sports.

Mike is the most naturally athletic person I've ever met. Skills I spend ridiculous amounts of time training to do—he just shows up and masters. Naturally. Swimming, golfing, cycling, bowling, skiing—on water and snow—racquetball ... hell, he's even the best-damned dart thrower I've ever seen! There's nothing he can't do.

His most helpful competency at the time, though, was with the Frisbee. This guy could throw a disc like no one else. He threw forehand, backhand, sidearm, overhead, upside down, behind his back, under his leg, and any other way you can imagine. His catches were equally dramatic. I loved to sit and watch the magic.

Mike became the default owner of Aspen, a dog abandoned by a roommate one summer. From a discipline standpoint, this animal was a wreck. I mean, he was raised by college guys. He chewed up half the furniture in the house. He was a big nuisance. But he could catch a Frisbee like a pro. Whatever Mike threw for him, Aspen would run and jump to catch it. Midair. Near the ground. Wherever. It was art. And Aspen was a magnet for dates. Shirtless guys, flying discs, and a talented dog—the girls in Auburn loved it.

A native Floridian, Mike got to know my family, too. When we needed a taste of home, Newnan was less than ninety minutes away. He became the brother I didn't have.

We shared an apartment during my senior year at Auburn. Mike had graduated and worked at a golf course, relishing the game he'd loved since childhood. He got me back into golf, too, which was fun. After college, we went our separate ways, him to Atlanta and me to Nashville, but we stayed in touch.

In Atlanta, Mike worked as a sales engineer before joining a financial modeling company, which kindled a deeper interest in finance and led him to grad school. Back in a classroom, my buddy thought about what he really wanted to do with his life.

Mike had grown up in Indian Harbour Beach, Florida, which he described as a small town where he had a great childhood. His mom was a kind soul who founded a community program for abused and abandoned kids. His dad was a math teacher who loved golf and gardening and made ends meet with a side gig in landscaping. The son evolved into a blend of his parents. He was a guy who loved people with all his heart, an analyst who ran numbers and scenarios like it was another sport he naturally excelled at, and a fun-loving person who enjoyed the simple pleasures of life.

One of those simple pleasures involves food. Devil's Hoagies, a sandwich shop in his hometown, set the standard in Mike's mind for what freedom and a great sub taste like. As a twelve-year-old, he admired the guy who made his living serving fabulous cheesesteaks to a beach-loving crowd.

This would be cool, he thought.

A dozen years later, in Atlanta, Willy's reminded him of his favorite childhood eatery and became his nearly everyday lunch spot. He loved it so much that he asked the owner if he would consider franchising. At the time, the answer was no.

While pursuing an MBA in finance at Georgia State, Mike attended classes at a satellite campus located in a shopping center. This is where he stepped into one of the earliest iterations of Moe's and thought, "Oh man, this place is just like Willy's!" The artwork, the music, and the vibe all hit him at once.

This is what I'm going to do, he decided.

He met with guys at the corporate headquarters of Moe's, conveniently located in Atlanta. Since he didn't know anything about restaurants and didn't have any money to invest, they paired him with a franchisee in South Carolina, where he went to work making $6.50 an hour as the steamer on the front line. Soon, he became a partner in Moe's stores in Greenville, Anderson, and Clemson.

Mike remembers us exchanging a few calls in his early restaurant days that sounded like this. "Hey, Doug, can you tell me how food costs work?" "How does scheduling work?" "How does insurance work?" He bounced ideas and questions off me while preparing business plans for the bank. He later said this was when he realized how grown-up this "fun little restaurant thing" could be. I don't remember these conversations, but I know he was elbow-deep in the day-to-day with little time for life outside home and work. If I understand anything, it's that.

Mike and I were on the same path in more than one way. Long before modern-day philosopher Ryan Holiday told us that obstacles were the way, we tested his theory. With my second marathon and two fires highlighting my tenth year in the restaurant business, I found myself ready for more. *What doesn't kill us makes us stronger, right?* I kicked off 2007 thinking about how to grow.

Operationally, our stores were stable. We were at a point where we had enough money to build a store. I was ready to bring a restaurant from groundbreaking to grand opening. I immersed myself in site intel, learning a new part of the business. When I pivoted to building a store, I quickly saw that I couldn't run operations and development.

The wisdom of Michael Gerber's *The E-Myth* had been simmering in my mind for nearly a decade. Finally, it was time to work on the business rather than in it. I had done all I could do on my own. To rise to the next level, I needed help. That's when I began reaching out to Mike, leaving messages until, finally, he returned my calls.

"Mike, I need a fresh set of eyes on the business. I can't get us any further than we are on my own. I need you."

I shared my vision to acquire and build more stores. His initial response was shock.

"Doug, I just opened my third restaurant. I don't know what the hell I'm doing, and I'm up to my eyeballs. This is absolutely crazy."

Mike's business was turbulent at the time. He was wrapping burritos in an environment where training and support were as thin as a tortilla. He and his partners were barely surviving, consumed by the strain of opening new stores, the internal and external pressures of the industry, and the day-to-day challenges of the business.

Plus, Mike and his wife, Holly, had a three-year-old and a baby on the way.

"Come see us," I said. "Let's just talk about it.

The natural next step after stabilizing a business is to grow. The natural segue from a marathon is the Half Ironman. Following the Disney Marathon, I fell in love with running again and, because of Danny Beck, rediscovered cycling, which was even more enjoyable. A Half Ironman is a triathlon that includes a 1.2-mile swim, a 56-mile bike ride, and a 13.1-mile run. Since I was already running and cycling, I just had to add swimming. Easy, right? Why not? So, in 2007, I began training for 70.3 miles of Type 2 fun, which, by definition, is anything that is more fun to read, write, or talk about than it is to do. It's something you want to have done more than you actually want to do.

Type 2 fun is where I thrive. Getting out of my comfort zone through athletic events is also my way of dealing with change or discomfort. I need the structure and discipline of training to counteract the chaos around me. Training served me in the same way that weightlifting did earlier in my life—as a pressure release valve for stress, anxiety, and depression and yet another proving ground for the power of incremental gains. Here was my daily reminder that you improve if you put in the work.

Preparing for a Half Ironman took six to twelve hours of weekly training for about six months. At the time, I thought this was merely the next progression in my personal endurance challenges. Looking back, I now see the process of upping the ante on my athletic game paralleled the protocols needed to grow the business. I also see how important it is to be sure that in the midst of all that Type 2 fun, you're having at least a little fun in the more traditional definition of the word.

Brian Frank invited Danny and me to return to the Highline Hammer in 2007.

"You guys have to come back," he said. "It will never be the same without you."

He was right about that, but just to be sure, Danny brought a little extra excitement to the next event. That first experience had schooled us. When we signed up for our initial Highline, we missed the fine print about four days of rides of various lengths, about three hundred miles total. The rides were all near Whitefish, Montana, the headquarters of Hammer Nutrition. Brian created the event as an endurance school. Amateurs like us joined athletes with credentials we could only imagine. I still cringe to think that in 2006, we stood clueless next to Race Across America champions and double and triple Ironmen.

This time, we knew what was involved. Since I was in the middle of training for a Half Ironman, I showed up much more prepared than I had the year before. Danny was also ready. He was laser-focused on the event's namesake, the Highline Hammer loop, 136 miles of breathtaking scenery along Going to the Sun Road in Glacier National Park. The ride crosses the Continental Divide twice and includes an elevation change of nearly nine thousand feet.

Danny had an idea to give us an advantage for the longest ride.

"Let's rent a motorhome," he said. "We can park near where the Highline begins."

It seemed like a brilliant notion to us. Waking up near the starting point would allow us to sleep later, saving at least a few hours by skipping the meetup and van ride in Whitefish. We could show up at six thirty, rested for the ride. So, we rented an RV, and the night before, around eight o'clock, we drove to the park entrance, where we encountered our first problem. The railroad goes over Going to the Sun Road, forming an overpass at West Glacier, the road we needed to take to arrive at the start of the ride. A yellow caution sign in the center of the overpass indicated the maximum height to clear the concrete bridge was thirteen feet, six inches. Our home for the week was too tall to enter the park.

"Okay," Danny said, "we'll stay next to this old train depot. It looks like it's been abandoned for years."

"Good idea," I said.

Before you begin thinking that a Google search could have led to better decisions, remember that in 2007, the iPhone was brand new. We couldn't thumb our way across the internet or ask for help from Siri, who hadn't been born yet. We didn't know that the train station's rustic look was a deliberate design to match the historic architecture in the area. We had no reason to suspect that trains would rattle the motorhome all night. But they did. It seemed like every hour, a train was passing within forty feet of our heads.

I managed to fall asleep but woke up around three to find Danny driving the RV with the slides out very slowly down the highway.

"What are you doing?" I stammered.

"I'm going to find a place where I can sleep," he answered. A few miles down the road, he pulled into the parking lot of a gas station, where we stayed for the rest of the night. Instead of being rested and ready, we both showed up sleep-deprived for the big ride. Still, we finished in under ten hours.

Unfortunately, Danny developed severe saddle sores while cycling through the park. Consequently, he decided against riding the eighty-seven-mile loop around Flathead Lake the following day.

"See y'all later," he said, popping a beer before eight in the morning.

When we returned, we found Danny on a ladder propped against the motorhome, which was parked next to Hammer Nutrition's warehouse. Tools were scattered all around the RV.

"What the hell is he doing?" Brian asked me.

"No idea," I said.

We walked over to the crime scene.

"Hey, buddy, what are you up to?" I asked.

"Man, you are *not* going to believe what happened to me," he said.

Honestly, I still don't. Danny said that around mid-morning, he realized he was hungry but had no food or car, so he drove the RV into town. On the way, people were honking and waving at him.

"I was thinking, 'Man, people are really friendly in Montana,'" he said. "Before I know it, I hear 'Bam! Bam! Bam! Bam! Bam.'"

He had left the awning out, and it was ripped off by a fresh planting of small trees along the roadside. By the time we came back from our ride, he had been working on the problem for four hours. It was "fixed," he said, as long as no one wanted to open or retract the awning again, which he figured hardly ever happened.

What happened in Montana stayed in Montana. Until now.

"I'd like to talk to the owner," an angry code enforcement officer said.

I heard these words while in the middle of a discussion with the contractor remodeling the dining room of one of our stores in 2005. Customers were being served through the drive-thru while the dining room was closed, so it was easy to see who was looking for me in the empty room.

"Can I see your permit?"

"Well, the general contractor is right here," I said. "You can talk to him."

Unfortunately, I heard my builder say, "Well, I don't have a permit."

"I know you don't have a permit because if you had a permit, I wouldn't be asking you for it," the guy replied.

My builder explained he'd done work in other nearby counties and had never needed a permit to remodel a dining room.

"You can't even replace a toilet without a permit!" said the officer, even more furious. "You guys have to stop right now."

And he meant the entire operation, not just the remodel. The drive-thru. The dining room. The whole restaurant.

"Look, we're not trying to avoid paying or any of that stuff," I attempted to explain. "We are just doing what we thought we could do."

During the three-hour interrogation that followed, I deployed my best diplomacy skills. Despite giving him our plans for review and buying permits, we were on the brink of jail the entire afternoon.

"We can't even review these plans for two weeks," he said.

We shut down operations for two weeks but, thankfully, avoided getting arrested. It was a crazy experience and one I never want to repeat.

So, by the time I had the funds to develop a store from the ground up, I had already had a few building adventures. The journey started where it usually does, with someone I trust recommending someone they trust.

In the mid-2000s, Patrick Mulkey was not only the best Taco Bell operator in the Atlanta area, but he was also growing his business, opening brand-new stores all over town. We had a good relationship, and I often sought his advice. He introduced me to the owner of the construction company that was building his restaurants.

Having done so much work for Patrick, the company was familiar with Taco Bell's designs and processes, which made the projects much easier for me. One of our first projects resulted in the memorable afternoon I just told you about. Despite this eventful beginning, we maintained a good working relationship and became friends.

In 2007, when it was time for my first ground-up project, this was the company I turned to for building the store. With Patrick Mulkey as his primary customer, he was a busy guy. There wasn't a whole lot of telling him what to do. He wasn't the cheapest vendor, either, but he never missed a deadline. I knew his work would be high quality and we wouldn't lose any time due to delays.

In essence, he had the proven experience I needed, and together, we built a new Taco Bell in Sharpsburg, Georgia, about six miles south of our original location. After our adventure with code enforcement a few counties away, choosing a spot on our home turf seemed like the best idea for our first ground-up project. My part of the process was to order the equipment package for the building design we selected, ensuring we had supplies when we needed them.

The location was chosen from Taco Bell's list of "A" sites. The company has every single trade area in the United States mapped out and graded A, B, C, or D. A sites were always more expensive, but they were also the highest volume stores. It didn't take me long to realize the value of better sites. The LaGrange remodeling project taught me the wisdom of owning the ground beneath the store. Paying more upfront improved the return on the investment and our likelihood of success.

The real estate we were able to acquire for our new store was an A site located at the intersection of a road that led to a growing residential area and the primary state road, which took them to grocery stores and other retail outlets and work, too, if they weren't commuting to Atlanta. We were buying the property alongside a Kentucky Fried Chicken franchisee who initially found the land. I reached out to him with a unique offer.

"Hey, I know you want to be on the corner, and I respect that," I said, "but I'm willing to pay more for it since Taco Bell is open later. It may make sense for both of us."

He agreed to what turned out to be a sweet deal for both of us and another precedent-setting decision for me. Customers love corner lots, Taco Bell loves corner lots, and I love them, too.

Taco Bell #23673, Sharpsburg, Georgia

I spent most of the year building the new store, training for a Half Ironman, and convincing Mike to join me as a partner in Georgia-Texas. The negotiation took time and patience, with brief communications punctuated by days of silence.

"Douglas, got your message ... sorry no call back," he said in an email one day. "Picked up five caterings today ... short employee ... mommy's first day without the in-laws to help ... very emotional evening ... long story short ... will call you tomorrow ... Thought I'd send a picture of Baby Bender."

Eventually, he and Holly made several visits to Atlanta during this time. He recalls walking into the Newnan store and thinking, "Wow, this is the nicest Taco Bell I've ever seen." Fresh paint and a crisp, modern feel were not what he remembered from the Taco Bells of his Floridian childhood. At this point, he knew enough about the industry and our training to see the store from an owner's perspective. He saw an operation he described as "really tidy" and "buttoned up."

Chatting poolside over lemonade one morning, we reached the pivot point.

"I'll do this under one condition and one condition only," Mike said.

I couldn't wait to hear what he had on his mind, imagining it might be some kind of monetary consideration. I knew we would be a good team. Our values were aligned, but we were different enough in our skills and leadership styles to complement each other. I was ready to do what it took to bring him on as a partner.

"None of that other stuff matters, Doug," he said. "I want to be your friend, and that's more important than anything else. You have to promise me that no matter what happens in this business, our friendship will be stronger than whatever we do together as business partners. If this is crazy and goes wrong, we just have to make sure that we don't blow up a friendship."

And so, we fixed our number one priority: friendship above all else. With this condition established, we began our grand adventure!

On September 23, I completed the 2007 Ironman 70.3 Cancun, crossing the finish line in five hours and thirty minutes. Meanwhile, Mike was running a different kind of race, deconstructing the life he had built in South Carolina, buying a house in a tumultuous real estate market, and packing up and moving with a three-year-old and a three-month-old. When I got home from Mexico, he was camping out in the home he and Holly had bought, painting the nursery, and getting ready for his family to join him in a couple of weeks. He exercised a different kind of stamina in the five months that brought him from Moe's to Taco Bell.

In our mid-thirties, we'd both trained our whole lives for what was next. Independently, we were strong. Together, we were stronger. Mike's first official day with me at Georgia-Texas was October 1, 2007.

*Mike and I attended his first Taco Bell spring
training in February 2008 in Las Vegas.*

CHAPTER TWELVE

Rock 'n' Roll

"The cave you fear to enter holds the treasure you seek."

— JOSEPH CAMPBELL

"MEDIOCRITY."

In giant letters, this word screamed silently from the whiteboard when Mike dropped into our monthly manager meeting a couple of weeks before his official start date. It was shortly before the opening of our Sharpsburg store, his first introduction to our team. And it was 2007 when we were all still sharing presentations using projectors. Business results were on the screen, with Enemy No. 1, the "M" word, close by.

I believe in always having a target, setting goals, then measuring outcomes. But I'm not emotional about data. As far as I am concerned, results are just results. They are facts that tell us where we are—no more, no less. Acknowledging reality is how we stay grounded.

Our meetings took place in the middle office in the building where Dad, Charles, Carla, and I had worked together a decade earlier. We had come a long way from those dicey days, but we had a long way to go. Those projections Mike saw were our monthly reality check. It was enough for him to know we had work to do.

Once onboard, Mike spent a few days at a training store in Atlanta, then jumped into the chaos underway at our newest location, which was a mess. Opening a store is no joke. Everyone is new and inexperienced. Demand is through the roof because customers get excited anytime a new eatery comes to their neighborhood. Neither of us was a newbie in the restaurant business, but getting an inexperienced crew and a shiny new store up and operating is a feat that makes endurance training look like the proverbial stroll in the park.

Mike's initiation was a shitstorm. Back then, we didn't invest the time to train a new crew that we did later. It wasn't that we didn't want to. Like they say, you don't know what you don't know. And we just didn't know. As a result, the turnover was tremendous. Two managers came and went within weeks. Soon, Mike decided the only way to conquer the madness was for him to learn and train every position in the store while acting as the restaurant manager.

Being willing to plunge into operations is one of the many values we share. If something's broken and we don't have staff to fix it, we know we need ground-zero knowledge of the challenges. He worked out the details and came to me with a plan that allowed him to train two people at a time. He asked that we fund double the number of hours that should have been required to run the restaurant. It was a whopping twice what Taco Bell's operating system allowed for a store this size. In terms of profit, it was the equivalent of setting money on fire!

Charles was convinced this move was a quick return to the road to bankruptcy, but without hesitation, I said yes.

"If that's what you think we need to do to get better, do it."

And voilà, a recipe for growth was born. It took years to refine and even longer to articulate, but this became the theme of our partnership.

Mike had to dive in and figure it out. And I had to let him do it. In a perfect world, he would have had more training and more people to help bring him along. But this was the real world, and it was not even close to perfect.

It's one thing to believe in people, but it's another to let go of the reins and let them do the job you've asked them to do. When I worked with my dad, he micromanaged everything.

"Turn left. Turn right. Go here. Do that."

It drove me crazy, and I was determined not to do that.

Instead, I walked away. I was prepared to step in if Mike got in trouble, but if he didn't, I knew it would be a win-win for us. So, I left him with that mess. Whatever he needed or wanted, I approved, and I let go.

It's hard to watch a trial by fire in progress. It's hard to resist jumping in to help. Mike went through hell, and it sucked, but our partnership wasn't about working side by side. We planned to divide and conquer. My role was vision and growth. He was operations. The only way it would work was for me to let him do it. And the only way I knew how not to interfere was to keep myself so busy, so preoccupied, so immersed in something else that even if I wanted to rush to the rescue, I couldn't.

I met Jeff Cuddeback because of that fateful decision that Danny and I had made to cycle through Glacier National Park with the Hammer Nutrition tribe. The Highline Hammer led to many relationships and experiences I would have missed if we had stayed home that week. Among these was access to a unique community of athletes.

Jeff was an official Hammer athlete, an elite group the company recognized as top in their sports. Unlike most brand ambassadors, Hammer's wasn't a paid endorsement. Instead, the Hammer spotlight brought a lot of recognition to amateur athletes who often coached weekend warriors like me.

A sought-after, no-bullshit kind of coach, Jeff let you know he was only interested in working with serious athletes, people who want to win races. Upfront, he told you his regimens were grueling, even intimidating. Fortunately, hard is my jam. When I hear a challenge will be Type 2 fun, it takes me back to the days when I followed Bobby Burgess around the Newnan Racquetball and Health Club, begging him to take me to Ben Green's gym. The "Grow or Die" challenge beckons me like no other.

After the Half Ironman in Cancun, I wanted more. With my sights set on 140 miles, I reached out to Jeff in October.

"Hey, Jeff, this is what I want to do. I'm willing to pay the price. I'm willing to train. You tell me how to do it, and I'm all in."

The first step was an interview. If he liked what he heard, you completed a college-like application, listing your goals and a whole bunch of other stuff. Then you hoped he accepted you. Fortunately for me, a week after I submitted my application, he said yes.

On Friday afternoon, November 2, I made the four-and-a-half-hour drive alone to Panama City Beach, Florida. Before seven in the morning on Saturday, I cheered with the crowd as more than two thousand athletes launched into the emerald waters of the Gulf of Mexico for a 2.4-mile swim. I applauded the competitors when they completed the swim and began the 112-mile bike ride and celebrated with runners crossing the finish line after a 26.2-mile marathon.

Sunday morning, I stood in line with hundreds of people registering for Ironman Florida 2008. On the drive home, I was nervous. A hangover would not have made me any queasier than I felt after signing up to race

140 miles. I was intimidated. Honestly, I was scared. This was not like hiking or weightlifting. I had a sense that I was jumping off a cliff.

What in the hell am I getting into? I wondered.

Triathlon training fanned the hot flames of my love affair with systems and processes. This next level of endurance training accelerated my drive for systematic, step-by-step procedures. The experience gave me a new perspective on the business. I saw a new way to set goals and then go after those targets. It allowed me to get really clear on what we wanted so we could all work toward that common objective.

My first goal was to acquire more restaurants. I wanted us to have a plan to work toward and to know where we were racing next. This was the vision I became clear on while running, biking, and swimming my way around the country.

Meanwhile, Mike took over the monthly managers' meetings and every other operational aspect of our company. Although I left him completely alone so he could figure out what the hell was happening and how to wrangle it, our checks and balances took place at those monthly meetings. Whatever was happening in my athletic journey, wherever I had been the weekend before, I was at every one of those meetings.

His role at these gatherings was to keep everyone abreast of the nuts and bolts of the operation. There was plenty to discuss. Among Mike's initial trial-by-fire experiences was a day he referred to as Black Saturday, a moment when every employee walked off the job at our newest store. Why did they quit? I don't remember. It doesn't even matter. What could we do about it? I had been in the business long enough to learn that the best strategy in moments like that is to hunker down within the narrow universe of things you can control. It's a small place, which means it's really not that hard. Sometimes, all you can do is focus on how to prevent it from happening again.

My job was to bring clarity, vision, and motivational philosophy while clearing the pathway for growth. Together, Mike and I built a base and solid foundation for the future.

I come up with all these crazy ideas when I'm running. It's my think time. It's when I mull over problems. It's when I figure out what to do next.

I'll come in from a run and share my thoughts with Andrea or pass them by Mike later in the day. Eight times out of ten, they give me a no-go.

"Okay, that's just dumb," I might hear. Or "No. Just no. That's not happening."

But sometimes, I get a positive response.

"That might work," one of them might say. "That's actually pretty smart."

Some of my crazy ideas solve problems.

A series of runs at corporate conferences provided the slingshot that propelled Mike and me into growth. In 2005, Charles and I flew to Dallas to take a weeklong class in franchise financing. Topics of discussion included how store values are determined.

Wherever I go, I sit on the front row, a holdover habit from childhood. My family always sat on the first pew at Mass. In school, since my last name began with an "A," I often found myself in the front row in class. As a small guy, I learned I could see and hear better closer to the action. Over the years, I discovered that I learned more and made better connections from this vantage point. You can't hide in the front row. You can't duck out a side door early. You have to be present. An extra benefit is that speakers are more likely to notice and respond to people at the front of the room.

In the franchise financing class, I definitely wanted to sit close to the action. This was not the time to hang back. If we were going to grow, I needed to know everything I possibly could about how this worked. From the front row, I asked lots of questions and got to know Cathy Johnson and Chris Armbruster, organizers of the conference. Cathy was the senior manager of franchise finance for Taco Bell at the time. Chris was the company's senior director of franchise finance and development. We formed friendships over chats about mutual interests outside of business. Chris and I shared a love of travel and had many conversations about our favorite destinations. Cathy loved running, so we also found a lot to talk about. Over the next few years, we often ran together before meetings. I talked about our operation and peppered her with questions during these runs. She taught me a lot about what to expect in the expansion process. She and Chris became invaluable sources of knowledge about business development.

Cathy and I finished an early morning jog at the annual corporate convention shortly after Bender came on board. That's when I let her know that I was ready to grow our company.

"I need stores," I told her.

She said she could do little to help with acquisitions, but she knew someone who specialized in this area.

"Meet me at my booth at eleven, and I'll introduce you to him," she said.

On the convention floor, Cathy escorted me over to Naveen Goyal. With a handshake and a phone date scheduled, this was when some of my wildest ideas found both an ally and a launching pad.

Naveen is the co-founder and managing director of Auspex Capital, an investment banking and financial advisory firm specializing in quick-service restaurants. They help people like me with mergers and acquisitions. A key service is their diligence in finding the best financing terms for their clients. They also examine data and market conditions to determine the value of stores and give strategic advice to buyers and sellers.

Naveen's a smart guy. At the time, he had ten years of experience representing millions in franchise financing and an MBA from Drucker School of Management. His credentials were impressive. What made the most difference to me, though, was what his customers said. On a conference call with Mike and me after the convention, Naveen gave us a list of approximately thirty franchisees they represented.

"Call anybody you want on this list," he said.

One of his clients was a guy named Nick Davis. Although I had never met Nick, I knew of him, and our paths had intersected in several ways. In the mid-'80s, he was an assistant manager of a corporate-owned Taco Bell in Huntsville, Alabama, where Charles—back when he had hair and people knew him as "Chuck"—worked while he was in college. Nick was on the team that helped my parents open the original Taco Bell in Newnan in 1988. He assisted with training our first crew. In 1991, Nick went to work for a Wendy's franchisee who owned forty-six restaurants. He returned to Taco Bell as a franchisee in 1997. With all these common connections, I called him first.

"Let me tell you about Auspex," Nick said. "They are not cheap, but they made me a pile of money." He added, "They are expensive, but they saved me a lot more money than they cost me."

This was the consensus of everyone I talked to in the franchise community. They all said the same thing.

"Auspex is not cheap, but they're great at what they do, and they'll make you a lot of money."

Their stories all sounded good to me. I knew Naveen was a guy I wanted on my team. When we began working together, we hit it off immediately.

"We want more restaurants," I told him.

"All right," he said. "Let's go after it in every way possible!"

Meanwhile, I began working with my new trainer.

"A lot can go wrong in an Ironman."

That's the first thing Jeff Cuddeback told me. He began our journey with this reality check.

"We can't have a time goal in mind, Doug," he said, "because anything and everything can happen in a ten, eleven, or twelve-hour race."

Weather. Injuries. Illness. Other competitors. The list of external factors he cited as outside our control was long.

"Our goal is to get you to finish and finish strong. That's our number one objective," Jeff said.

How long it might take to complete the race fell behind the priorities of avoiding the medical tent and finishing well. He made no promises for a finish time—none—and no apologies for not doing so.

"If you're willing to accept that objective, I can coach you."

"A lot can go wrong" was a familiar story, the classic parable of risk. A lot can always go wrong, but things can go right, too.

"I don't really care what my time is as long as I do my absolute best," I told him. "I just want to be all in. I want to race the distance."

And off we went. Because once I commit, quitting is not an option.

CHAPTER THIRTEEN

Running Down the Dream

"We must undergo a hard winter training and not rush into things for which we haven't prepared."

— EPICTETUS

BEFORE THE VIRTUAL RELATIONSHIPS we take for granted today, before Zoom and the many other ways we meet now, Jeff and I talked on the phone all the time, but we never met in person. He devised weekly training plans for me, regimens that took anywhere from twelve to eighteen hours. I emailed him my results, and then we'd discuss what happened that week.

We'd talk about progress, run times, pace, obstacles, injuries—whatever should be factored into the program. Then, Jeff adjusted the next week's plan to accommodate the challenges we identified. Our relationship was deep and dynamic.

But I knew it was vital to take care of my most important relationships, too. There's a reason Ironman athletes have the highest divorce rate of any sport. The goal attracts high achievers, people already working sixty, seventy, or eighty hours a week. Then they spend another twenty hours training, which leaves no time for family.

When you're married to an Ironman triathlete, your spouse rises at four in the morning for a two-hour workout before work, spends a long day on the job, and logs another hour-long workout at the end of the day. Then, they fall into bed early to get enough sleep to repeat the routine the next day. No energy remains for anything else.

The weekend is no better. A typical Saturday includes a 100- or 150-mile bike ride. Sundays are for running, at least three hours of it. It's easy to see how the sport wrecks relationships. I saw a lot of marriages, including those of some of my friends, dissolve.

I determined that the only way I could protect my family was to train during the day when the rest of the world was working. I did that long bike ride on Fridays and the weekend run on Saturday, out by six a.m. and back home in three hours. That's how I mitigated the divorce rate.

Most people can't do that, and I could not have done it without Mike. But he was fully engaged, and I needed to stay out of his hair. He gave me the ability to balance my family and my endurance journey.

Plus, Andrea and I had a deal. She agreeably tolerated my triathlon training in exchange for traveling to destination races.

"You can do this," she said, "but we gotta go to some cool places."

This was a treaty we could both live with.

On January 13, 2008, eight days before stock markets plunged around the world, I ran the Rock 'n' Roll Arizona marathon, finishing in three hours, twenty-two minutes—fifteen minutes faster than two years earlier at Disney. It was the first in a series of races Jeff had me do in preparation for Ironman Florida.

While the rest of the world was glued to the news of market crashes, the subprime mortgage crisis, and a looming global recession, I was geeking out on the science of fitness. In hindsight, I see the extraordinary value of this obsession. Rather than worrying and focusing on the myriad of issues I could do absolutely nothing about, I dialed into what I could control—my own actions.

In endurance training, these races leading up to the Ironman are known as "B" races. You never give them everything you've got. You don't race them all out. Instead, each is a gauge of your fitness level. They are an opportunity to gain strength in specific areas to get your body and your mind ready for the big event. The idea is to prevent overtraining while identifying what you need to work on.

So, the Rock 'n' Roll marathon was really just a training day. I wasn't trying to break any records. My only goal was to see how well I could do while staying as close to my maximum aerobic heart rate as possible without exceeding it.

Aerobic (with oxygen) versus anaerobic (without oxygen) is the fine line runners skirt in training and finishing races. Your Maximum Aerobic Function (MAF), a term coined by Dr. Phil Maffetone, is typically 180 minus your age. Depending on your fitness, your MAF may be five or ten beats higher. The important detail to know is that with proper training, an athlete—and Dr. Maffetone believes everyone is an athlete—can sustain an aerobic pace nearly indefinitely.

However, even the fittest athletes in the world cannot maintain an anaerobic pace for long before slowing down or stopping. You can only be in that anaerobic zone for a limited time before your body says, "Mercy. I'm done. I can't go anymore." Whenever you go anaerobic, you're on borrowed time.

Our goal with that first marathon was to stay right around my heart rate threshold without going over it. We didn't know what kind of pace or time I was capable of doing, but the plan was to hold that threshold throughout the race. This is not to say that staying just under that magic number is easy. It's hard, but it's doable. I learned to trust the science. I knew I could hover near my maximum heart rate for an entire race without slowing down or walking.

Here's the irony: You have to go slow before you go fast. That's what's really hard. When everyone is passing you, the peer pressure is on, and the ego screams, *Oh, hell no!* the most important thing to do is hold your pace. There's a reason the fabled tortoise won the match against the hare. There's a reason for the Ecclesiastical warning that the race is not to the swift. There's a reason Jeff told me that if I hold the heart rate, I could run a pretty good time.

Those hares flame out. They slow down, and that's your moment.

"Don't worry about how many people pass you," Jeff said. "But at the halfway point of the race, start counting how many people you pass, and by the end, you won't even be able to keep up with the number."

And that's what happened. I ran my best marathon time ever and felt great at the end of the race. I left the finish line to catch a plane to Montana, where I joined my family and skied with my son the next day.

Another term often applied to this type of training is periodization. This progressive conditioning program takes the long-term goal—in my case, to finish strong in the 140-mile race—and breaks it down into periods and events that focus on different variables. With periodization, you train hard for three or four weeks, and then you scale back the intensity to about 50 percent. This allows your body to absorb the change. You need a rest before you can add another layer to the base.

Varying "B" race lengths also helped me prepare for the Ironman. They were an audition—you could even call them a rehearsal—for the big performance.

But for the "B" races, you run them as part of the training for that week. You don't taper or rest ahead of race day. In fact, you run them tired, really tired. Jeff wanted me to go into these events absolutely smoked.

In March, when I ran the Berry Half Marathon closer to home in Rome, Georgia, it was just a Saturday long run. But our plan was for me to run it fast.

"I want you to run above your aerobic threshold," Jeff said, "but make sure the first half is slower than the second."

It's called a negative split, and it's really, really, *really* hard to do. You have to be disciplined to go slower than you're capable of so that you can go faster later. The hare in you wants to follow all the bats flying out of hell at the starting line. He wants to race with them, but you have to hang back. You have to check your ego at the door when the guy you know you can beat zooms by.

Fighting back all those speeding demons, I ran the first half at threshold but the last six and a half miles in an anaerobic state. I finished third in my age group in an hour and twenty-nine minutes, stoking the private embers of my secret desire to run a sub-three-hour marathon. When I doubled the distance and the time, I knew I had the potential to finish twenty-six miles in under three hours. I was ecstatic!

Jeff and I were building the groundwork for Ironman Florida. You can't have a solid fitness level without a healthy aerobic base. You just can't. But if you lay that foundation, when it's time to go up, you can ascend quickly.

After the Berry Half, I spent the spring and early summer training for the Vineman Half Ironman, which takes place in Northern California's wine country. Andrea was pleased. This one met the conditions of our treaty.

Jeff planned for me to run this as an "A" race. An "A" race is followed by a couple of weeks of light training. So, in addition to spending a long weekend in Napa Valley, Andrea and I could hang out in San Francisco without worrying about me having to go out on long runs or bike rides every day. We were both looking forward to the downtime.

The spring training schedule included a Thursday night ride with my buddy Danny Beck and some other friends from high school who were into cycling. Most of these guys did not swim or run. Cycling was everything for them. Anywhere from fifteen to thirty people would join us for these rides.

One of these guys, my friend Josh Shields, was also a triathlete. He's actually the person who got me into the sport. He was a hell of a competitor, and Josh and I would jump into these Thursday night groups and put the wood to the rest of the cyclists. Our mutual goal was to push the pace and blow up anyone who tried to hang with us. We were all like kids again. People chased us, but no one caught us. Those fifty- or sixty-mile rides were a highlight of the week.

Keep in mind that I followed this with a long ride on Fridays and then a long run on Saturday mornings. As you can imagine, I was tired. Tired as hell. All the time. In fact, that whole year was about managing fatigue. It was about showing up and doing the workout anyway because in the real deal, in a 140-mile race—*and in life and business*—you're going to get tired. The key is to learn how to absorb that fatigue and manage a constant state of bone-weariness.

Before an "A" race, you scale back training for ten to fourteen days, working at about 50 percent of the normal rates. Fewer miles, slower paces, fewer days. For the first time in weeks or months, you're getting some rest. It's called tapering, and it works like a slingshot. By the time you get to the starting line, you feel like a caged animal. You're ready to rip the head off anything around you.

Zig-zagging across the country again, I arrived at Johnson's Beach in Sonoma County on Wednesday, July 16. I was confident, prepared, primed, pumped, and intensely focused. Despite Jeff's warning—any and everything can go wrong, remember?—I had internal goals to meet. I wanted to break five hours that weekend, which would put me in an excellent position to finish the full Ironman in less than eleven hours. I had done the work. I was fit, trained, and ready. Why not?

When the fog rose from the Russian River on Sunday morning, it was fifty-three degrees, and I had nothing to keep me warm. I was so cold my teeth were chattering. At that moment, pros and amateurs alike understood why someone would say the coldest winter they had ever spent was a summer in San Francisco.

The water was cold, too, cold enough that Ironman rules allowed participants to wear wetsuits. The extra warmth and buoyancy made plunging into the seventy-two-degree water much more pleasant than freezing on the shore. The air was still fifty-three degrees when I emerged from the nearly one-and-a-half-mile swim and peeled the insulating wetsuit off my body. When I got on the bike, I was so frozen that my feet felt like bricks. I couldn't move them. It was not fun.

A good time for the fifty-six-mile bike ride would have been three hours or less. I finished that part of the race in three hours and fifteen minutes. By then, the sun was hot, and on the unshaded course, I went from freezing to burning up.

Okay, I thought, *I am not going to do as well in this race as I had hoped.* And then the second-guessing started.

Damn, this is half the distance of Ironman, and it is really, really hard, I thought. *What the hell did I sign up for?*

Meanwhile, the pros were crossing the finish line. They were gathering in the cooldown area as I began my run. It took me five hours and fifteen minutes to finish. I was demoralized.

"Jeff, there's no way I'm going to be able to do an Ironman," I told him afterward.

"Doug, it was fifty-three degrees in the morning," he countered. "You didn't have any warm layers, so you were burning a tremendous number of calories just to stay warm. And the course was hilly."

It was true. The course was much harder than I expected. The elevation profile on paper looked easy. The reality of climbing those first fifteen miles was not at all like I thought it would be.

"Florida will be completely flat," he said, continuing to tell me why it was a good race.

My heart had been set on a sub-five-hour race. I wanted the confidence this would have given me heading into the Ironman. Double my time, then add thirty minutes. *I should be able to finish the Ironman in less than eleven hours. Really, I should.* These preconceived ideas of what I should be doing messed with my mind. Even though I knew that moments like these are when you have to trust the process and listen to the coach, I drove myself crazy with the calculations.

In October, I got closer to my goal with another Half Ironman on Florida's Amelia Island, my last race before the full Ironman. By then, I was training fifteen to eighteen hours a week. For this race, we didn't taper, so I was exhausted. Worn out. And when you're fatigued, your emotions are all over the place. I wasn't even sure I wanted to go to Amelia.

"Man, just jump in and do it," Jeff said.

I listened and left on a Tuesday. At the last minute, Andrea and Grant came with me. Then, her dad and stepmom drove up from Tampa. We'd never been to Amelia Island. It ended up being a fun week hanging out with the family.

I appreciated that aspect of the experience, but on race day, I was freaking out. The wind was howling, so much so that I wondered if they might cancel the swim part of the triathlon. The waves were up to four feet.

Shit. Not only am I tired and really not wanting to do the race, but this is going to hurt.

Sure enough, the swells were major. I was constantly swallowing big gulps of salt water. People were swimming on top of me. There's a reason they call it a human washing machine. The swim sucked.

Then, it seemed like I raced against a headwind the whole bike ride. The island was barren and ugly. I was miserable, beyond tired, and getting scared, really scared, about the upcoming Ironman.

When it came time to run, I was so mad at myself that I couldn't do it. I walked, the thing you never, ever want to do in one of these races. Once you start walking, it's so hard to run again. It's like Kryptonite to Superman. But many people end up walking, and this time, I was one of them.

Soon, I was crying, and then I shot Jeff's nutrition rules to hell and drank a Coke that someone handed me from the side of the road. Then I drank another. And another.

"I'll show him," I thought.

Amelia turned out to be the hardest race of my life, but I finished three minutes faster than Vineman, at five hours and twelve minutes.

"I don't want to do the Ironman," I told Jeff afterward. "I think I'm just going to quit."

"Look," he said. "Everything that happened is good. This is all normal. All this stuff you're going through is normal."

Why on earth do people do this? I wondered.

"It's about overcoming adversity," Jeff said. "This is as hard as it's going to get. You just experienced it. You were walking through hell. That's the Ironman right there. But you did it, and you can do it on race day. You're going to be tapered. You're going to be great."

A few weeks later, I was tapering, slowing down before the race, and I was nervous. Once you start tapering, you worry you're losing fitness. I was running in our neighborhood for the last time before Ironman Florida, and all my fears were running with me. Not paying attention, I twisted my ankle on a curb.

Oh shit, I thought. *Here it is. This whole year gone.*

I had to sit down—I couldn't even walk!—and had only a week to heal.

"Ice and rest," Jeff said. "Don't do anything else. Just ice and rest."

Four days before the Ironman, and I was injured, unable to walk or pedal. Still, the family loaded up with me and headed to Panama City. My mom came along, and Andrea's dad was there, too.

Triathletes often get together for rides before the race, but I had to skip that to rest and nurse my ankle. At the pre-race meeting, a mandatory gathering, it was getting real.

"Every single one of you in this room is an Ironman or Ironwoman," the race director said. "You've done the work. You're sitting here. You. Are. Ironmen. You've already made it. Tomorrow is just a matter of going out and having fun."

I realized he was right. We were all fit enough to do the distance. We just had to show up and do it.

I didn't sleep well the night before the race—no one does—but I rested really well on Thursday, two days before, which is very important. And I continued to take care of my ankle.

The morning of November 1, 2008, was cold, but this time, I wore layers. I bundled up, watched the sunrise on the beach, said the Pledge of Allegiance with 2,600 other athletes, and waved to my family. It was an emotional moment.

I decided to take my time, enjoy the swim, and have some fun. To avoid the human washing machine, I kept to the far right of the pack. The course was two laps around an orange buoy a mile from the start. My ankle was hurting, but otherwise, I felt terrific. The swim was easy. Soon, I was in a flow state, not watching where I was going. When I looked up, I was two or three hundred yards off course.

Panicking, I headed left to the buoy, realizing I'd lost at least ten minutes just by being an idiot. The second lap went well, though, and I felt good. I was grateful for the volunteers who helped me out of my wetsuit. Recentered, I got on the bike, thinking, *I'm just going to carpe diem this day.*

My ankle was sore, but the pain was manageable. A headwind opposed the bike ride, but people all along the way cheered us on. One hundred and twelve miles and about five hours later, I felt great when I got off the bike. Invincible even.

I was nailing the nutrition and hydration and decided to run based on how I felt. I didn't care about heart rate. I was just running. As I headed out, the race leaders were coming in. I couldn't believe they had finished the whole race when I was starting the marathon.

One of the most challenging aspects of Ironman Florida was the running course, a six-mile out-and-back through beautiful St. Andrews State Park. The emerald waters of the Gulf of Mexico and the dunes and white beaches were stunning. We ran through the park, came back to the finish line, then turned around to do it all again. I cannot describe how hard it was to leave the finish line to run twelve more miles.

Cheers from the sideline helped.

"Hey man, you look good! You're running fast, and you're strong. You got this!"

They gave me some confidence, but I struggled on that second loop.

With no spectators in the park, it was just me and the rest of the runners. I started thinking about my time, realizing I would not break eleven hours. And the negative thoughts took over.

I can't … I won't … I'll never … Why am I even here?

At a breaking point, I started walking. I was feeling sorry for myself when another competitor came alongside me.

"Hey, is this your first Ironman?" he asked.

"Please leave me alone," I said. "I don't want to talk to anybody right now."

He didn't leave. I couldn't get rid of him.

"Hey, this is my twentieth Ironman," he said. "This happens. You're going to be all right."

"I was hoping to finish in under eleven hours," I said. "That time goal is out the window. I'm just going to walk it in."

"Why?"

"Because I don't even care anymore."

He stopped me then and looked me in the eyes.

"You look great right now, and there's no reason you can't start running again," he said. "Here's what I want you to do. As soon as we finish this conversation, I want you to run all the way in. You can do it."

He continued, "You're going to finish under eleven and a half hours, and that's an awesome first-time goal," he said. "For most people, just finishing is great, but I think if you take off running right now, you'll beat eleven and a half hours. That needs to be your goal right now. You've got this!"

"Man, I appreciate the confidence," I said, "but I can't."

We walked and talked for thirty more minutes. He was from Colorado, in his mid-forties, I'm guessing. I don't remember the specifics of our conversation, but we went deep into life wisdom and experiences, kids, all of it. I started feeling better, and he brought us back to the beginning.

"You need to go," he said. "Right now."

"Come with me," I said. "Let's run together."

"I can't," he said. "I'm done. I'm walking in, but you don't need to be walking. You can do it."

In a minute, I was running as fast as I could, turning fifteen-minute miles that felt like five minutes. I was giving it all I had, hardly moving, but seeing myself in *Chariots of Fire*. I remember hearing the crowd in the distance and the announcer saying, "So and so, you are an Ironman." "So and so, you are an Ironman." "So and so, you are an Ironman." And on and on.

I kept my head down, sprinting toward the finish line as fast as I could, and then I heard my own salute: "Doug Augustine, you are an Ironman!"

I finished strong in eleven hours, twenty-nine minutes, and twenty-eight seconds, avoided the medical tent, and ranked 125th in the men's 35–39 division.

When I crossed the line, my family was there. Andrea, Grant, Andrea's dad, my mom—everybody. They were hugging me and cheering, and it was a crazy, wonderful experience.

"Take me to Wendy's," I said. "I want a freaking hamburger. Like right now."

And they did. At the drive-thru, I ordered a single with pickles and mustard. It was the best hamburger I've ever had in my life.

"Doug," you may be asking, "what does this have to do with running restaurants?"

Only everything. Every. Single. Thing.

With Andrea at the starting line of Ironman Florida November 1, 2008

CHAPTER FOURTEEN

Breakthrough

*"Even if some obstacle comes on the scene, its appearance
is only to be compared to that of clouds which drift in
front of the sun without ever defeating its light."*

— SENECA

MORE THAN ONE KIND OF ENDURANCE TRAINING was underway in 2008.
Naveen launched a methodical growth campaign, and we spent the entire
year trying to buy more restaurants. If I had to describe Naveen in three
words, they would be "very well organized."

First, we approached Taco Bell with proposals we thought made
sense for the franchise and for us. We asked for the opportunity to buy
some of their corporate stores in the Atlanta market, but they weren't
interested. They had nothing against us; they just didn't want to sell any
of their stores.

"If we ever decide to sell corporate stores, you're going to be the first person we call," we were told.

Naveen also called other owners. We were willing to buy anywhere in the Southeast. Without disclosing the identity of his client, he said he had a franchisee who was looking to grow.

"Are you interested in selling?" he asked repeatedly.

Over and over again, the answer was "no." Naveen kept telling me good things were going to happen.

"Just hang in there," he said. "Be patient."

He was conservative. He never proposed an acquisition that might stretch us financially.

"You never know what will happen with the economy," he said.

If a situation didn't make sense for us, he didn't even tell me about it.

"I wouldn't be able to sleep at night if I put you in a deal that went south," he said. "Any deal that I put you in will be a home run."

At the Taco Bell convention that fall, we were still stalled on the growth front, but I hit a home run in a more important arena. I was wearing my Auburn shirt when I bumped into Nick Davis, who was also sporting an Auburn shirt.

"War Eagle!" we cheered simultaneously.

This may have been the first time we had ever met in person. Neither of us is certain about that, but I had no idea he was an Auburn grad, and I don't think he knew I went to school there, either.

"Hey, if you ever want to go to any games, I've got tickets," he said. "You just let me know."

"Man, that's really kind of you," I said. "I haven't been to a game in a long time. I may take you up on that."

A few weeks later, I had a break in my Ironman training schedule, so I followed up on the conversation.

"My son, Grant, is five years old, and he's never been to an Auburn game," I told Nick. "I'd love to take him if you have tickets this weekend."

"I do," he said, "and I'm going to be in Auburn. I've got a garage apartment behind my house. You guys just go to the game and have fun and stay there."

I accepted his generous offer, and a few days later, on a beautiful fall Saturday, Grant and I were seated in the scholarship section. I didn't even know such a place existed, but as I talked to folks around us, I realized they all had a kid on the field.

"See number fifty?" one woman said, pointing to a player on the field. "That's my grandson."

I was blown away. It was such a fun place to be sitting, especially when Auburn won and we all lost our minds! Grant and I joined in the fun tradition of rolling the oaks at Toomer's Corner after the game. The weather was awesome, and we had a great day together. At home the next evening, Grant and I engaged in our favorite bedtime storytelling routine. I would make up a story, and he would make up a story, and we went back and forth while the sun set. The room was getting dark when, between stories, Grant said, "This was the best day of my life, Dad."

The next morning, I made a call.

"Hey Nick, I don't care what those tickets cost. I want two tickets right there," I said. "Forever."

He laughed.

"Doug, first of all, those seats aren't for sale," he said. "And second, I've had them a long time."

He proceeded to explain how the "good seats" are reserved for donors. Noted.

At the end of 2008, I remained in a holding pattern. Despite Naveen's best efforts, our attempts to grow were not successful. I felt like the athlete who qualified but was too far back in the registration line to get into the big race. It would have been easy to be frustrated. Year one of our expansion campaign was a bust.

I could have second-guessed my decision to work with Naveen, but trusting the process was my default response. The voices of Ben Green, Scott Curson, Roy Benson, and Jeff Cuddeback played in my head. The backs of fast runners early in the race passed before my eyes. I knew not to rush, not to force the timing. I waited.

On December 31, I had the same six restaurants that we'd had at the start of the year, but an Ironman medal hung in my office and new friendships were blooming.

Early in 2009, Brian Frank was on the phone.

"Hey, you guys want to go riding with me for a couple of weeks in Italy?"

Wow. And ugh. I had a lot of balls up in the air. Naveen and I were in constant back-and-forth discussions on potential acquisitions, and Andrea and I had a five-year-old at home.

Andrea, always my voice of reason, implored: "Are you kidding? Don't be an idiot, Doug! You have an opportunity to ride bikes in Italy with Brian Frank, a guy who speaks fluent Italian and at least three other languages. You'll never have a chance like this again!"

She assured me that she and Grant would be fine.

"Don't even worry about us," she said. "You're going to have a great time, and you'll come home with more great stories!"

She was right, of course.

Cycling in Europe is a lot like boxing in the United States. It's a bit of an underground sport, but a national presence and pride surrounds it. In the same way that we have boxing clubs in large and small cities across America, many communities in Italy have cycling clubs. Like boxing, cycling is hard, mentally and physically. Cyclists worry about

everything from being hit by cars on the road to the logistics and endurance challenges of long-distance rides. It's a tough sport that attracts
tough participants.

When Danny and I joined Brian Frank in Italy in 2009, we rode with
the Bertis, a hundred-plus-year-old men's cycling club based in Cuveglio,
Italy. Every year, the group, made up mostly of men in their fifties and
early sixties, sets off in June on a two-week cycle across the country. They
choose a place they haven't been to recently, or ever, and plan a trip around
it. For two weeks, Danny, Brian, and I meandered across Northern Italy
with this Italian cycling group. And we had a blast.

We arrived in Italy a few days before the tour began in June. This gave
us time to meet our hosts and acclimate to the time change and new
terrain. We spent those first days in the province of Varese. From there,
one afternoon, Brian, Danny, and I biked into Switzerland, where the
town of Lugano took my breath away. Stopping next to a marina at the
base of a mountain, I made a pledge.

"I'm coming back here with my family at some point in my life," I
told Danny. "I have to bring them to this place."

The 2009 Bertis bike expedition would follow the southern tip of Italy,
down the heel of the boot, all the way to the toe, and back. On Sunday
morning, we loaded our bikes into the Bertis crew van, which traveled
ahead of us, serving as transport, repair shop, and chuckwagon for the
trip. A few hours later, we joined more than two dozen cyclists, including
several other Americans, and flew to Brindisi to begin the tour.

More than twenty riders clad in matching red and white set out
each day around eight in the morning to cover 100 to 150 kilometers
before evening. The excursions were long but relatively easy. These were
non-drop rides, which means everyone stayed together. No one was ever

left behind. Our goal was to make about two-thirds of the day's distance before stopping for lunch.

We hugged the east coast from Brindisi to Lecce and proceeded through coastal towns all along the Adriatic and Ionian seas. For twelve days, we pedaled by blue-green waters, groves of olive trees, and rocky brown-brush hillsides to the brick and paved streets of small towns across Southern Italy. We wandered through ruins, resorts, bike shops, cafés, and waterside pubs.

The Bertis van followed our peloton, fixing flats, providing support, and buying provisions along the way. Around midday, we paused in a picturesque spot and unloaded tables, tablecloths, and an amazing spread of Italian meats, cheese, fruit, bread, and—most importantly—bottles and bottles of wine, which flowed freely for the rest of the day. We lingered over the meal for up to an hour and a half, hunting down a nice cup of coffee in cafés when available. I looked forward to this relaxing highlight of each day. Back on the road, we usually arrived at our destination between four and six in the afternoon, grabbed a quick shower at our hotel, and headed out sightseeing if interesting spots were nearby. We reconvened later in the evening for dinner, a rowdy, joyful four-hour event powered by endless toasts, tales, and sing-alongs. Danny and I were 5,300 miles from home but a million miles away from the day-to-day concerns of business.

Italians laugh at American cyclists. We're too serious, they say. We ride with our heads down so we can go fast and avoid hitting obstacles. We're obsessed with training plans, intervals, and pace. It's all about our speed and whether you can keep up with us. In comparison, they are the complete opposite. They ride with their heads up. They don't care how fast they're going.

Now we understood what Brian Frank meant in 2006 when he said we would be cycling the Highline Hammer *European-style*. The Italians are all about the ride and the scenery, about being together and having fun. Don't get me wrong. They're strong cyclists. They'll race you to a street sign or another spot ahead, but then it's back to the party. They're heads-up riding again. Their water bottles were filled with wine, and they made fun of Danny and me for our frequent stops.

"You guys stop drinking all that water! We're stopping all the time for you to pee!"

My first trip to Europe made a big impression on me. We weren't accidental tourists on this trip. We were embedded, spending time with our cycling group and people we met as we traveled through small communities. Relationships transcended language barriers. We communicated. We connected. I was amazed at how friendly people were, how much they loved their country, and how chill everyone was.

The contrast between the cultures was impossible to miss. Americans go through life in a hurry. We're always trying to get to the next level. We're in a hurry to finish the ride, the project, the book, or whatever we're doing so we can move ahead to another goal. We go, go, go, go, go.

In Italy, no one was in a hurry. Shops were closed in the afternoons when people rested and napped, and no one seemed anxious. Traveling with more than two dozen people, you can imagine how many things could go wrong, but no one worried, and everything turned out okay. Better than okay. Everything was wonderful.

I came home with a renewed appreciation for relationships—the ones we made on the trip and the ones we brought with us. I marveled at how my nearly lifelong friendship with Danny brought me back to cycling, how that reunion took the two of us to Montana, and how our crazy adventures led to meeting Brian Frank, which is how we found ourselves making friends all over Italy.

Later that summer, I got a call out of the blue from Nick Davis. We had not talked since the game that Grant and I went to the year before. He told me that after being on a waiting list for twenty years, he had been awarded a suite at Auburn's Jordan-Hare Stadium.

"I'll never forget that story you told me about Grant," he said. "Would you like to go in half with me?"

"I think my CFO would probably appreciate it if I were to have a partner," he laughed.

I couldn't afford half of the suite, I told him.

"What if you just take four of the twelve seats?" he offered.

"That would be great!" I said, and I've missed very few home games since.

If a moral can be found in these tales, it's this:

When you're taking yourself too seriously, go have some fun. Life is short and best lived heads-up.

Back at home, I eased off training, which was causing a tremendous amount of inflammation in my body. (European-style cycling does *not* count.) I realized that the more rigorous the activity, the more my body broke down. I wasn't sleeping well and frequently injured myself. Ironically, the harder I worked, the less healthy I became.

I began to think about where I wanted to be in twenty years. *What would make me physically and mentally better in two decades?* I knew the answer wouldn't be found in triathlons. On November 26, 2009, I finished the Atlanta Marathon in three hours and twelve minutes, ranking fifth in my age division and thirty-third overall. Still active. Still competitive. More strategic. With one more race on my bucket list, my goal was to remain fit enough to run it. The Atlanta Marathon finish qualified me for Boston.

The long-term horizons in business and health were on my mind. *Where did we want to be a fourth of the way through the century?* Late in the year, after a disappointing string of roadblocks, Naveen called with a surprising question.

"What do you think about getting into Burger King?" he asked.

"Hell no!" was my first response.

I wasn't a fan of Burger King operations. Besides, Georgia-Texas runs Taco Bells. It's who we are. It's where we started. It's what we do. Bender didn't like the idea either.

"Hear me out," Naveen said and proceeded to tell me about four stores in the Atlanta market with good volume and a lot of room for operational improvement.

"I can get you a good deal on these stores if you want to get in the Burger King system," he said.

The thought felt wrong, but with respect for Naveen, I did my best to keep an open mind.

"He knows what he's doing," everyone had told me. "He's good at it."

Listening to experts who know more than you do, then *following their advice,* is a simple concept. Otherwise, you're wasting everyone's time. It's the cornerstone principle in my life, the practice that took me from Ben's gym to Olympic weightlifting. It carried me through a business turnaround to the negotiating table. Knowledgeable mentors and advisors had served me well. It seemed like a good practice to continue.

Naveen pointed out that the Burger King situation was similar to what I had faced in the past. The stores were dirty, service was slow, and employees were rude.

"You know, it sounds like exactly what you did after your dad died," he said.

He was right about that. I'd been there, done that before. He upped the ante by pointing out that real estate was included.

"I can get you a good deal on these stores if you want to get into Burger King."

"Hey, Mike, we just bought some Burger Kings."

"Wait, I wasn't done analyzing this!"

"Well, tough shit, we own them now."

This is how Bender remembers the story. We were going into the third year of our partnership, and this pivotal moment sums up the roles we assumed in the business.

Mike takes a measured, pragmatic approach to decisions. He calculates data and variables through a very ones-and-zeros brain. On the other hand, I trust my gut. I'm not reckless or risky, but I have courage. I may be afraid, but I do it anyway. We make a good team.

In fairness, Mike's hesitation was understandable. It was the early days of our relationship with Auspex. Neither Mike nor I had anything other than the recommendation of other clients and my gut feeling to base our confidence upon. Auspex specializes in helping owners of franchise restaurants grow their businesses. They are known for working with clients of all sizes, but we only had six stores. Would they really represent us in the same way they did people with dozens or even hundreds of restaurants?

My attorney didn't think so. An eternal pessimist, Brian Wooldridge was conservative and always my protector. He and Naveen butted heads fiercely in the beginning. I often found myself in the referee position with those two. Lawyers don't get paid to trust people, and he was far from forgetting what we went through with Atherton. After that experience, who could blame him for zealous caution?

But the two companies were dramatically different. Atherton was essentially a bank, whereas Auspex is a full-service financial advisory company. Auspex doesn't lend you money. They negotiate on your behalf, find the best deals from lenders, and then watch your back as contracts mature. They go after the devil in the details, where hidden fees and other easy-to-miss and expensive pitfalls wait to creep up on you later.

Clients love them. Banks? Not so much. That fact alone helped me sleep at night.

So in 2010, we went from owning six restaurants to ten, nearly doubling in size.

Taco Bell was less than thrilled. A corporate emissary came to Atlanta to talk to me about the situation.

"Doug, we're not real happy that you're in the Burger King business," he said.

"I'm not that happy about it, either," I told him.

"What?" he asked, looking puzzled. "Then why did you diversify?"

"Do you know why I'm in the Burger King business?"

"I have no idea," he said.

"Because you guys won't sell me any stores," I said. "Y'all made this decision. If it was my decision, we wouldn't be Burger King franchisees. We'd have more Taco Bells."

Despite how we arrived at this juncture, Mike and I were on the same page with the new stores once we got there. Naveen was right. Sloppy operations were familiar territory. We both knew how to turn that around. Fixer-uppers were our jam.

The owner of the Burger Kings we purchased held more than seventy restaurants in the Pacific Northwest and only four stores in Atlanta. Geographically, that's a challenge. It's easy to understand why the stores were hard for his company to run and why they were for sale. At the time of purchase, the real estate was more valuable than the operations.

Under Mike's leadership, we cleaned up the new stores, fixed all the broken equipment, and began improving the physical properties. Customers noticed. Once we started remodeling, the sales increases were astronomical. No one was complaining about that.

Life was busy but good.

In May, I completed a Half Ironman in White Lake, North Carolina, in five hours and twenty-eight minutes. I went back to Europe that summer with Brian and Danny, cycling for a couple of weeks in France. On November 7, I crossed the finish line at the New York City Marathon in three hours and fourteen minutes, fast enough again to qualify for my top marathon bucket list, Boston. A qualifying time does not guarantee you'll get into the race, but it does enter you into the lottery for a limited field of participants.

On November 26, Auburn met Alabama in Tuscaloosa for the Iron Bowl, the rivalry first played between the schools in 1893. At halftime, Alabama led 24–7. The Tigers scored twice in the third quarter while Alabama made a field goal, closing the gap to 21–27. Then, in one of the greatest comebacks in the history of the rivalry, the Tigers scored a touchdown and then the extra point in the fourth quarter for a final score of 28–27. Victory is even sweeter in enemy territory.

The following week, we beat South Carolina to end a perfect 13–0 winning season and clinch the SEC Championship.

There's nothing, *nothing*, like ending a year on a winning streak. We had momentum, and then some, going into 2011.

Look who we ran into at the 2010 National Championship weekend! "Sir Charles" Barkley, All–American Auburn alum and former NBA power forward. War Eagle!

CHAPTER FIFTEEN
Heads Up

"You fight it when it don't look good, you fight it when everybody counts you out, you fight it when there's no way that anyone thinks you can do it but you, you keep fighting and at some point you're going to win it."

— GENE CHIZIK

THE SAME YEAR WE BOUGHT FOUR Burger Kings, Nick Davis sold thirty-two Taco Bells. He retained the real estate on twenty-two stores with twenty-year leases. It was a sweet deal, followed by an even sweeter chain of events.

Nick is a third-generation Tiger. In honor of his parents and grandparents, when Auburn headed to Arizona to face Oregon for the college football national championship title in January of 2011, he bought twenty-eight tickets to the game. He took nearly everyone in his family, plus a few lucky extras, including Andrea and me, to the University of Phoenix Stadium for the national championship playoff. Five of his six brothers and sisters and his mother were in the stands. The only time Auburn had ever won a national title was in 1957, so this game was a big—*big*—deal.

Like the 2010 Iron Bowl, the championship clash was another nail-biter. Neither team was ever very far behind or very far ahead. Neither team scored in the first quarter. The second quarter was juicier. At the end of the half, Auburn led 16–11. The Tigers made a field goal in the third quarter, ending the period ahead 19–11. But in the fourth quarter, Oregon scored a touchdown, then a two-point conversion within the first two and a half minutes, tying the score at 19–19. The tie held until Auburn made a nineteen-yard field goal with triple zeros on the clock, clinching its second national title in the school's history with a final score of 22–19.

Nick vividly remembers the intensity of this game. No one was chit-chatting or having side conversations. No one was talking about the weather or any concern outside of the stadium. Most of us never left our seats or visited the concession stand. At the end, we stood and cheered, but we really didn't talk to each other.

"It was the most bizarre thing," he recalls. "I remember looking back, thinking, 'This is surreal.' We were certainly excited, but we were all stunned and introspective. It was not the celebration you would expect," he says. "It was more like, 'Oh God, this finally happened!'"

The game left us speechless, and the weekend proved life-changing.

The following day, four inches of snow fell in Atlanta. Thousands of flights were canceled. None of us were able to fly home as planned. We couldn't stay in Phoenix, either, because every hotel room in the city was already booked. Nick came up with the idea to rent a fifteen-passenger van and shuttle everyone to Vegas, where a friend of his brother's managed the brand-new Cosmopolitan hotel. We all were able to get rooms there, so the post-game celebration took a road trip.

A few weeks after the national championship game, I was still on Cloud Nine. Andrea and I were having our coffee one morning when I realized she was crying.

"Babe, it's six o'clock in the morning," I said, bewildered. "What on earth?"

"You know that championship football game we went to?" she says. "You know how expensive it was?"

"Yeah, and worth every penny," I said.

"Well, it just got more expensive," she said. "I'm pregnant."

"What?!"

We were both forty. We hadn't thought this would happen for us again. Andrea was in shock, but I was so excited! I started tossing out ideas of what to name the baby. Gene Chizik was head coach at Auburn at the time.

"We could name him after the coach and my dad!" I suggested.

The quarterback, Cam Newton, won the Heisman that year, so I proposed, "Cameron sounds nice for a boy or a girl."

If looks could kill, I would not be writing this book.

We didn't choose either of those names, but the happy arrival of another son brought so much joy to our home. James, who will always be our championship baby, was born in September.

Before the year ended, we added another Burger King in Atlanta, a single-ton held by a franchisee getting out of the business. We closed the year with eleven stores. Not only was this nearly twice as many stores as we owned two years before, but we also posted twice the revenue and twice the profits.

If I were asked to identify a breakthrough era on my personal and company timeline, the period between 2009 and 2011 deserves consideration. This was when Mike and I collectively found our strides in our roles in the business. He was crushing it in operations. I was crushing it with new store acquisitions. We were learning how to set goals for growth, and our pivotal connection with Auspex and Naveen began to pay off. We had the right advisor for leveling up.

It's when I really learned to appreciate the value of taking a break and how new experiences in a new place can be exactly what's needed, especially when you're trying so hard to do something that isn't working. During this period, my intellectual understanding of why I should work *on* the business instead of *in* it became real. I couldn't have done it without Mike, and I think he would say the same about me.

It's when, once again, we proved the difference between costs and investments. Making things better is a capital investment, whether or not you see results on a P&L or balance sheet.

And it's when God sent us a gift, reminding us that a new person can make an exponential difference. We had no idea what we were missing until there, in our nursery, we snuggled a joy we had never imagined. Our family became not just bigger but stronger, both at home and at the office.

It must have been all those wins that inspired me to go for the medal I didn't have yet. A month before James was born, I began training for Boston. Having qualified several times, I decided it was time. I was fortunate to work with Tim Waggoner, an ultrarunner and elite amateur triathlete. Like my experience with Jeff Cuddeback, getting to work with Tim was a privilege. He was highly sought-after by professionals. I was honored that he made time for a weekend warrior like me. He was similar to Jeff in that he approached training very scientifically.

"I want to break three hours in Boston," I told Tim. I knew if anyone could help me reach that goal, it was this guy. His personal mission was to break the two-and-a-half-hour threshold, so we were on a similar track. The first leg of our journey took place on Thanksgiving Day at the 2011 Atlanta Half Marathon. I crossed the finish line in an hour and twenty-eight minutes, fourteenth in my age group and 133rd overall.

I had a lot to be grateful for.

In the spring of 2012, a record heatwave was underway in Boston. Typical highs were below sixty in the city during this season, but temperatures soared to eighty-eight degrees on April 16, the day I ran one of the world's best-known marathons. It was so hot that many runners sat it out, choosing to defer to the next year. Fewer than twenty-three thousand of the twenty-seven thousand registered runners entered the race. Having trained with Tim for nearly nine months, I felt ready and stayed the course.

My family was with me. Grant, age nine at the time, was studying the Boston Massacre and Paul Revere in school and loved hearing about the history from the guides on the Freedom Trail. He fell in love with the city. The atmosphere was intoxicating. The marathon takes place on Patriot's Day, which commemorates the first battles of the Revolutionary War. The holiday is observed on the third Monday in April each year, and everyone you meet is happy. The spring weather and long weekend electrify the setting for one of the most famous athletic events in the world.

Unfortunately, the heat affected every runner. My buddies who could run a sub-three had times like three forty. I finished in three hours and twenty-three minutes, which was probably the equivalent of running a two-fifty, fitness-wise, even though the clock didn't reflect that. I was ecstatic with these results, and so was Tim. But he had another idea.

"You're so fit right now," he said, "and you didn't hit your time. Let's knock out a sub-three marathon right after Boston."

A month later, I was headed to the Pocono Mountains for the Run for the Red Marathon. To use a baseball analogy, I was ready to knock the cover off the ball. The Pennsylvania race is known for being a fast marathon. The run was held on Sunday, May 20, and I was scheduled to fly out on Friday. But on Thursday, I contracted food poisoning. I felt deathly ill, and I was throwing up all night.

"I'm not even going to do this race," I told Tim on Friday morning. "It's not worth it."

We were both bummed. This was my chance to break that three-hour barrier. Tim pushed back.

"Look, you've already got your plane ticket," he said. "Just go out there. Listen to your body. If you feel good, go for it. If you don't, well, then don't."

"Oh, all right," I said.

Sigh. This is why you work with a coach.

The morning of the race, I woke up feeling pretty good, so I went for it. At the halfway point, I was at an hour and twenty-eight minutes. My heart rate was low, and I was rolling. I was in a flow state.

Hey, this is easy, I thought.

But as the miles rolled by, it got harder and harder. And harder. And I was no longer feeling good. Around twenty-two miles, I started walking. Pretty soon, I had to sit down on the curb, where I entered the beating-myself-up stage. But then I looked at my watch and realized that if I just stood up and started running again, I could make it in around three hours and fifteen minutes, which was what I needed to earn a chance to run in Boston again.

I got off the curb and limped in at three hours and twelve minutes—fast enough but a huge disappointment. So big that I decided I was done trying to break three hours. I didn't feel like doing it anymore.

The number of runners admitted to the Boston Marathon is limited. Qualifying does not guarantee admission, only the opportunity to apply. Since I qualified for it, if my application was accepted, I would tackle Boston once more, but I would run it easy. Heads up.

Celebrating Boston 2012 with James and Grant

Back at work, it became clear that we needed more administrative support. We still ran the company from the original office my dad had rented, but the building belonged to us now, and we took up all the space. With eleven restaurants, Charles was maxed out as the only full-time person at our headquarters. Mike spent much of his time in the field supporting operations. I was busy steering the ship, looking for new opportunities.

Occasionally, I made trips to the bank for Charles. We had an exceptional local bank. Their niche was accessibility and exquisite customer service. Teller windows opened at seven in the morning and closed at eight at night on weekdays, and at three on Saturdays. The culture must have been great because turnover was low. I was accustomed to seeing the same friendly faces whenever I visited.

One day, I was chatting with the teller operations manager at the drive-thru window.

"I'm looking for somebody to fill an administrative assistant position at our office," I told her. "If you know someone who might be a good fit for us, let me know."

"Well, I might be interested," she said.

"Really?"

"Yes."

She was upbeat and energetic, and I knew she would be an asset to our organization.

We met for lunch and swapped stories. She was twenty-three, about the same age I was when I came to work with my dad, and she had a toddler at home. She wanted shorter days and an opportunity to grow but had worked at the bank for five years and enjoyed some great benefits she didn't want to lose.

"I work part time, and I'm really not interested in grinding it out forty hours a week," she said. "I have four days off every week and get six weeks of vacation. It's a pretty sweet deal."

"No problem," I told her. "We can accommodate that."

She came on board in the summer of 2012 and gradually began offering to help in areas where she noticed inefficiencies. For instance, at the time, we were manually inputting documentation from employees in two different systems. Taco Bell had one way of doing things, and Burger King had another.

"Hey, I can help you with that," she said.

We had five operating companies at the time. Matching credit card invoices to the right company was time-consuming.

"Hey, I'm kind of bored," she said. "I'll do that for you. I'll help."

Mike and I began to think of her whenever a task was bogging us down. Insurance renewals and all the related meetings were tossed her way. She caught that ball and many more like a pro.

And this is how Abigail Bishop became part of the leadership team at Georgia-Texas.

Grant and I caught a Red Sox game at Fenway in 2013.

The next year, we returned for the 117th Boston Marathon. I was there to sign off, to turn off the lights on my endurance career. I hadn't trained for the race like I had for other marathons. This was my farewell tour. I didn't care about time anymore. We flew in on Friday, ready to enjoy ourselves. I wasn't worried about sleep or nutrition, just having a great time with my family.

Grant and I watched the Red Sox beat the Cleveland Indians at Fenway Park. James toddled around in the plazas in an adorable little red jacket. We had dinner at Atlantic Coast Seafood, where I talked about my plan for the race.

"Look, I am just going to carpe diem tomorrow," I said. "This is my tenth marathon, and it will be my last. I'm going to seize the day and enjoy it."

Heads up.

Grant was stunned.

"Dad, you're not even going to try?" he said. "I love coming to Boston, and I really want you to come back."

"I can't come back, buddy," I said.

"Why not?"

"Because I have to finish fast enough to earn an entry next year. I'm not going to race that kind of race. I'm not here to qualify."

He looked puzzled, like, *Who is this man? Is this my dad?* And then, a bit stern.

"I think you should try to qualify," he said.

I preferred an easy exit, but his voice resonated in my head for the rest of the day. Before I went to bed, I promised myself I would show this kid. Not only would I try, but I would qualify.

I woke up to beautiful blue skies, cool temperatures, and light winds. The perfect day to run a fast race. I was fired up. When the gun went off, I took off and eased into a seven-minute, twenty-six-second-per-mile pace, knowing I had to repeat this twenty-six times in a row to qualify.

Unlike most marathons, Boston is not a loop. It's a linear course. Runners are shuttled to Hopkinton, twenty-five miles west of the city, to begin the race. What most people don't understand about Boston, what makes it so hard, is that the first sixteen miles are downhill. It takes a lot of skill and discipline not to go out too fast, because the last ten miles are uphill.

Feeling good and pacing well, I had banked a little time coming into the dreaded four miles known as Heartbreak Hill. I had not prepared well physically, but mentally, I was strong. I had been here before, knew what was coming, and understood how to press through the darkness ahead. Soon, the iconic Citgo sign was visible, the signal that gave every runner hope. I knew I didn't have far to go. I crossed the finish line in three hours and thirteen minutes. I saw Andrea and the boys right away and jogged over, giving Grant a high-five and a bear hug.

"That was for you, buddy," I said. "That one was for you."

Back in the hotel room, I maintained the tradition that started with my Uncle Steve at the Marine Corps Marathon. I ordered a pizza and a six-pack and had just popped the top on my first beer when my cell phone rang. I looked down and saw that it was Abigail from the office. *So sweet,* I thought. *She's calling to see how I did in the race.*

"Hey, Abigail, what's up?"

"Are you okay?"

I chuckled.

"Yeah, I'm okay. My legs are a little tired, but I'm okay."

"Is your family okay? Are you okay?"

Why did she sound so worried?

"Doug, turn on the television. A bomb went off at the finish line of the race. Are you guys okay?"

I immediately went from a state of euphoria to panic and then despair. Soon, our hotel, like the rest of the city, was locked down. No one came in, and no one left. The lobby and common areas were filled with desperate people on their phones, trying to locate loved ones. Most runners check their phones with race officials or leave them with a friend or family member during the race. Once the bomb went off, the race shut down, and wherever a runner was on the course, that's where they stayed. It was nearly impossible to find them. The whole scene was the stuff of nightmares.

Outside, the city was still, eerily quiet. Authorities asked people to stay home while they looked for the bombers. It was the first time I had ever heard the phrase "shelter in place."

It was one of those moments in life when you realize nothing matters but your people. Is your family okay? Is everyone accounted for?

On our way home, an FBI agent approached me at the Atlanta gate at the airport.

"Did you see anything unusual?" he asked. "Anything weird?"

"No sir."

"I don't care how trivial it seems to you, any detail could help us," he said.

"I'm sorry. I can't think of anything."

It was a short exchange. Federal agents were talking to many of the people around us. I left with a new appreciation for law enforcement. If they were talking to random people like me, I knew they would catch the guys responsible for this evil act.

Looking back, I am so grateful to Grant. He challenged me to go for the win. He wore a Boston Marathon T-shirt in a photo capturing the moment, which, according to the metadata on the picture, was taken at 1:30 p.m. If I had run the race I originally planned, I would have crossed the finish line in four hours and twenty minutes, and my family and I would have been at Copley Square when the bombs went off at 2:49 p.m.

Heads up, but do not settle.

Grateful – Boston 2013

CHAPTER SIXTEEN

Catalysts

"Nothing really worth having comes quickly and easily. If it did, I doubt we would ever grow."

— EKNATH EASWARAN

NOT LONG AFTER WE BECAME Burger King franchisees, a private equity group bought Burger King Worldwide Holdings. Neither Mike nor I was excited about the change in leadership. Many people we had met and established relationships with had been replaced, and a nervous case of buyer's remorse settled on both of us like a blanket.

I called Naveen.

"We want out of Burger King," I told him. "We are not enjoying this anymore."

"Just hang on," he said. "Trust me. I'll tell you when to sell. Just keep doing what you're doing."

So we did. Not joyfully. Not without some agony. Not unlike running a marathon in a heatwave, but we stayed the course.

In 2014, Naveen called with good news.

"I've got a buyer for the Burger Kings," he said. "And I've got a seller on the Taco Bell side."

Naveen negotiated a deal that made us enough profit to buy the new restaurants outright. By the end of the year, we had sold five Burger Kings and bought four Taco Bells in North Georgia. We did it all within the same year in a 1031 exchange of assets that satisfied the IRS requirements to defer capital gains taxes.

With Naveen's help, we had borrowed the money to buy the Burger Kings. In three years, we improved the operations and increased the value of the stores enough that the profit on the sale paid for four restaurants. Outright, without using any of our own money. The deal was absolutely brilliant. And unforgettable.

We owned ten Taco Bell restaurants at the end of 2014.

Heads up.

"Congratulations, Doug!" Nick's voice boomed over the phone.

"Congratulations for what?" I said, puzzled.

"You guys are being recognized as one of the fastest-growing companies led by alumni," he said.

It was April 24, 2015, and Nick was calling from Auburn University, where the school was hosting the first-ever Top Tiger awards ceremony. The day-long event included a keynote address by Kevin Harrington, one of the original *Shark Tank* judges, and an Entrepreneur Hall of Fame gala. It was a big deal.

"Oh my gosh," I said. "I had no idea!"

Georgia-Texas ranked number six among mid-sized "Top Tiger" companies that day. We were among sixty stellar businesses representing nine states, with an overall average growth rate of 34 percent. I was blown away!

A few months earlier, I had filled out four or five pages of paperwork applying for the award but forgot about it as soon as I submitted the application. I had planned to attend the ceremony, but a conflict came up, and I couldn't be there. I didn't think anything else of it until Nick called me.

"I can't believe I missed the event!" I said. "Wow!"

My whole life, I have wanted to be the best that I could be at whatever I do. I don't care about being better than anybody else. I just want to be the best I can be. Still, the recognition was validating and a catalyst for our most significant business improvement.

Thanks to my fellow Tiger, Nick Davis, for always cheering me on!

In the same year, I threw away my office phone. One morning, I ripped it out of the wall, took it outside, and threw it in the garbage can.

"What are you doing?" Abigail asked, wide-eyed.

She was accustomed to following me around with a trash bag when I went on a cleaning rampage. Accumulating stuff suffocates me. If I haven't touched or used it in a month, I get rid of it. I do this with everything. Clothes. Books. Shoes. Cycling gear. Nothing's safe. (Except my family.) If you look in my car, it's absolutely empty because I can't stand clutter.

Periodically, I come into the office and start throwing things away. I might clean out the fridge, or toss an aging vacuum cleaner, or donate every item in the "junk" room. That day, it was my phone, which I admit was a little more dramatic than anything I'd done before.

"I don't need it anymore," I said. "I'm not taking calls on my office phone."

"Okay," she said and immediately reprogrammed the phones so calls were no longer transferred to me.

I should note that our work environment is tidy. Perhaps the team takes cues from me, but in general, they are also fastidious. My impulsive cleaning is about clutter, but it's also about my relentless need to improve. I know I drive a lot of people crazy with it.

"Why can't you just relax?" Andrea has asked me.

I don't know, but I can't. It's not who I am. I'm always learning, always growing, always reading, always figuring out how to level up. Whatever was next, I didn't see the need for a landline office phone for me anymore.

Soon after, we moved from our original headquarters to a larger, new building.

"Hey Abigail, where's my phone?" I asked, settling into my new office.

"We didn't give you one," she said.

I may have gotten ahead of myself that time. Fortunately, a phone was on my desk for the next important call.

"Hey, I was down here at this Auburn thing, and I noticed your company was recognized as one of the fastest-growing Top Tigers," the caller said. "I'm a business coach, and I'd love to talk to you about what I do."

"Your timing couldn't be better," I said, "because I would like to hire a business coach to take us to the next level. I'd love to talk to you."

I hadn't shared my idea of wanting a coach, let alone needing one, with anyone on our team, but I knew it was the next step.

When I said, "Hey, I'm thinking of hiring a business coach," everybody dug in their heels. Human nature resists asking for help.

"We don't need a coach," they said. "We're fine."

"I'm not saying we're going to hire a coach," I said. "Let's just talk to the guy and see if he can help us get to the next level. I'm looking for someone who can push us and guide us and put some structure and discipline around our routines."

When Ken DeWitt came to our office and gave a ninety-minute presentation on the Entrepreneurial Operating System (EOS), the whole team fell in love with the idea. EOS is based on the methodology presented by Gino Wickman in his book *Traction*. Running a business on EOS involves setting annual goals, which are then broken down into quarterly deliverables called rocks, and those rocks are broken down further into weekly to-dos. If you can do it in seven days, then it's a to-do.

Rocks and to-dos are benchmarked and reported at structured ninety-minute weekly staff meetings. Any issues that may have arisen in the last week are also discussed at the weekly meetings. Short-term issues may become to-dos, but if they can't be dealt with in seven days, they may become a rock or annual goal.

Implementers like Ken help a company identify its niche and establish a foundation of values, focus, and targets. These philosophies guide every decision and every operating practice, ultimately creating a company's culture. You can run anything with EOS principles—a business, a home, and even your life. Everyone was on board. Not only do we need this, they said, but we have to have it.

But they changed their minds when Ken told us the cost.

The investment was around thirty thousand dollars for eighteen months and included implementation guidance and unlimited access and use of EOS materials.

No, I heard. And not just no, but *hell no*.

"We're not spending that kind of money for a business coach," they said.

I called Ken to relay the message.

"Look, everybody loves the system," I said, "but they don't like the fee."

Ken stood by his fee but offered to introduce us to other nearby EOS implementers whose fees may be negotiable. We ended up going with one of those. We didn't like him as much as we liked Ken, but we committed to a year and moved forward.

When we sold the Burger Kings and bought four Taco Bells in North Georgia, we brought in the operations manager of the four stores, Mark Grabowski. Mark had been running those stores for a while, and the operations were consistently number one in the Atlanta market. Our six stores and those four stores had been neck and neck in the rankings for a long time. It drove me crazy that we couldn't beat their scores.

"Why are we hiring Mark?" Mike asked.

"Because, first of all, he's beaten us in the market," I said. "And secondly, we need him."

"What do you mean we need him?" Mike asked. We had just sold five stores. We bought four. Mike was sure we had the capacity to run them.

He wasn't wrong. We had the infrastructure and people in place to handle those stores. We could have easily run them without an additional person, and most people would have done that. But I saw something in Mark that I liked. He was a great operator.

"We're growing," I said. "We're going to own thirty restaurants, and Mark will be a part of our team."

This moment may have been the first time I said the thirty-unit goal out loud, but the idea of owning thirty stores had been a simmering vision for a long while. Why thirty? I was inspired by Nick Davis, for one thing. I admired his success. And I knew we needed a goal. Thirty was a solid aspiration, something to reach for. We were only a third of that size, even with the new stores, but I knew we could get there. I was looking ahead, expanding the team to handle the growth. To scale that peak, we needed the best people in our camp.

Would an operations manager be an extra weight to carry? Yes, and in the short term, the profit and loss statements would reflect that, but I don't make decisions based on money. I don't want to say that I don't care about money, but my actions are based more on intuition and on people. I know the money will come. And if it doesn't, we will figure it out.

Also, to satisfy Taco Bell, as part of the sales agreement, we agreed to fulfill the previous owner's promise to build a new store there. It's a beautiful part of the state, but the population is low, and so were our expectations. It was likely to be a loss leader. A good operator in that location would maximize our chances of success.

The new stores in North Georgia gave me a fresh opportunity to double down on my mission to own the ground under our restaurants. As part of the deal, I had agreed to build a new store in Hiawassee but found myself in a tricky spot with a builder we inherited from the previous owner. This guy wanted to do a build-to-suit, a situation in which somebody buys the land and builds the building for a tenant, which in this case would have been us. There was no way I would agree to that scenario. Brian Wooldridge and I teamed up for a tough negotiation.

We good-cop, bad-copped our way through a few dicey moments before ultimately extricating ourselves from the situation.

In 2015, my perspective reflected nearly twenty years in the business. From this vantage point, I could look back and see how far we had come. When my father died, we didn't have any money. You could even say we had less than "no money" because the debt obligations were so steep. Guys who get paid to play it safe told us to pack up and make a living another way, but we persevered. A lender threatened to call our loans, but we found a way around their demands. We had conquered these and many other obstacles, pushing past fear and shysters at plenty of other junctures. We were strong and I knew we were ready to grow.

Five people—Charles, Mike, Abigail, Mark, and I—were around the table when Georgia-Texas began our EOS odyssey. The first day in the process is known as Foundation Day. In this pivotal step, the person we hired to help us implement the system led us through a process of defining who we are and who we want to be. We spent a day and a half throwing words we thought would resonate with our vision onto a whiteboard. By the second day, we whittled the list of maybe a hundred words down to just a few.

Taco Bell has an acronym, RPRP, which means "right people, right places." Our core values happened to fall in line with these four letters. In our case, we chose the words respectful, passionate, reliable, and personal best, which reflected the acronym, then added the word honest. At the end of the day, we defined who we wanted to be using these words.

Our Core Target

Build a company that is among the best in our industry at developing people both professionally and personally.

Our Core Values

Respectful –
We listen first and have support for one another.

Passionate –
We are eager and show enjoyment for our work.

Reliable –
We follow through on our commitments.

Personal Best –
We consistently strive to give our best.

Honest –
We tell the truth and solve without blame.

Our Core Focus

Just Cause –
Create a great restaurant company by embracing a people-focused culture.

Our Niche

We run great restaurants that we are proud of.

These basic tenets cleared the way for a culture that led us into the future. Every decision we made from that day forward came back to this creed. When we weren't sure what to do, we found the answer here.

The next task the implementer asked us to do was to rate our above-store leaders on these core values. In EOS, this is known as the people analyzer.

In the restaurant business, a general manager runs the store. This person and everyone who works for this person are considered to be on the store level. Everyone above this level is referred to as "above store." We were asked to examine ourselves and our above-store managers to determine how well we exhibited our core values. A plus-and-minus rating system was used. Am I reliable? Passionate? Respectful? Giving my personal best? Am I honest?

If we demonstrated these character traits all the time, we earned a plus. If we didn't, we earned a minus. We rated team members using secret ballots so none of us knew what scores others assigned.

In the first round of ratings, every one of us gave one of our above-store people a minus on honesty.

"Woah, this is a problem," the implementer said.

"What do you mean?" we asked.

"Tell me about this person," he said.

We proceeded to relay that the person was responsible for half our stores and got great results as far as numbers were concerned.

"But you gave minus ratings on honesty and integrity," the implementer said. "You don't trust this person."

It was true. We didn't trust this person. However, we couldn't argue with the results. And this was where EOS became so powerful.

"Do you hear what you're saying?" the implementer asked. "You've got someone you don't trust in your company, and that's one of your core values."

Silence.

"You know what you have to do, don't you?"

We had no idea.

"You have to let this person go."

As a team, we were unanimous in our response.

"Have you lost your mind? We can't let our best performer go!"

"Well, then," he said, "let's rip up these core values because they don't mean anything to you."

Using the people analyzer, when someone earns a minus on core values, especially when the negative rating is unanimous among the leadership team, EOS recommends termination. Coaching may be an option if disagreement occurs among the people giving the ratings, but when everyone agrees that someone fails to represent what we believe, action must be taken.

Did we believe in these core values we had just spent a day and a half on?

"Time-out," I said. "Before we start firing people, give us a couple of days to think long and hard about this one."

Turns out, we did stand by our beliefs, and in the end, we let the person go. It was scary. We were sure that Armageddon was about to rain down on us. We expected the stores would flounder, but as soon as we did the right thing, my phone started ringing. Not the one which may or may not have been on my desk, but my cell. I have always given this number to store managers, telling them not to hesitate to call me when they need to. Every single manager who was subordinate to the person we let go called to thank me. One of them was even crying.

"Doug," he said, "thank you. This is the best decision you could have ever made for me."

I was flabbergasted.

"Tell me more."

And he did. The person we fired had been stealing money from that store and covering it up by making the store manager report it as a shortage from the safe.

"I couldn't say anything because he told me if I did, he would fire me," the manager said. "I needed my job, but it made me feel dirty. I didn't like it."

As I heard similar stories from other managers, the real power of EOS emerged. Making that difficult decision changed our culture immediately. In six months, we were stronger and more cohesive. We knew who we wanted to be, and we understood our goal.

To be the best company we could be, we needed the best players on our team. We had no place in our organization for anyone violating our fundamental values. The people analyzer gave us a fair, consistent way to make important personnel decisions. When someone is dishonest, when they don't operate with integrity, nothing else matters. We told people when we hired them that the only way they could lose their job was by violating our core values. The people analyzer removed the emotion from difficult personnel decisions. We didn't fire people. They fired themselves.

"I wish I had something like this when I was a store manager," Charles said. "It's so easy. If you're not reliable, if you're not showing up on time, if you're not being respectful, you're out of here."

If you think the core beliefs we established through EOS are just another corporate mission statement, think again. How many stories can you tell me about a mission statement changing a culture? I'm betting not many.

From 2015 forward, every decision we made and every action we took was processed through our EOS system. Every objective was either a goal, a rock, or a to-do, and problems were issues. And people either represented our core values, or they didn't. That's how we ran our business.

Another component of operating with EOS is having a ten-year plan. Our team developed a strategy for the next decade that included my goal of owning thirty restaurants. That was our target, and we quickly began aiming for it.

In the fall of 2015, we added another franchise to our company, opening two Einstein Bros. Bagel stores, one in our hometown and one in Opelika, Alabama, which is less than ten miles from Auburn. Burger King was behind us, but we hadn't given up on diversifying our company.

Einstein had been around for twenty years, beginning in 1995 when Boston Market purchased and merged four small bagel chains into a franchise. The idea of operating bagel shops in affluent areas where the iconic New York roll was a relative novelty seemed good to many entrepreneurs back then. Even though the chain had a rocky history, optimistic corporations still liked the concept twenty years later.

The year before, a new holding company bought the brand from its second owner. The new owners sold us a great picture of how profitable the brand was. Bagels and coffee seemed uncomplicated to us, especially compared to tacos, we thought.

I ran the idea by Naveen.

"It's a long driveway to a small house," he told me, advising against it.

Translated: the return on the investment might be small.

But Mike and I believed these would be simple operations and nice profit centers for us. We signed up anyway.

The markets, buzzing with excitement, also responded well to the idea. Who doesn't love a new breakfast option? And what college town doesn't love more options for carbs, the ultimate hangover fix?

In 2015, Georgia-Texas grew from ten to fourteen restaurants. In addition to the two Einstein locations, we built new Taco Bells in Hiawassee and McDonough, Georgia. Thirty stores, here we come!

In hindsight, was the "Do Not Enter" sign an omen?

CHAPTER SEVENTEEN
Course Correction

*"All men have fears, but the brave put
down their fears and go forward."*

— DALE CARNEGIE

AS THE NEW PRESIDENT OF TACO BELL, Emil Brolick influenced me
as much as anyone in those early years after my father died. He took the
helm of the franchise as the fiery aftermath of the StarLink Crisis was
still raining down on the brand. When he came onto the scene, the fateful
"We can't meet payroll" call was only four months in my rearview mirror.
We both had our hands full.

He stabilized the company and put the "rack and stack" rating system
in place. Using this scoring metric, every restaurant earned an A, B, C,
or D. The mission was to move stores that were below the "A" rating up

one letter, focusing first on the Ds. Emil showed us what it meant to put people and processes first, knowing that sales and profits would follow.

When I met him for the first time at a franchise convention in 2001, he looked the elephant in the room in the eye and addressed the toxic relationship between franchisees and the corporation.

We have to have a partnership, he told us. That was priority number one. Without it, he said, nothing else worked.

He then invited every one of us to come up and talk to him, and he proceeded to chat with each person until the cue was empty. Physically, he had so much presence. He was a big guy, tall and skinny like a basketball player, with hands that engulfed mine in that first handshake. When we began talking, he was locked in as if no one else mattered. I stood there as a little guy with five stores in Atlanta, yet he listened to me. He actually listened to me! I remember feeling that he really wanted to hear what I had to say, what each of us had to say.

After that first encounter, I made it a point to seek him out whenever we were at a meeting.

"Hey Emil," I'd say, and he'd remember me.

"Hey Doug, how's it going? I hear you're doing great things in Atlanta! Keep up the good work!"

He was famous for handwritten notes and stamped, signed Christmas cards—gestures that showed he genuinely cared. I became his disciple, learning from him about how relationships create culture. The results of his influence permeated our operation forever.

Emil spent ten years at YUM! Brands before returning to Wendy's as president and CEO, which is where he was when I reached out to him in early 2016. It was a simple correspondence. I let him know I was thinking about him and congratulated him on the success he was having at Wendy's.

I hadn't talked to him in years, but he responded to my email within thirty minutes. Like he wasn't busy. Like he still had time for the little guy.

"Hey Doug, it's great to hear from you," he responded. "I'm glad you're continuing to do well."

Then he asked if I had any interest in becoming a Wendy's franchisee.

"I'm intrigued," I said. "Maybe?"

Emil invited me and Mike to come up and visit the company headquarters in Columbus.

"Let me show you around," he said.

Mike and I decided to accept the invitation. In May, we chartered a plane, something we had never done before. We gave ourselves a nice break from the office, and enjoyed a pleasant change of pace and scenery.

"I'm taking you to meet Emil at the flagship store," the young woman who met us at the airport said. "I'm so excited you're going to see him. I've never met him myself." Then she asked, "Who are you guys? He just told us you're Taco Bell franchisees and to give you whatever you want!"

Later, my mom told me that my dad had researched Wendy's when they first moved to Newnan. The company had closed franchising then, but the research opened the door to my parents' entry into the quick-service restaurant industry.

"Your dad always wanted a Wendy's," she told me when we bought six of their stores in 2016.

I had that feeling you get when life comes full circle, when you land where you're supposed to be, even though you never expected it. A seed I never knew my father planted had sprouted thirty years later.

If I've learned nothing else, it's not to argue with fate. Or destiny. Or whatever you want to call her. She has her ways, and she loves relationships. Maybe above all else.

*Hello, Wendy's! Mark, Abigail, Mike, and I attended
our first Wendy's conference in October 2016.*

One reason EOS worked so well for me is because it mirrors the kind of training it takes to win a race. Like periodization, EOS builds momentum by breaking a long-term goal into periods and acknowledging variables. With EOS, you break down objectives into manageable tasks while simultaneously dealing with unforeseen events. And both methodologies focus on building a foundation before you grow.

We followed EOS for a year with an implementer. We made great progress with his help, and after that first year, we thought we were smart enough to use the tools and run the program ourselves. Honestly, his personality was not a great fit for us, and we also figured we could find many other ways to use the money we would save, so we continued without his guidance.

Getting into Einstein Bros. Bagels turned out to be a bad decision. It was the first and last time I failed to follow Naveen's advice. It still hurts.

We didn't know what we didn't know. We believed in the idea. We believed in ourselves. We believed in the markets. Despite everyone's enthusiasm—well, everyone but Naveen—the reality was far from what we expected. It reminded me of those three Taco Bell Express units Dad operated in convenience stores. Déjà vu. Again.

But now we knew. The stores were in decent locations and we were good operators, but we couldn't make it work. It was a good model for mom-and-pop operators but not for us. We were able to get out of the lease in Alabama but were stuck with the hometown location, which sat in a column of bad investments for years. Still, we cut our losses, and I didn't worry about it.

Similar to Einstein but more complicated, we had no idea what we were getting into with Wendy's. We went in blind. We liked the brand and the corporate team—we loved Emil, of course—but we didn't fully understand the condition of the equipment and facilities. The brand had not been reinvesting in the restaurants. It seemed like nothing worked. In one store, a box fan blew over the line to keep employees cool because the air conditioner was broken. Similar nightmarish situations were pervasive.

Also, Wendy's was behind the technological eight ball. We were accustomed to Taco Bell, an industry leader in adopting technology. Direct deposit, pay cards, and electronic applications were becoming the norm. All the brands had employee apps. Wendy's, however, had too many systems and a painful lack of integration.

Geographically, we had moved farther south and east than we'd ever been, making the territory much more difficult to manage. Three of our

Wendy's were located in middle Georgia, in Madison, Monroe, and Forsyth. One was in North Georgia, in Clayton, and two were in North Carolina, in Franklin and Cashiers. From store to store, we covered an area three hundred miles north to south and 120 miles east to west across the state of Georgia and into North Carolina. It was impossible to avoid going through the worst of Atlanta traffic to get from one area to the next. A maintenance issue could be an all-day, or even multiday, ordeal.

In the beginning, we didn't have a head of operations for our Wendy's stores. Both Taco Bell and Wendy's frowned on the idea of a single operations director overseeing all the restaurants. As usual, it wasn't easy to find the right person for this position. We interviewed a lot of people who had worked with Wendy's, ultimately hiring a corporate guy with thirty years of experience. Unfortunately, his idea of managing a team was to do so by sitting behind a computer. That never works.

Even more challenging, as a company, Wendy's was under new ownership. Just before the leadership change, corporate raised menu prices and wages. Pricing and wages go hand in hand. Historically, we're conservative on raising either, but we had no pricing options to increase sales.

To say Wendy's complicated our lives is an understatement. All of a sudden, it wasn't fun. We weren't cash-flowing. In fact, we were losing a ton of money. Like a gambler, we faced the dilemma of whether to throw good money after bad.

"What are we doing?" Mike was saying. "This is too hard. We've got to get out."

His frustrations were shared by the whole team. Everyone was feeling the pain.

In the Einstein situation, I folded and left the table. But in this case, despite the challenges and resistance, I believed we could turn things around.

"I'm not looking at it as losing money," I told Mike. "I see it as investing money. Investing in people and facilities."

Cleaning up operations, "fixing stuff," is what we do, I argued. Sales volumes for these stores were good based on the shape of the facilities. Demand for the product existed despite conditions and the brand image. I felt confident we would see the fruit of our labors.

It wouldn't happen overnight. It wouldn't happen without a lot of effort. But if we could just get a little better every day, if we played the long game, I believed it would work out.

Knowing when to hold and when to fold is as much an art as a science. Intuition versus the P&L. My gut told me to hold. And that was also Naveen's advice. He had been right about Burger King. He was right about Einstein. I believed he was right about this as well.

I felt twitchy, though. On paper, absorbing six Wendy's wasn't as dramatic as Dad going from one to seven restaurants overnight, but now we had seven hundred employees, more than three times the two hundred we had when I came to work with my father. This was familiar and not in a good way.

Charles suggested later that winning can make you blind. When you start to have too many good things going on, you think you know what you're doing and that you can do no wrong. Not for the first time, he was right.

Looking back, I'm mindful of what Bill Gates said about success being a lousy teacher: "It seduces smart people into thinking they can't lose."

We had nineteen restaurants at the end of 2016, twelve Taco Bells, six Wendy's, and one Einstein's. Essentially, we had doubled in size again in two years. Accountants love to say that numbers don't lie. Maybe they don't, but they sure can sound a lot better than they really are.

A lot of people in this world, and many in the restaurant business, don't want to change. They want to be comfortable. They want life to be easy. People like that don't last long with me. I'm on a mission. Either you get on board, or you travel with someone else.

I do not settle.

Which is not to say that I won't adjust my plan.

Heading into 2017, I was concerned that we were losing our focus, that numbers were becoming more important than people. Also, it turned out that we weren't that great at self-implementing EOS. We needed to slow down in order to speed up. We needed a new coach, a Jeff Cuddeback for business. It was time for me to pick up the phone again.

"Hey Ken, we made a mistake," I said. "We should have hired you from the get-go. We were being cost-conscious, penny-wise but dollar-foolish."

Ken's warm response was welcoming.

"I'm humbled and grateful," he said.

"I think you'd be a great fit for our organization," I told him. "We need you to take us to the next level."

"The good news is that I'm still here, and I can help you," he said. "The bad news is that if you thought I was expensive in 2015, my price has doubled now."

Clearly, his services were in demand.

"Ken, I don't care what your fee is," I said. "We need you."

We hit the reset button with Ken with a two-day retreat. Mike, Abigail, Mark, Charles, and I drove a few hours to a golf resort in Sylacauga, Alabama, for this event. Away from home. Away from the office. Away from our comfort zone.

Monday was nice. The first day of an EOS annual retreat is all about team health. We get to know each other better. We talk about what's going well for each of us, personally and professionally, and what we're working on. This process is mirrored in the first fifteen minutes of a weekly EOS meeting, but on a retreat, we spend all day on this. Through a series of exploratory exercises, we learn more about each other and ourselves.

I'd known Charles for more than thirty years, but at one of our annual retreats, he told us something about himself that I never knew. This happened with every team member. At the end of the day, we were more in touch with ourselves and had a much more holistic picture of each other.

I believe you can create anything with the right people, but the relationships between these people need to be solid. Teams depend on each other for success on and off the job. The more we knew about our individual goals and vulnerabilities, the stronger we became as a team.

Tuesday was not as pleasant as Monday. This is often the case on the second day of an EOS retreat when we take a hard look at the company. We talk about what we're doing, where we're going, and how we're going to get there.

"We've got to get rid of this stupid target of thirty stores," I told the team. "We are starting to do things that don't make sense. We're compromising, and I don't like the direction we are headed."

It hurt to say these words, but it was true. No one disagreed. Once a number becomes more important than people, you lose your culture. Your values deteriorate.

"Our core target is to run great restaurants by embracing a people-focused culture," I said. "That's what we want to do. Chasing stores is not people-focused."

This uncomfortable moment launched a four-year charge to live up to being the kind of people we say we are. The goal was to be the best version of ourselves and to strike a chord with people who want to do the same.

Music connects a lot of dots in my story. Mike and I had spent most of our college careers chasing bands around the South. Andrea and I first bonded over bands and music we both loved. I can't remember a time when tunes I love were not playing in the background of my life.

I can remember the first time a guitar mesmerized me, though. I was maybe eight or nine years old, visiting my grandparents in Texas. My Uncle Jeff and his two young kids lived there after his wife died. He was always into music. I suspect it was important therapy for him at that time, but of course, I wasn't thinking about that as a kid. I was just happy to hang out with him, glad to hear whatever he was spinning on the turntable.

He was playing the Rolling Stones album *Sticky Fingers*, and the song "Can't You Hear Me Knocking" changed my young world. At that age, I had no idea a song could last for more than three minutes, but here was a seven-minute-long song, essentially a jam session, with at least a three-minute guitar solo, depending on the version. My young mind was blown, and my fascination with the guitar was born. I remember going home, buying the album, and playing it for all my friends.

I never got over my love affair with the Stones—to this day, they are my favorite band—or the guitar. I had always been afraid to learn to play because I wanted to be good immediately, and I knew that wouldn't happen. I don't like to do anything I can't be good at.

I was forty-one years old before I saw the Stones in person. And I was forty-six before I picked up a guitar, knowing I would be horrible for a very long time before I would be any good at all.

In 2017, Andrea and I were visiting our friends Angie and Jody in Florida. Jody, a lifelong guitar player, is pretty good. He can play rhythm and strum chords. He doesn't know notes or theory, but if he hears a song, he can play it. What a gift! I don't have that ability, but if you teach me something, I'll practice.

That weekend, he taught me two chords, and I proceeded to play those two chords the rest of the time I was there. Nonstop, strumming mostly a C chord, for seventy-two hours. My focus was insane.

"You were driving me absolutely crazy," he told me later. "I knew you were either going to get it or going to be just god-awful."

After Jody's tutorial, I began taking lessons, and today, he'll tell you I am ahead of him, even though he's been playing his whole life. Now he strums rhythm, and I play the lead. All the notes.

What I love about music, what it's taught me about life, is how important it is to pay attention. It's made me a better listener because before I began playing, I was never able to even hear chord changes. When I liked a song, I couldn't tell you why. Maybe I enjoyed the rhythm or the melody, but I could not have told you more. I have read many books on music theory since then. Now I understand how scales work and how the seventh resolves back to the chord tone. I know how it's all supposed to go together when I'm playing.

Music also taught me the value of the beginner's mindset. Learning a skill from scratch takes courage. When I let go of the fear of being god-awful, to my surprise, I enjoyed the process. I discovered that although you can learn to play better, you never master a musical instrument. You never perfect it, but with deliberate practice, you improve. When you focus on the smallest, incremental details, two or three measures at a time, you gain ground. As far as I know, this is a universal truth. It certainly applies to running great restaurants.

Music also helped me define great people. Someone once asked me what this means. What are great people?

It's hard to articulate, but we all know them when we meet them. It's kind of like hearing a great song. You may not understand the technical aspects of the music, but you know you love it. The rhythm, melody, chords, key changes, and dynamics mix with the tone and texture to create an experience you want to repeat. You want to listen again. And again.

People give off energy. If you doubt that, take a trip to the Department of Motor Vehicles. You'll see what I'm talking about. In most DMVs, you immediately feel the tension and negative vibe. Great people are the exact opposite. When you're around them, they generate cheerfulness.

My cousin, Colin Hilley, comes to mind. He came to work with us as a general manager when we opened the Einstein store in Auburn, a bright spot in that otherwise bad deal. Colin is the most positive person in the world. He has so much energy. When he walks into a room, people's eyes light up. He has an abundance of joy, love, compassion, and acceptance. It's almost tangible. You can feel it, and you're attracted to it.

You want to be in a room with great music and great people.

The core values we established with EOS were the guiding principles for identifying great people. When someone is respectful, reliable, passionate, trustworthy, and doing their personal best, they're great people. And they want to get better. If you give them a little love and encouragement, if you build them up, it's amazing what they can do.

As we grew, we doubled down on training and our people-focused culture, promising people who came to work with us that we would engage with and support them in their careers with Georgia-Texas. And we kept that promise in many ways.

We showed appreciation for them with recognition, gifts, and celebrations. We responded when team members were in crisis. Whether it was time off for personal situations or help with expenses in tough times, we were there when we could help.

We offered benefits you would not find in other companies, full-time hours rather than part-time, and health insurance benefits for all full-time employees. Georgia-Texas established a 401(k) program back when Andrea sold us payroll services. Employees who worked for us for a year were eligible for a 401(k) program with a 6 percent match. A few decades later, Charles was a millionaire because of it, and he was passionate about making sure people understood the opportunity. On a quarterly basis, he walked people through the math of how investing a little every month funds retirement.

With EOS and Ken's help, our culture became more affirming and supportive. We took care of our team. We educated them. We loved them. We promoted and supported personal development, helping people move from good to great, and we set ourselves up for healthy growth.

Eventually, we bucked the brand resistance and promoted Mark Grabowski to director of operations over Taco Bell and Wendy's. We brought in two great guys to manage the individual brands and work with him. We also upped our training game with frequent off-site training sessions and implemented an important focus on shift leaders. The idea was to grow our own, to develop a bench of store managers and, as much as possible, to promote from within.

Everything about this strategy resonated with me. In the quick-service industry, restaurant managers are often underappreciated. I've always had a soft spot for them. Most are not college graduates. Some have not finished high school. Many have been dealt a tough hand, but when you peel back the layers, these are really good people. I want to come alongside them like the guy did for me in the Ironman and say, "You got this! You can do it!"

How do I know? Because *(here we go again)* the secret to running great restaurants is doing what needs to be done. It's simple. Focus on cleanliness and hospitality. Get a little better every day. Repeat.

In creating an operations hierarchy and growing managers, we became top-heavy. While we weren't chasing a number anymore, we still planned to grow. And to prepare for that, we created more infrastructure than we needed for a company of our size. The idea was to build the foundation before we acquired more stores. We wanted to be ready to hit the ground running in a new store with a manager hungry for opportunity. We wanted the brands and lenders to be confident that we could handle the growth.

Most people do it differently. The norm is to bite off more than you can chew and then constantly play catch-up. I think that's backward, and I didn't want to do it that way. It's much easier to get a thumbs-up from corporate on an acquisition or location when you have people who are hungry and can move immediately into a position of leadership. Our aim was for a seamless transition, to be ready to take over a store and not miss a beat.

In June of 2017, we purchased seven more Wendy's stores in the southern part of Georgia. Americus, Cordele, Moultrie, Douglas, Fitzgerald, and Tifton were new names added to the mix of conversation at our weekly EOS meetings.

In North Georgia, we built a new location for our Taco Bell in Dawsonville. At the end of the year, we had twenty-six stores, within shouting distance of our prior goal of thirty. But I didn't care about the number anymore. I cared about whether we were getting better.

Wendy's #3172 Americus, Georgia

CHAPTER EIGHTEEN

Unfinished Business

"We waste our time waiting for a path to appear. But it never does. Because we forget that paths are made by walking, not waiting. And we forget that there's absolutely nothing about our present circumstances that prevents us from making progress again, one tiny step at a time."

— ANGEL CHERNOFF

I NEVER GRIEVED FOR MY FATHER. As a family, we never mourned together. We never talked about his death. We didn't talk about how we felt, what we feared, or what we were worried or mad about. It was twenty years before I realized we should have.

No one knew how disturbed and upset I was when he died. No one knew that for the first two weeks, I was so angry I raged in my bedroom closet at night, punching the lifeless shirts and pounding the floor while I cried. The next day, I would emerge from these secret fests of fury as if everything were normal. It was Oscar-worthy.

In 2018, twenty years later, I still hadn't forgiven him. I didn't even remember those dark nights. Some kind of protective eraser had removed those memories from my mind. It took two decades before the scab began to fall off those wounds.

With a physical injury, a scab can facilitate healing, preventing continued blood loss and infection. It's a healthy process. I don't think that's true for the mind.

When my dad died, I went into fight-or-flight mode, doing whatever I could to protect my mom, the business, and our people. No road map showed me how to get us from devastation to safety. I had to figure that shit out every single day. And I was so mad at my father for putting me in that position.

I'm old enough and wise enough to be grateful for the opportunity he gave me, but I hate that it came at the expense of his life. I also know there are things I could have done differently. My mom and my sisters could have done some things differently, but we were doing the best we could, given the circumstances. Isn't that always true? Looking back, who wouldn't say the same thing? Most of the time, most of us are doing all we know how to do.

I remember a conversation from one of my Appalachian adventures. Bob, my hiking buddy, had a young son at the time. This was before Andrea and I had children, before we were even married. I'm not even sure if we had met yet.

"One day, you're going to have kids," he said, "and you're going to want to be their friend. But your number one job is to make sure you're their parent first. Your kids don't have to like you. It's not your job to make them like you."

My dad was definitely a parent first. We became business partners, but he wasn't my friend. He was always somebody I was afraid of. I worried that I would not level up, that I couldn't meet his expectations. To be fair, that was a weight I put on my shoulders. I wanted to make him proud, but I didn't know how to do that. I always wanted to please him, but I felt like I was never enough.

Three or four times a year, I have these recurring dreams in which my father reappears in today's world. He's been away for a long time, but he's back. I'm not sure where he has been or why he was away, but he's here now, transported from 1998 to today.

When he shows up, he looks around and begins drilling me with questions.

"What have you done? What are you doing? What's going on?"

The confrontation is intimidating.

"Oh my gosh," I say. "Are you happy with what I've done?"

Fiercely, he just keeps questioning me.

"Why did you do it this way? What is that about? What are you thinking?"

I still seek his approval, and he's still not giving it to me.

Looking back, I can also see how the universe had my back. A few months before my father died, I met Andrea. Soon after, I met her father. You may remember that my first attempt to impress the man resulted in me dumping him into the water. Also, recall that he had had a recurring dream in which his wallet got wet. Apparently, it was my destiny to make his dream come true, and despite our unsettling beginning, his destiny was to become a father to me.

Joe loved Andrea and her sister and would do absolutely anything for them. His daughters were his world. He was happiest doing things for them, from helpful tasks as simple as taking care of household chores, even cats, to preparing lavish meals and planning summer camping vacations. Remarkably, he folded me into the family and treated me like a son, being there for me in the same way he was for his girls.

Even though we lived more than four hundred miles apart, we spent a lot of time together. He was with Andrea and me when we took Grant to camp for the first time. Joe comforted us when we bawled our eyes out as we were leaving our baby behind.

Our first meeting set the tone for years of antics that I somehow passed down to my sons. Our boys were known to play silly tricks on Joe, like when Grant put a cup of water above the door so that when Joe opened it, he would get soaked. James hid in the pantry so he could jump out and scare his grandfather. James also loved to tell funny jokes that always made Granddaddy laugh.

On a whitewater rafting trip in Montana, Grant and I purposely put Joe behind us so he wouldn't get wet. *(Wink, wink!)* Just before we hit the large rapids, we would duck on cue, and Joe would be the recipient of a glacial facial as Montana's super cold waters drenched him. By then, I think he had learned not to bring his wallet on any water excursions with me.

Joe was generous with his praise for me, just as he was with his daughters. Yet he was unafraid to give judicious counsel. Once, on the night before July 4, Joe let me know that he thought it was a bad idea when I decided to launch fireworks, with no tube, directly from our pool deck. When they went off like a bomb in our backyard, rattling windows and setting the bushes on fire, he was by my side with the water hose.

One summer, he and I spent an entire day in the car, visiting some of our restaurants and employees. He asked me questions about my childhood as we drove to pick up Grant from camp again. It was a particularly memorable day for both of us.

We often discussed the business over the years. As the company grew, so did our debt. When you decide you want the corner lot as often as possible, and then you decide you have to own the real estate or the deal is off, the numbers get high. Around the fifty-million-dollar mark, Joe asked me, "How do you sleep at night with all that debt?"

"Joe, it's just a number," I replied.

"What do you mean?"

"Well," I said, "if you don't have a hundred dollars, then what's the difference in not having fifty million of them? I mean, if you don't have it, you don't have it. I sleep fine."

I'm sure I explained, as I often do, that a laser focus on running the business solves most worries. If food costs, labor, and maintenance percentages are in line, then we'll make money. When we make sure we're hitting these numbers, when we uphold percentages, the money takes care of itself.

Risk is uncomfortable. It's not for everyone. My father-in-law preferred safety. We understood and respected each other's positions.

The man who favored playing it safe was known for answering his phone no matter what time it was or what he was doing. In one case for me, he took my call while he was up on a roof. His selflessness had no boundaries.

One time, he and his wife took Grant camping in Tennessee. Joe and Grant rode every roller coaster at Dollywood. Joe never complained about feeling sick or nauseous despite this exhausting experience.

Joe also took great care of himself, which, in my opinion, is another example of his selflessness. Taking care of ourselves is a gift to our families and the people who rely on us. One time, when we were visiting him, he invited me to come to the gym with him, and he amazed me with his strength. He bench-pressed his body weight and did ten pull-ups like they were easy. I was in awe.

The day we found out that he had brain cancer, he and I rode in the car together from the hospital. It was just the two of us, and he was telling me how happy he was that he was the one who had cancer. He said he wouldn't be able to deal with anyone else he loved having to face a diagnosis so devastating.

In March of 2018, saying goodbye to him was shattering, but in a different way than when we lost my father. The circumstances, in nearly every way, were different than twenty years before when, on a random day in November, with no warning, my dad was gone.

For one thing, we had time to prepare. You're never ready to lose a loved one, but a heads-up does help. Three weeks before his death, I spent the night at the hospital with him. We watched the Olympics and talked about life. He was so positive and grateful that day. It's a memory I treasure.

Also, when Joe died, his house was in order. He didn't leave me or anyone else with any more than the unavoidable details to attend to when someone dies. He certainly didn't leave a flailing business to be salvaged. You may say that when and how we die is out of our control. You're not wrong, but we can live in a way that a sudden loss doesn't threaten to cripple the people we love. We can't avoid dying, but we can take care of ourselves and our affairs with the understanding that our actions and inactions affect everyone in our lives. We can be cognizant of the wake we leave behind. The way my father-in-law lived showed that he knew this.

In comparison, for several years after my father's death, we continued to uncover more information we needed when he died. We discovered documents and excavated the details of operations and deals for longer than I can remember. It was perilous and absolutely no fun. This experience marked me in ways I continue to process. Every day, I make decisions as a result of what I went through so that my family and our company will not endure this heartache.

Finally, my relationships with Joe and his relationship with his family were different, too. He never missed an opportunity to tell us he loved us and how proud he was of us. I always appreciated this, and in hindsight, I see how priceless this was for me. He loved me. He approved of me. I always knew I was his favorite son-in-law. The fact that I was the only one did not diminish the pure joy this gave me.

With Joe Salemi, my father-in-law and a great friend

The year that Joe died, I stared down a stubborn company that held the ground lease on one of the stores my father had bought. I had been asking them to sell me the property for years and years, but they would never even discuss it. As many times as I broached the topic, their answer was "Nope."

"Nope, nope, nope, nope, nope, nope, nope."

But I never stopped asking.

As the company evolved, so had I, and so had the roles my attorney, Brian Wooldridge, and I played together at the negotiating table. We were a long way from the days when I hid under my desk before and after difficult calls with a lender. Countless times, Brian and I sat across from people who did not want to cooperate with my vision. These scenes became a stage upon which we honed acting skills that Academy Award winners might have respected.

When fate dealt me a card I had never even hoped for, I could hardly wait to call Brian.

"This is our chance!" I told him. "We got 'em!"

Our landlord was selling the property adjacent to us to a company that planned to build a large gas station and convenience store. They needed me to agree to an easement so that our new neighbors could put an entrance which they couldn't build anywhere else. Without this easement, there was no deal for them.

First, I raised the ante.

"I'm not signing anything unless you sell us the land," I told our landlord.

That didn't go as well as I hoped. They tried to bypass us and the Department of Transportation with a scheme to eliminate the need to cross our lot. Thankfully, that did not work.

Next, I tried a sympathy card.

"Listen, if we give up this easement and they come in here and build a temporary driveway, they are selling food, too, so that's going to impact our sales," I told them. This was true, but I may have made a bigger deal out of something than it was.

"We may need some concessions for that," I said.

Then I pulled the wild card.

"If you don't sell us the land, we'll move when our lease is up in two years."

Theoretically, we could have done that, but it was not the best option. We had a good location.

"But if we don't leave, will you sell us the land?"

Many calls and messages were exchanged, during which Brian persuaded them to agree on a price for the property.

"Okay," I said. "Deal."

But then they backtracked and refused to sell.

Eventually, Brian and I took this high-stakes game to his conference room with the landlord and their attorneys. We wanted to buy the property, and they wanted to stall, probably hoping they could avoid a sale, but they needed my cooperation for the bigger deal. Finally, the landlord agreed to sell the property to us if we signed the easement, but then Brian balked at their price.

"Well, I don't know if Doug wants to pay that much for it," he said. "Doug, let's talk about it away from here."

In my mind, I was doing backflips, but my poker face held. We left the room. The high-fiving commenced as soon as we were out of sight.

We won the deal and many others over the years. Some required spilling some blood, metaphorically speaking, of course, but we almost always prevailed, and the ramifications were far-reaching.

In 2018, we bought that property and rebuilt one of my father's original stores. We also built a new Taco Bell on one of the busiest roads in our hometown, where growth skyrocketed after the turn of the century. The store was on a corridor that connected a major residential area to medical and retail centers. Property, in general, was hot, hot, hot in Newnan. Getting the lot we needed for that store was challenging, to say the least. We also scraped and rebuilt a Wendy's in Monroe. Many miles and hours in traffic were logged, managing these projects, which spanned ninety miles from the southeast to the southwest of Atlanta.

As we grew, I often wondered, *What would my father think?* And I still don't know.

In 2019, however, we made a deal that I know my dad would have loved.

Back in 1996, when Taco Bell was putting packages of stores together for franchisees to purchase, the original deal they offered my dad included two stores in Griffin, Georgia, a town about thirty-seven miles east of Newnan. It was simple to get to from our base of operations, with an easy-to-drive state highway connecting the two towns. My father was excited about having these stores.

Another franchisee also wanted them, though, and corporate changed the package so the other company could buy them. The other franchisee, it turned out, was very risk-averse. He ended up holding just the two stores from Griffin from the deal. My dad always regretted that he had lost the opportunity to own those restaurants.

Years later, around 2006, I began to let the guy know I would love to buy his stores. He was not interested in selling, but I made him offers all the time. It became an ongoing joke between us. He would say yes, then change his mind. Or he'd say no, or maybe, before settling on "If I ever sell, I'll sell to you." Finally, in 2019, he sold his stores to us. Then, in a serendipitous twist of fate, a relative of this franchisee also offered us his Taco Bell. He only had one store, and since his brother was getting out, he decided to sell too. We ended up buying his store, which was located right next to our Wendy's in Monroe.

It was one of those situations where we were thinking we'd buy those stores when pigs fly. And then, pigs finally flew.

The way we handled deals like these, and the way we did business in general, is that, with Naveen's help, we negotiated from a position of "we don't need it." If the deal made sense, and the price was what we wanted, then we did it. If it didn't, we let it go. This strategy takes courage. It's easy to get caught up in what everyone else is doing or not doing. When an attractive opportunity is on the table, it's easy to forget your policy. But it's easy to stay the course when strategy drives tactics. When we bought the seven Wendy's restaurants in 2017, I only agreed to the deal when the seller promised to let me buy the real estate to go with these stores within twenty-four months. In 2019, we added those properties to our portfolio.

We bought a Taco Bell in Clayton, Georgia, in 2019, as well, exceeding my original goal with thirty-one restaurants. Twelve years into our partnership, Mike and I had tripled the business. In an audio version of this story, I might cue the marching bands and fireworks here. If you're reading this, perhaps a pause to imagine the effect will suffice.

In 2019, we purchased our thirty-first store, Taco Bell #36722.

In hindsight, we could have grown faster. We could have been bigger. There were stores we could have bought and deals we could have made that we passed on. In each case, there was more risk involved or other factors that didn't work for us, and we held our position. When you make a plan and work that plan, it doesn't matter what the rest of the world is doing. It doesn't matter what anyone else is thinking or saying. And it doesn't matter what your father would have done.

That summer, I kept the promise I had made to myself on that first cycling trip to Italy. My family and I spent a week in Lugano, Switzerland, exploring the stunning scenery I had fallen in love with ten years earlier. One day, while hiking a mountain there, we got lost and ran out of food and water. We were tired, hungry, and thirsty, and I was getting worried. And then, we stumbled onto a bed and breakfast. The kind people there were getting ready for dinner and generously brought out food, water, and wine for us. We ended up having the best time, taking off our shoes and resting for a while. After a couple of hours, we followed their directions to a ferry that took us back to town.

I often think about how we would have missed this experience if we had stayed on course.

I kept the promise I made to myself to bring my family to Lugano, Switzerland.

On November 10, 2019, twenty-two years after my father's death, the Georgia-Texas senior leadership team hunkered down for our annual

EOS retreat. Ken asked us to meet on his home turf in Tuscaloosa, Alabama, for this pivotal event. He sweetened the deal by offering his personal houseboat overlooking a beautiful river for the meeting place and giving us a fee break if we agreed to convene in Tuscaloosa.

As an Auburn alum and die-hard fan, Tuscaloosa was enemy territory for me. Alabama's Crimson Tide has flowed like sewage from T-town since the school's inception in 1831. One hundred and eighty-eight years later, this Tiger had never set a paw on that battleground. I had never been to Tuscaloosa. Ever.

It's possible there was some trickery and collusion in this negotiation. The team was on board. I think they may have purposefully chosen this location to see how I would react. Reluctantly, I came along, but I can't say I was looking forward to it.

The anniversary of my father's passing is always a somber time for me. I'm never quite myself on November 10. Between that and being in Tuscaloosa, I was out of sorts.

We spent Monday, the first day of the retreat, reconnecting with each other. We all had our stories. We were all fighting our own internal battles. For me, my buried grief was surfacing, but I had found a healthy outlet for these feelings. I took the opportunity to remember my father and remind us that we stood on his shoulders. Acknowledging his leadership and expressing gratitude for what he poured into the company relieved my uneasiness. When we got down to business on Tuesday, I felt centered and clear about what I had to say.

At this same meeting two years before, we exchanged an arbitrary goal of owning thirty stores for a mission to grow by developing and supporting a great team. As president of the company, I know it's my job to be the visionary, to set a course and keep us on track. Straddling a delicate line between cheerleader and commander, I must be willing to speak up when I think we're not on target.

"I feel like we're missing an opportunity to truly go all in on people," I told the team. "We talk about it, but we have not fully embraced a people-focused culture in the way I want to."

The pushback was familiar.

"This will cost a lot of money, Doug," they said.

I heard my father's voice: *You'll bankrupt the company!*

And my rebuttal sounded the same as the one I gave to him: "What if we invest in people and our sales increase by 10 percent? Instead of protecting our P&L, what if we open it up and encourage, support, and coach people who genuinely want to run great restaurants?"

"I'm the one who is always saying we have to get out of our comfort zone," I said. "Hey, I'm in Tuscaloosa. If anybody's out of their comfort zone, it's me right now!"

So, we rallied together, unanimously agreeing that next year, once and for all, we would be all in on people. We brainstormed ideas for pay increases, incentives, and other reward systems, including a company cruise for managers who meet their targets. I could not have been more pleased.

"We're playing an infinite game," I told the team. "We can't get stuck on the short term, and we can't have this finite game where we have an opening, a middle, and a close. I'm trying to set this company up for generations to come. We're in it for the long haul."

Back in the office, three days after the retreat, I began a new tradition. I wrote a message for our leadership team and store managers that became *Do Not Settle*, a weekly newsletter sent out on Fridays. The next week, I signed nine hundred Thanksgiving cards, and we distributed gift certificates to all the salaried employees in our stores.

We ended the year with a nice holiday party for all our store managers and their guests. Nearly eighty people were in attendance for this elegant affair. A live band played, and they even let me join in with my guitar on a song or two. A sky full of stars reflected on the lake view outside the venue's floor-to-ceiling windows.

At the end of the year, my *Do Not Settle* newsletter summed up nearly everything I believed in with a rally cry for bravery. Our vision to be the best, embrace people, stick to our core values, and run great restaurants we are all proud of had never been stronger. Courage would be required to meet these lofty goals.

"We can move mountains," I said. "Who's with me?"

And then, it was 2020.

PART THREE
THE SUMMIT

CHAPTER NINETEEN

Unsettling

"One can choose to go back toward safety or forward toward growth. Growth must be chosen again and again; fear must be overcome again and again."

— ABRAHAM MASLOW

GREAT TEAMS DON'T JUST HAPPEN. You can never take one for granted.

At our quarterly EOS meeting on February 4, 2020, we celebrated our progress, noting wins in communications, sales, operations, and talent recruitment.

"It feels like we're going in the right direction at the right speed," Mike said.

All day, I couldn't stop thinking about how grateful I was for the people sitting around that table with me. EOS had been the real game-changer for us. The system drove how we solved problems and focused on what really mattered in the business.

The biggest challenge we discussed was how to keep score.

"What does a great restaurant look like?" I asked. "My perception may be different than others. How do we all get on the same page?"

We agreed this was the most important priority for the next quarter. Mike took the lead with a goal to clarify benchmarks and find a way to automate objective scores.

After lunch, we discussed upcoming visits to the restaurants and the metrics we might use to determine how store managers would qualify for the company cruise in the fall.

In the last hour of the meeting, Ken asked if there was anything else we wanted to discuss. He mentioned that he had spent a full day the week before helping a company develop a coronavirus strategy. None of us knew what to think or say about that. A month later, I was pretty sure we should have given that topic some attention.

At the end of February, we knew more, but still very little, about this mysterious virus. I checked the Centers for Disease Control and Prevention website daily while trying not to get sucked into the growing media dialogue. A decision by the Fed to lower interest rates worried me. Were they concerned about the economic impact of people isolating themselves? This could be huge.

Two important bellwethers were on my radar. First, my mother canceled her plans to travel to Italy in April. The franchises, however, were still relatively quiet on the matter. They would let me know when we needed to worry, I reasoned.

Second, on March 2, the governor of Georgia formed a coronavirus task force. A day later, the first two cases of coronavirus were confirmed in our state. That same day, the Fed dropped rates by fifty basis points, and Taco Bell corporate canceled a franchise forum meeting scheduled for March 16.

Meanwhile, I was reading more and more about how to battle viral infections, including the importance of handwashing and getting enough sleep. *Would supplements be helpful? What were the best protections against an enemy we could not detect?*

We celebrated Mike's birthday on March 6, and our banker came to town for a golfing weekend.

Three days later, on March 9, four more cases of coronavirus were confirmed in Georgia, and thirty-four cruise ship passengers were quarantined at an Air Force Base in metro Atlanta. The school system in our home county reported a family member of one student was exhibiting symptoms of what became known as COVID-19.

Sources I trusted were predicting that we would all get this virus at some point. Endless discussions about the ramifications of the crisis flooded traditional and nontraditional media streams.

On March 10, Fulton County schools, which encompass most of Atlanta, closed. That same day, I received an email from Mike Grams, president and global chief operations officer of Taco Bell, inviting us to a call the next day, beginning a process for daily and sometimes hourly updates and communications.

Restaurant General Manager Blake Chira and his team showing us why the Summerville Taco Bell was consistently #1 on the weekly ranker!

Despite these increasingly alarming reports, we made the decision to keep our plan to visit stores in the northern part of our territory on March 11 and 12. We followed our custom and rented a minivan from my buddy who owned a Toyota dealership in Newnan.

Perhaps I should say we followed my custom.

"No, don't get the minivan," Mike and Abigail both said. "Get a cool ride, Doug. A minivan's not cool."

"The minivan's comfortable," I said, "and easy to get in and out of." And every time we did this, I wanted to buy a minivan when we got home.

"We're not buying a minivan, Doug!"

The disapproval was always universal. It's a little reassuring to have the same arguments when the world is unraveling that you have when it's chaos as usual.

Mike, Abigail, and I rode together from Newnan. The store visits were encouraging but awkward and less authentic than they might have been. Was it okay to hug people? No one really knew.

The first evening, our executive team stayed at a hotel in Young Harris, Georgia. In the bar, everyone was glued to their phones and the TV, where bad news continued to fall like dominoes. That day, the first family in our home county was quarantined when a parent of a student tested positive for the virus.

The next day, while driving in Floyd County, we ran into a detour because someone who lived on the road we were driving on had tested positive and was in quarantine. Someone behind closed doors, in a house we never saw, was sick, and as a result, we had to drive miles out of the way to Hiawassee. Was this real, or were we in an episode of *The Twilight Zone?*

That same day, March 12, the first two deaths in Georgia from the coronavirus were announced. At the time, a total of nineteen cases were suspected and twelve confirmed across the state. The governor requested one hundred million dollars in emergency funds, and the first patient was sent to a Georgia state park designated as a quarantine site. We got an email from Wendy's, unveiling a pandemic communications hub. Also that day, in what may have been the first move of its kind in America, Starbucks announced drive-thru-only service.

All these ominous data points crowded into the car with us on the drive home from visiting the stores. We tuned in to Atlanta's WSB radio, which was like having CNN in the car. Ominous updates filled the airwaves every fifteen minutes. Anxiety was so palpable that it might have been a passenger whispering the scariest worst-case scenarios from the back seat. When I thought it was impossible to be more tense, Naveen called.

"Doug, go to the bank and withdraw as much money as you can."

What is going on?!

When the person you count on for fiscal clarity is concerned, it's hard not to panic. When my father died, we discovered numerous places where he had stashed cash. Maybe that hadn't been such a bad idea after all.

The weekly newsletter I wrote on the way home from the tour of stores was the first to mention the virus. Whatever I was thinking or feeling, my New Year's battle cry for bravery and being our best was as relevant as ever. Our priorities were clear:

> *"As we get daily updates regarding the COVID-19 virus outbreak, let's make sure we are staying safe by following proper handwashing procedures, cleaning and sanitizing our dining rooms, and not allowing anyone experiencing flu-like symptoms to work in the restaurants. Your health and safety are our number one priority!"*

Any other year, I would have been ecstatic about the promise of spring on the nearly sixty-degree sunny afternoon in March. Perfect weather for a bike ride or a run or relaxing in the backyard with my guitar. On that day, though, I didn't feel the temperature and couldn't think about anything pleasant. At all.

I could only hear the voices in my head, each with a worrisome piece of news to report. *What was true? Who knew?* I didn't know what I didn't know—and neither did anyone else—but I knew this for sure: above all, we had to protect cash.

When I opened the car door in the driveway after the store tour, the nightmarish realities I had been processing on the way home climbed out with me. Andrea had spent the day in Atlanta. We arrived home at nearly the same time but in very different states of mind.

Fear poured onto the grounds of my sanctuary. Finally, with the person I could always count on for reassurance and stability, I couldn't get out the tsunami of words fast enough.

"Oh my God, Andrea, we're in trouble," I said, near tears. "I don't know if we'll be able to keep the restaurants open. I don't know how we're going to take care of our people. No one knows how this will play out. We've never been in a situation like this before. I'm not taking a paycheck. Mike's not taking a paycheck. We cannot spend any more money. Zero. None."

At this point, my rock-steady, always-encouraging partner blinked, glancing toward a few packages from her favorite boutique.

"You mean after today, right?" she said.

You don't have to be superstitious to get nervous when, on Friday the thirteenth, schools close for two weeks, and *The New York Times* and the *Wall Street Journal* both run headlines about possible government quarantines. *The Times* asked, "Can you be forced to quarantine?" while the *Journal* reported, "US Considers How to Enforce Quarantines."

I had a talk with our lender that morning. We owed them fifty-five million dollars, after all. I figured it was a good idea to be proactive and check in. We may need some extra goodwill in the weeks ahead. They were encouraging, assuring me they were empathetic with the situation and said that if a quarantine forced the closure of our stores, we did not have to worry about being out of compliance with our loan agreement. Mike and I determined that with the cash we had on hand, we could meet payroll for the next seventy-five to ninety days before we ran out of money, even if we were forced to close the restaurants.

At that point, business was continuing as usual for us. In one of our stores, an employee reported that a family member tested positive for the virus. He quarantined, and after we closed the store for a thorough cleaning, we returned to full strength. Other than that, operations were normal. So far. We were getting reassuring updates on the strength of the supply chain from Taco Bell and Wendy's. That night, the White House called

David Gibbs, CEO of YUM! Brands, and invited him to a briefing with other restaurant leaders. It was comforting to know that the challenges we faced were being heard at the highest levels.

Three days later, on Monday, March 16, 2020, Georgia-Texas closed the dining rooms and began drive-thru-only service in all our stores.

On Wednesday, March 18, the Georgia governor and the Georgia Department of Labor began talking about how quickly they could get unemployment benefits to workers. The governor also asked the Small Business Administration to provide economic injury disaster loans to businesses. That same day, the Red Cross called for Georgians to give blood.

By Friday, March 20, information from Taco Bell, Wendy's, and the government was coming in hourly. I thought my father's death had taught me everything I needed to know about beating fear. I was wrong.

Embracing challenging activities has always been how I deal with change. Leaning into discomfort as a way to cope may be the most constant thread in my story. When the going gets tough, I double down on structure. The routines and schedules of weightlifting, marathons, triathlons, cycling, guitar, or whatever I'm learning or doing have always given me regimens that trumped my fears. The only way I've ever been able to feel grounded is to tackle what I can control, especially when chaos swirled around me like a tornado.

When my father died, my whole world—money, operations, emotions—was bedlam. Fixing it all at once was impossible, but I had a sense of making progress. When I woke up in the morning, I knew that even though what I did today might not make a difference tomorrow or next week, it would make a significant difference in a year. I looked for what I could do each day that would get us closer to the outcome we were aiming for down the road. The certainty that day after day, I was making small improvements was my salvation.

Everything I thought I understood about surviving was upended in 2020. The pandemic was a global crisis, nothing like losing my dad, of course, but it is natural to compare any hard situation to tough times we have endured in the past. I think we all did that, whether consciously or unconsciously. My father's death was apocalyptic to me, my family, and our company, but it wasn't an international event. In 1998, I could not have imagined a scenario like the one we faced in 2020.

The business challenges were staggering. Our number one priority at the company, come hell or high water, was our employees. We wanted to keep them whole. We wanted to keep them safe. We wanted to keep them healthy, and we wanted to keep them paid. How? This was the top priority we addressed every day.

In response, we followed protocols recommended by the Centers for Disease Control and guidance from the franchises. Providing a safe place to work and eat was paramount. We intensified our commitment to our core value of operating clean restaurants. We took extra steps to ensure food safety procedures were followed by all. When people were sick or at home due to exposure to the virus, they were paid until they could return to work. When a store closed briefly for quarantine cleaning, crews were paid for any hours they may have missed as a result.

The next question we asked ourselves every day was how we would get through this situation without running out of money. This cash flow question fell hardest on Mike, Charles, and me. The three of us calculated, collaborated, and recalculated the numbers ad nauseam. The results validated the back-of-the-envelope estimate Mike and I had theorized. We could fund payroll for ninety days if the restaurants were closed, maybe even six months if we got lucky.

"Your paycheck is not going away."

This was the message employees heard from Mike and me.

It was a good feeling to be able to tell a thousand employees that if we had to close the restaurants for a while, they would continue to be paid. I didn't want anyone working with us to add financial concerns to pandemic worries. People knew from experience that they could trust us. This scenario was no different, but I felt the pressure. We had to make this work—for ourselves and for everyone who worked for us. It was a heavy burden, and I would be lying if I said I was not scared. Honestly, I was freaking out.

What if this lasts a year or eighteen months? I had no idea what we would do. Our best efforts to preserve cash would only take us so far. It literally made my stomach hurt to think that we went from thriving to survival mode overnight. I couldn't think of anything we could do that might make the outlook better for any of us in a year.

But what I could do, after following the guidance of the best advisors for taking care of our people and our business, was to cultivate a new set of daily routines that kept me grounded. Practicing the guitar was a great stress reliever. So was running. I remember days when getting outside for a run kept me from losing my mind.

On the weekends, I postponed responding to emails or texts that could wait until Monday. I often paid a price for it at the beginning of the week, but it helped me maintain balance. Every day, I called my mother and reached out to at least one friend or other family member I had not spoken to in a while just to see how they were doing. I think it helped me more than them.

Similarly, the weekly discipline of writing a newsletter to the leadership team and managers proved encouraging. In the March 27, 2020, edition of *Do Not Settle*, I addressed the elephant in the room—anxiety and fear. Whether anyone else benefited, I was reminded that fear is rational. It's based on facts. Anxiety, however, is not rational. Anxiety feeds on what-ifs, on all our middle-of-the-night thoughts about scenarios that have not happened and may never happen.

Cooler heads also reassured me. Nearly every day, Mike said, "I'm so grateful for what we've done." And he was right. Our strategic planning and careful growth positioned us to weather this crisis. We knew many people whose situations were vastly different. I was grateful for Mike. If a storm was coming, there was no one I'd rather face it with.

On April 3, when the governor ordered people to shelter in place and closed bars, nightclubs, gyms, and so many other businesses but exempted take-out, curbside pickup, and delivery of food, Andrea checked me.

"Why are you so anxious?" she asked. "Most businesses are closed. Ours is open. What's your problem? Stop worrying!"

As always, she was right.

Someday, someone may read this story who wasn't alive during the pandemic or who wasn't old enough to remember or understand how events unfolded. The further this era in history appears in the rearview mirror, the fuzzier the details get. Many people became sick, and many people died. The rate of the spread of the virus was only exceeded by the rate of disagreement among experts over what should and should not be done.

When I think back to that quarterly EOS meeting in February when we blinked at the idea of a coronavirus contingency plan, I don't fault us for not creating one. No one could have predicted where we would be two months later. No plan we might have devised could have covered all the scenarios that occurred. It was the definition of uncharted territory.

If you had told me that two months later, the United States Congress would fund a nine-hundred-billion-dollar program to provide low-interest loans to protect the payroll of small businesses, I would not have believed it. If you had predicted the National Guard would be deployed to nursing homes and that enormous drive-thru testing sites would be opened, I would have been incredulous. And if you had said that the weakest link in the supply chain would be toilet paper, I would have placed you on my list of known lunatics.

In a prophetic tweet on January 15, 2020, James Clear, author of *Atomic Habits*, identified three things that affect results: luck, strategy, and habits. Only two of these variables are within our control, he pointed out. But when we master strategy and habits, he said, the odds that circumstances will work in our favor improve.

Life has taught me that there is no benefit to worrying about what might happen. Hurricanes are going to come. And fires, and earthquakes, and pandemics—and more events we haven't even imagined yet. We have no sway over the unpredictable. We can't control what's happening around us, and we can't control luck.

We can only control whether we're prepared to respond. We do that by having a plan and a daily process for achieving our goals. We figure out where we want to go and create a road map for getting there. Then, when the worst comes, we are more resilient, more agile, and more stable than we would have been without a game plan.

I am forever thankful for the way the Georgia-Texas team embraced discomfort so that when we faced the scariest enemy any of us had ever known, we were strong. We didn't have a handbook for an apocalypse. We had a strategy for creating a great restaurant company by embracing a people-focused culture. While our philosophy might not qualify as a disaster-preparedness plan, when the world turned upside down, it didn't take us long to find our "new normal."

We conquered our anxiety by acting in spite of fear. Every day. One day at a time.

CHAPTER TWENTY

The Promise of Victory

*"The more we value things outside our
control, the less control we have."*

— MARCUS AURELIUS

A FUNNY THING HAPPENS ON THE WAY to a twenty-five-year career in the franchise restaurant industry. You meet a lot of people, and if you stay alive—*literally and fiscally*—eventually, you meet some of the best people in the business. In 2001, I was fortunate to connect with Emil Brolick when he was president of Taco Bell, but it was a long time before I connected again with the top tier at Taco Bell corporate.

In 2017, on the last day of the convention in Hawaii, Mike Coccia, my franchise business coach, asked me for some help.

"Hey, Doug, I need you to do me a huge favor," he said. "There's some

YUM! Brand folks on their way to Atlanta, and I would like you to meet with them."

YUM! owns the trifecta of franchises: Taco Bell, Kentucky Fried Chicken, and Pizza Hut. It's rare for an operator to have a chance to meet anyone from the parent company.

"This guy's going to be in Atlanta, and he wants to meet some of the franchisees," Mike said.

Despite the unique opportunity this presented, I did not want to say yes. I was not looking forward to driving into Atlanta after just getting home from the conference. Other franchisees in our area were feeling the same way. We had all been away from our offices for days. Everyone wanted time to get home, catch up on business, spend time with family, and rest.

"Will you help me out?" he pleaded. "Take one for the team?"

So, in another one of those "weak" moments, I said "no" to my comfort zone and "yes" to my friend. Back in Atlanta, on the day of the meeting, I drove around frantically looking for a parking spot near the restaurant where we were scheduled to meet. The store was downtown, where parking was scarce. When I came in thirty minutes late, several franchisees were already taking a tour of a Taco Bell Cantina, the first of its kind in Atlanta. Cantina locations are restaurants with limited parking and seating, designed for high-density areas. They are often open later than traditional Taco Bells, and the menus offer a few surprises, including alcoholic beverages.

I made my apologies and then, lo and behold, ended up spending half a day with David Gibbs. At the time, he was president and chief financial officer of YUM! Brands, a multibillion-dollar company. And I was late for the meeting!

I had no idea this was the person I would be meeting in Atlanta that day. If I had known where he was headed professionally, I hate to admit it, but I probably would have been a little more professional, a little more buttoned up. But instead, I was just myself. I came in thirty minutes late, super chill, and we had a very relaxed meeting. The conversation was casual, small talk, a couple of guys just shooting the breeze. He told me he worked for Taco Bell in Atlanta in the late '80s and that he remembered my dad.

"Are you kidding?" I said.

"No, I totally remember your dad. I remember when he got into the system."

I spent half a day cutting up and having fun with him. When I left, I had his cell phone number and email address.

Later, when I told Naveen I had spent the afternoon with David Gibbs, I could hear his jaw drop.

"How in the world did you get face time with that guy? People would pay to spend half a day with him, and you're just hanging out in a restaurant with him? He is going to be the next CEO of YUM! Brands!"

Two years later, at the convention in 2019, I returned to my seat after a break, and David was sitting in the chair next to me.

"Well, hey, David, it's great to see you again!"

"Hey, Doug, how's it going in Atlanta?"

Because of our time together in Atlanta, David knew my name and my face, and I believe he was genuinely glad to see me. The conversation was easy, the connection real, as he sat with us for the next hour and a half.

We heard a presentation on operations from Taco Bell's chief operating officer, Mike Grams. A few months before COVID, Mike was all about food safety, speed of service, and clean stores—like a football coach telling his team, "Hey guys, we need to block better. We need to focus on the fundamentals."

The basics never change. Mike Grams was saying the same things we had heard thirty-one years ago. He may have said it in a different way, but at the end of the day, we want to run great operations by having clean restaurants with friendly people, quick service, and great food.

I'm small potatoes when it comes to Taco Bell franchisees. We've been franchisees longer than probably 95 percent of other owners, but there are companies with hundreds of stores, and they get a lot of attention at these conventions. Before the awards dinner, though, Mike sought me out.

"Hey, Joey Pierson's looking for you," he said.

Joey was the CEO and President of Tacala Companies. He came into the system right after my father did. Based in Birmingham, Alabama, Tacala has more than three hundred stores. Joey and I had become friends through our mutual love of our alma mater, Auburn University. Joey is very well respected and was at the convention in 2019 to support the founder of Tacala as he accepted the Glen Bell Award, the highest honor a franchisee can be given.

"Go find Joey," Mike said.

So I set off to find him, but before I did, Joey called me on my cell phone.

"Hey Joey, where are you?" I asked.

"I'm up here at table six," he said. "Come see me."

When I found his table, Joey introduced me to Mark King, the brand-new CEO of Taco Bell.

"Hey Mark, this is Doug Augustine," Joey said. "He's a great operator in Atlanta. We need to help Doug get more restaurants."

I had a great conversation with Mark. In his keynote speech earlier in the day, he revealed himself as a huge Green Bay Packers fan. I told him about my dad and about the time he took me to meet the Packers in Detroit in 1978. Mark loved hearing how I had my picture taken with half a dozen players when I was six years old. Turns out he is also a big golfer. We had a lot of common interests and could have talked for hours if we'd had the time.

The stars aligned for us that night in a way I never could have orchestrated. When I did my coach a favor and agreed to show up for a corporate visit in Atlanta, I never imagined the opportunities or connections that would ripple from that single "yes." Often, people and opportunities come into your life when you least expect it, but it only happens when you put yourself out there.

Naveen called it. In January of 2020, David Gibbs was promoted. David became CEO of YUM! Brands.

Looking back, I appreciate that we entered the pandemic having real, authentic relationships with people at the highest level of the corporate structure. It was comforting to personally know the folks who signed off on the hundreds of emails we pored over during the pandemic. It was reassuring in those emergency meetings when the voices I heard and the faces I saw on the screen were friends I knew that I could call if I needed to.

Every time I think about Mike Grams's spotlight on fundamentals at the 2019 convention, the timing feels amazingly uncanny. The basics trump every other tool in the kit. This is always true, but in a crisis, they are usually the first, and sometimes only, tools you need. We built a business on the basics—consistency, cleanliness, and caring for our team, our customers, and our community. We survived one of the most dangerous periods in modern history by practicing these core values. We drew courage from knowing that the people we looked to for guidance were following them, too.

When I think about 2020, so many images come to mind, more than I can articulate, more than we have time and pages to share. It was a long year. For the sake of relevance, I am filtering some of these scenes through the lens of our company's core values.

I see drive-thru delivery servers greeting customers warmly at the window, eyes smiling above their masks. **Respectful** of the Centers for Disease Control and health department guidelines, our employees diligently guarded the safety of our customers as well as their coworkers.

I see store managers and team members delivering numerous meals to healthcare workers, **passionate** about the communities we serve.

I see the elderly couple who came through our drive-thru, parked their car, brought out camp chairs, and had a picnic outside one of our restaurants. When they needed to get out of the house for a while, they felt safe with us. We were a **reliable** sanctuary of normalcy in an otherwise crazy, upside-down world.

I see all the moms, dads, daughters, sons, sisters, and brothers who gave their **personal best**, showing up for work despite juggling new and difficult personal demands. Many were suddenly homeschooling or caring for extended family, but they bravely overcame the chaos to stabilize our stores. They faithfully stood with their fellow team members and comforted the communities we serve.

I remember more than a few **honest** tears over losses, frustrations, and fears. We cried, and then we carried on.

I see the faces of our senior leadership team, sometimes in person, sometimes on the computer screen, engaging in some of the best EOS meetings we ever had. We ended the year together, profitable, stronger than ever, and confident that we could endure whatever came next.

2021 EOS Quarterly Meeting with Ken DeWitt

I keep a scale tucked away in our laundry room. Every morning, I tiptoe out of bed, slip through the kitchen to the laundry room, and weigh myself.

"Do you ever use this?" Andrea asked me one day. I don't know if it was in the way or if she was just curious.

"Andrea, I weigh myself every single day," I said. "I've been weighing myself every single day for the last eight years."

She gave me this crazy look.

"Why?"

"Because I want to know."

Back in the day, when I toured our stores following Taco Bell's "success routines," I drove around with a food scale in my car. Following the checklist, which began by placing an order at the drive-thru, I used that scale to weigh the food I received to be sure we were meeting product standards.

On February 4, 2021, our Above-the-Line scorecard debuted in my weekly newsletter. A year after the EOS meeting in which we prioritized finding a way to objectively measure how a store was performing, we finally had a rubric everyone agreed on. Initially, we set out to solve this hotly debated puzzle by the second quarter of 2020. However, it took longer than we anticipated to get there. It's easy to see how the challenge may have been sidelined by the pandemic, but that's not the only reason it took a while to create this scorecard. The feat required drilling down and determining which metrics were the most important indicators of the health of an operation.

Our Above-the-Line tracking system included nine areas of operation from each of the two brands. We set weekly goals for scores from variables such as sales, overall customer satisfaction and dissatisfaction, speed of service, accuracy, cleanliness, and how many hours of labor it took to run the store. We mapped these results in a graph. Scores falling below the goal were highlighted in red. Scores at goal or above were in green. To achieve "Above-the-Line" status, stores were required to meet or exceed objectives in at least seven of the nine areas measured. That first week, ten of our seventeen Taco Bells and three of our ten Wendy's achieved Above-the-Line status.

Red scores gave a particularly helpful visual to areas and stores that needed to improve. It's not unlike assessing your personal health with your doctor. A range of numbers related to your weight, blood pressure, and lab results are considered during a wellness exam. Any numbers that are outside the normal range get attention.

Finally, twenty-five years after joining my father in the restaurant business, I had a concrete way to know for sure how to answer Scott Curson's questions, "Are you getting better, or are you getting worse? Or do you even know?" Half a dozen seasoned industry professionals, many of whom had been in the business as long or longer than me, contributed to creating this metric. The debate on objectives—what to include, what goals should be, and even how to represent the results visually—was contentious.

Why did it take so long and so much experience to get here? Because a question may be easy to ask, but that doesn't make it easy to answer. The goal of running restaurants we can be proud of is simple to state, but it isn't simple to do. It's hard. It's really hard. Like many other uncomplicated goals, it is a difficult one to achieve.

Standing on the scale is easy. Moving the number? Not so much. But when you have a score and you know which way you want it to go—*up or down*—then you can set clear and specific steps to meet your goals.

When you need to lose weight, you and your doctor decide how many calories you should consume in a day. If your blood pressure is high, you might choose an exercise regimen to help lower it. You might decide how often and how long to walk, jog, or swim.

In a restaurant, you plan shifts, days, weeks, and periods around specific actions needed to achieve the objective. If staffing is an issue, how many people do you need to interview in order to make a good hire? Once you know this number, you set a goal to talk to a specific number of candidates every week. Every standard can be reverse-engineered in this way.

The Above-the-Line scorecard also gave our senior leadership team a road map for planning. It was clear that finding good people, training our teams, and communicating our mission would be critical to our overall health. Our goals for 2021 included focusing on these areas, and several related projects landed on my to-do list as a result. Launching a new website with an emphasis on recruiting was one of my EOS rocks. I also signed up to create personal knowledge management training programs for our managers, area coaches, and senior leadership teams, as well as a development program for shift leaders.

Telling our story and communicating our vision through my newsletter, training programs, and website were my highest priorities. Launching a podcast was also on my radar. I had no idea how dramatic some of those stories would be. Or how much the scale would move.

We took our development programs to another level with personal knowledge management training programs for our managers, area coaches, and senior leadership teams in 2021.

On February 18, 2021, after vaccines became available and people were beginning to travel more, I was invited to dinner in Atlanta with the executive team of Taco Bell: Mark King, CEO; Mike Grams, president; and Nikki Lawson, chief brand officer. They met with me, my franchise coach Mike Coccia, and Bob Carlucci, another franchisee who owned fifty-eight stores in Atlanta. The conversation was warm, optimistic, and promising.

During dinner, Mike Grams blew my mind. Mike said that based on our OPS (Operations Performance Scorecard) results, which is an internal metric that Taco Bell corporate uses to grade stores, we ranked in the top ten operators in the country. Until that moment, I had no idea we held this status. We had been heads down, focused on training, culture, and philosophy, just trying to be the best we could be. We weren't even thinking about our competitors or where we stood on a national basis. Before that night, I knew we were good, but I didn't know how good.

Twenty years before, a pair of company envoys told me to quit, to go home and get on with my young life.

"You're not going to make it," they said.

I had been conditioned to think our relationship with the parent company was a classic "us versus them." It was how my father saw it. It was how a lot of other franchisees saw it. It was how I felt when they told me to give up. Even after we improved, after we grew, even when healthy financials said we were winning, a stern voice was always whispering warnings of disaster in my ear. Failure was never an option, but it lurked like a menace just around the bend.

All of a sudden, I had finally arrived. If twenty-five years can be called "all of a sudden." That night, I felt like a part of the team. I wasn't on guard. I wasn't watching every word I said. I wasn't reading between every line that was spoken. It was a real conversation about real life and real "in the trenches" business. Corporate hadn't come to town because they wanted something from me. I wasn't there because I needed something from them. They invited me to the table because they liked the way we operated and wanted to spend time with me. If they wanted anything, it was to hear about our best practices and to talk about how we run restaurants that perform as well as they do.

I came away feeling valued, validated, and even victorious in a way I still can't describe. I represented an amazing team and knew that we had earned a seat at the table that night. The pigs were not only flying, but they were also gaining altitude. We knew what we were doing and had valuable information to share with people who needed to understand the challenges in the field.

Georgia weather will tease you. She'll give you a taste of what's coming, sometimes when you need it most. It was sunny with a high of fifty-seven degrees that day in Atlanta. I drove home under a partly cloudy sky, with a temperature still in the high forties. Spring was coming. I could feel it. Smell it. Hear it. She was making me a promise, the kind you feel when you hear the faint sounds of a finish line. In running lingo, we were headed to a PR, a personal record.

Five weeks later, however, the weather in Georgia got serious as hell and hurled one of the worst storms in state history at our hometown. Around midnight on March 25, 2021, a tornado charged through our county, leveling neighborhoods, snapping power lines, destroying schools, ripping hundred-year-old trees up by the roots, and leaving a trail of destruction that can only be described as catastrophic. Winds peaked at 170 miles per hour in a storm that the National Weather Service classified as an EF-4 in intensity.

Miraculously, our team members were all safe and our stores were minimally damaged. The next day, we provided bagels and burritos to relief efforts. The following week, Taco Bell sent a food truck to help us feed volunteers, first responders, and displaced residents who were continuing to clean up debris. It was gut-wrenching to see the nearly indescribable devastation the storm caused but inspiring to see how the community stood together and how our teams rallied to support our neighbors and friends. We had been feeding hungry families in our hometown for more than thirty years, and I had never been prouder to serve.

But it was hard to miss the fact that spring, barely a week old, was not exactly keeping her promise. Still in the midst of a pandemic, we found ourselves also literally in the eye of a storm. *What else can happen? What more do I need to know about things I cannot control?*

I attended my first FRANMAC convention with my parents in 1997.

CHAPTER TWENTY-ONE

Party's Over—Or Is It?

*"You must build up your life action by action, and
be content if each one achieves its goal as far as
possible—and no one can keep you from this."*

— MARCUS AURELIUS

MY GRANDMOTHER HAD A REPERTOIRE of powerful proverbial sayings.
Remember this one?

*"Never ask a lady to marry you until you spend four seasons
with her, Doug. You've got to make it four seasons."*

Even though I knew after our first date that Andrea was the one for
me, I honored Grandmother's counsel. Whether her advice was right or

not, I can't say, but it certainly worked for us. Andrea and I celebrated our twenty-first anniversary in May of 2021.

Another one of my grandmother's cautionary adages also came to mind that week.

"Doug, you can't be greedy, and you can't look back."

I remember her saying this to me often when I was in my twenties, but I never really knew what it meant. Now I know.

This means you can't have your cake and eat it too. You just can't.

In the early '90s, my dad had served on the board of the International Association of Taco Bell Franchisees (IATBF), a group of renegades who felt they needed more representation with the home office than they were getting from Taco Bell Franchise Management Advisory Council (FRANMAC). At the time, Taco Bell was growing fast, and there was a lot of friction between operators and the parent company. The two organizations, FRANMAC and IATBF, merged in 1997, the year before my father died. The relationship between Taco Bell and franchisees has improved dramatically since then.

On May 13, 2021, I was invited to join FRANMAC as a member of the Operations Committee. It was an honor to be asked to serve this organization. In a way, I was following in my father's footsteps. Not only was that a good feeling, but it also seemed like another sign that good fortune was smiling on our company that year.

A couple of weeks later, one day after my wedding anniversary, I was in my office when Naveen called on a Friday afternoon.

"Hey, Naveen, how's it going?" I answered, happy to hear from him.

It was the last day of the school year, around four o'clock, and I needed to head home soon. Andrea, the boys, and I were leaving the next morning for a two-week Caribbean vacation. I was ready for a break and more than a little excited about this trip, but I still needed to pack. So, although I always enjoyed talking to my most trusted advisor, I didn't have much time.

"What's up?" I asked.

"Doug, we need to talk," he said. "Are you sitting down?"

He's been to my office. He knows I have a standup desk.

"Really, Naveen?" I laughed. "Do I need to sit down?"

"Yeah, I'm serious," he said. "Sit down." I'd never heard this tone in Naveen's voice before, but I had learned to do whatever he told me.

Our headquarters is a modest, two-story building, the renovated former home of a company that owned golf courses. My workspace is at the top of the stairs, to the left. There's no door. Standing at my desk, I faced a slightly larger than door-sized opening in the short hallway wall. Mike and Abigail worked quietly in their offices to the right of the stairs. The wall to my left opened to a large breakroom. Across that room, behind the opposite wall, Charles was wrapping up the week. I could hear muted getting-ready-to-leave-for-the-weekend noises coming from beyond his door.

Four upholstered swivel armchairs guard a coffee table just inside the break room next to where I work. I walked over and sat down quietly in one of those chairs, turning to face the windows. Across the parking lot, traffic was as heavy as you would expect on a main thoroughfare at four o'clock on the last day of school.

"Okay," I said, still thinking this would be a fun call. "I'm sitting down. What's going on?"

"It's time to sell," he said. "This can't happen fast enough."

All end-of-the-week, day-before-vacation good spirits dissolved. My skin went cold.

There are moments in life you never forget. On the morning of 9/11, I vividly remember driving thirty miles of eerily deserted freeway to the East Point Taco Bell. When my father died, time stood still as I watched the ambulance leave the restaurant parking lot for the hospital. On Friday, May 28, 2021, tall pine trees filtered the afternoon light, casting shadows outside the window where I sat, feeling all the dèjá vu. It felt like almost everything stopped. Unplugged. Colors turned black and white.

"Why?" I asked, struggling to breathe. "What do you know that I don't?"

Nightmares careened through my mind. We were still in a pandemic. The world as we understood it was already upside down. *Was another apocalypse coming? What could it be?*

At that moment, what I wanted most was to rewind the clock twenty minutes, gather up my things, and go home to my family without having this conversation.

On my way out the door, I stepped into Mike's office.

"I just got off the strangest phone call with Naveen," I told him. "I don't even know how to react right now, but I want you to know that he told me we need to sell the business. I don't know what that means, and I hate to tell you right now because I'm leaving for two weeks, but I need to put that thought in your head because it sounds serious. I'll let you know more when I know more."

As I drove home, my emotions were a mixed bag. I was still processing the conversation, trying to comprehend the situation. My thoughts were spinning out of control. I was scared. Freaked out. And, deep inside, a little excited.

"Naveen says we need to get out." Those were the words I said to Andrea when I told her about the call. "I don't have any answers right now. I'm just telling you this is frontline stuff. I need you to start thinking about it."

Mama Bears don't always need to think. Her response was instantaneous.

"No! Are you crazy?" she said. "What about our boys? What do you mean? No! You can't get out!"

Grant was emotional when I told him, too.

"Dad," he said, "this is something I thought I might want to do down the line. It's not even fair to make this decision without talking to me about it!"

Mike, Andrea, Grant, and me—we were all blindsided. Looking back, I don't know if this was the right way to tell them, but I didn't want to sugarcoat it. Naveen hadn't sugarcoated his words to me. He did make sure I was sitting down. If he hadn't, I probably would've been knocked off my feet.

I'll never forget those next two weeks. It was good that I was out of the country. It made it easier to be fully present on the numerous calls with Naveen, with Mike, or with Naveen and Mike. It was easier to focus, but I can't think of anything else about this juncture that was easy.

Over the years, I have learned to listen very closely to Naveen because what he says is always important. I also focus carefully because sometimes I struggle to understand him. My brain filters his Indian accent through a Midwesterner-turned-Southerner strainer. Occasionally, the words collide and tumble around in there. This has been true since we first met. One way I have honed my listening skills is the practice of visualizing words. So, on that fateful Friday afternoon call, I not only heard his words, but I also saw them. They scrolled through my mind like a news ticker.

TIME TO SELL was the bold red header.

It's hard to articulate how radically different this was from all I had ever heard him say. From the beginning of our relationship, Naveen laid down a strategy for the long term.

"You're a serial acquirer, Doug," he said. "Like Warren Buffett. We buy, and we hold. That's the game we play. We never, ever sell."

He had drilled this principle into me from day one. These were the words he used all the time. This reversal in policy amplified the shock I felt as he began to explain why he was changing the rules.

"I'm advising half of my clients, the ones that can, to get out," he said. "You're one of them."

Naveen outlined several factors affecting market conditions that placed us in a golden window for selling, and he emphasized that this opportunity would not last long. In subsequent conversations, I learned more.

Private equity groups sitting on nearly a trillion dollars, as later reported by analysts, topped the list of reasons the window opened. These groups were looking for good investments and were keenly interested in quick-service restaurant (QSR) franchises. The supply of willing sellers was well below their demand to invest. Low interest rates and favorable lending options fueled the flame of this hot, hot climate.

Additionally, the looming expiration date on capital gains tax rates, particularly those governing real estate exchanges, meant the third and fourth quarters of 2021 were going to be a very favorable time to sell. The time it took to close a deal was expected to compress to thirty to sixty days. Trust me. That's quick! I have been involved in plenty of negotiations that took most of a year to close.

Another important factor in the "now's the time" decision-making rubric was higher profits in 2020. Running drive-thru-only service during the pandemic positively impacted the bottom line of most QSRs. I expect this to affect how restaurants operate for years to come. As stressful as operating was during COVID, profits improved. Business values are historically based on profits times a multiple that generally reflects demand. In 2021, both of those numbers were high, possibly even a peak. Furthermore, because of where we were in the debt cycle, we could expect to gain more from a sale. The more I thought about what Naveen was telling me, the more it made sense financially to make this move.

"You could work the rest of your life and not accomplish this," Naveen told me. "You're going to thank me later."

But I was fifty years old. I wasn't ready to be done. Mike and I were both as busy as ever moving projects forward and growing the business. We had so much synergy, so many great people, so many good things going on. Mike was heading up the opening of a new store in LaGrange, about thirty miles south of our home office. We were both engaged in interviews, video shoots, and reviewing content for our new website. I was actively creating and delivering training workshops on personal knowledge management and productivity for our managers and senior leadership team.

Despite all this positive momentum, though, Mike and I talked candidly about the upcoming labor pressures predicted in ominous daily headlines. Mike assured me that most of our store-level employees would cross the street for an extra dollar an hour, and it wouldn't take much more to entice managers to leave. I heard the word "rowdy" over and over again in our weekly meetings.

"It's hard, really hard, out there," I was told.

No one was expecting workforce challenges in the restaurant industry to improve anytime soon.

I scratched writing a State of the Company Address off my to-do list. How could I tell an authentic story about strategies and plans for the future when every goal we were working toward was, all of a sudden, completely up in the air?

On our first date, Andrea and I went to see the documentary *Everest* at the IMAX theater. I'm still fascinated with what it takes to stand at the top of the world's highest peak above the sea. The feat requires years of training, a trainload of confidence, and all the courage in the world.

Only the most skilled climbers even attempt it. The summit window, when winds and temperatures increase the odds of success, lasts only a few weeks. Yet no amount of skill, audacity, preparation, or ideal timing will save them from bad luck or bad weather. And if they do get to the top, celebrations are short. They've got to turn around quickly and get back to camp before a storm comes.

I will always remember the words Naveen said that made the most sense to me.

"Nobody's got a crystal ball," he said. "Nobody knows what twenty years from now is going to look like, but there's a good chance that you could spend the next twenty years doing what you're doing and sell these stores at this same price."

It reminded me of another piece of advice my grandmother gave me.

"Be grateful for what you have and where you are, Doug, because you never know what's coming."

And you don't.

At the end of the year, everything I had imagined for the future was overturned.

"I'm giving you twenty years of your life back," Naveen told me.

Now, the question was: What would I do with it?

CHAPTER TWENTY-TWO
Lessons Learned

"Don't explain your philosophy. Embody it."

— EPICTETUS

I BEGAN WORKING ON THIS BOOK in October of 2019. At the time, I was gazing up at a mountain of opportunity with the confidence gained from more than twenty years in the peaks and valleys of running a business. Our company was secure, well-insulated from setbacks, and far beyond that moment when the corporate delegation told me to pack up and go home, that we wouldn't survive.

I believed I had some valuable insights to share about what it took to succeed when no one thought we could. I thought I knew how it felt for *everything* to change in one day. In 1998, I had buried my father—my leader—with no time to cry, then turned to face a frightening uphill battle.

The story was timeless. Me and my tribe of misfits had gone on a quest. We met some challenges, learned some lessons, and made some changes. I was back at base camp, reflecting on the journey.

In March 2020, six months after beginning this book, a dragon was at the door again. Catastrophe loomed. Events over which we had absolutely no control threatened to destroy all that we had accomplished in thirty-two years in business. After surviving so many scary expeditions, a bigger storm than I had ever seen or even imagined came with what seemed like only one purpose—to end us.

Two years later, we were stronger than ever.

I learned so many lessons while scaling these entrepreneurial mountains for a quarter of a century, lessons I hope are translated through this story. As I sifted through them all, six principles topped my list of the most important guidelines for business and life. Not one of these ideas is new or original. All that I know, I learned from someone who understood something better than me.

Focus on the smallest, incremental details and improve those, just a little, every day. From my friends at Ben Green's backyard gym, I learned that "Grow or Die" was more than a slogan on a T-shirt. This was sweat-bathed truth. Add a little weight; get used to it. Add a little more. Repeat. The results add up.

You don't know what you don't know, but you better figure out the right questions to ask. Are you getting better, or are you getting worse? Or do you even know?

Learn from the best. Listen to *and follow* the advice of proven experts. Imitate the hell out of their processes and best practices, then improve them.

Work with great people. Recruit individuals who are trustworthy, who share your values, and who will embrace your vision. Put that band together to create a culture in which everyone can thrive.

You can accomplish anything you set your mind to if you're willing to work hard. Wise words from my father, who added a few corollaries. "The harder I work, the luckier I get." "Never take no for an answer." And, like Jeff Tweedy and many others have also said: "When you don't ask, the answer is always no." (Unless it was "That's on a need-to-know basis. And you just don't need to know.")

Strategy trumps anxiety. Figure out what moves the needle most for you in the long term, craft a strategy with this knowledge, and then stick to it. When you're clear on your strategy, you can be kind yet fierce. This is how you negotiate without fear. This is how you say "no" when the pressure is on to say "yes." It's how you remain calm at the table when the second-guessing critic in your head says, *"You're going to bankrupt the company!"*

Someone asked me if I ever wanted to quit. I honestly never even thought about it. Not when my father died. Not when Charles called to say we couldn't meet payroll. Not when the corporate hitmen said to get out. Not when the pandemic rolled through.

Too much was at stake.

In the beginning, my number one goal was to save the company in order to secure my mom's future. I'm not sure the stakes were ever higher than that, but the well-being of hundreds of families was also at risk. Eventually, Georgia-Texas employed more than a thousand people at one time. Cumulatively, over the years, thousands and thousands of hardworking people depended on us in order to support their families, just as we depended on them to succeed. And always, there was my father's legacy to preserve.

So the answer is no. There was never a time in my entire career that I ever considered quitting. My philosophy was more like the Willie Nelson song: the party wouldn't be over until someone turned out the lights.

But there were plenty of times when I asked myself why I wasn't better, why I wasn't further along or progressing more than I was. That's when most people quit. When I hit that wall of resistance, when I couldn't see the difference I was making, I learned to ask myself two questions: *What is this telling me?* and *How far have I come?* Once I sat with the answers for a while, I doubled down and went back to work. I did whatever was on my plan for that day. And I continued to do it, and do it, and do it, and do it. No, I never thought of quitting.

If you look at all the greats—the best musicians, athletes, teachers, writers, artists, moms, dads, entrepreneurs, etc.—they've all been through this progression. Every one of them. No one is exempt. They all have times when they ask themselves why they're falling short, but they're not falling short. They're moving toward excellence and away from mediocrity and failure. Moving forward an inch at a time or an hour at a time. It all adds up.

It's not sexy. The only way to succeed at anything is to focus on the fundamentals, to do the things nobody wants to do. When I took over the company after my father died, I wanted to run clean restaurants with fast, friendly service. Everyone wants profits, but nobody wants to mop the floor and clean the bathrooms. Guess what? You can't have one without the other.

How does Eric Clapton make it look so easy when he plays the guitar? The answer is simple. Because he's been doing it for seventy years, that's how. The methods of this self-taught legend, everything from the way he holds his pick to the way he strings the guitar, have been the subject of profound and prolific analyses, but it all comes down to this: He played for hours and hours every day for years and years. He mimicked riffs he liked until he played them as well or better than the original artists. There was a day when he played no better than me or you, but over time, his relentless efforts catapulted him to an elite level of expertise. When I'm playing scales on my guitar, it's not like Eric Clapton ripping away on a solo in front of fifty thousand people. It's nothing like that, but it's how he got there.

The secret of success is that there is no secret. You can't fake seventy years of experience. You can't work for a week or a month or a year and expect to catch up to tens of thousands of hours of practice. You certainly can't stay up all night cramming for the test. You can only do it an hour at a time, but when you look back, you'll be shocked at how far down the mountain the starting point is.

So when you feel like giving up, give yourself some grace instead. Tell yourself, "You're right where you should be." Because you are.

Don't quit.

Until it's time.

And that's the hard part about quitting. There's never a good time. It never feels like it's the right time to go. Especially if you've been trained to stay.

When we moved to Newnan, Dad, like a pseudo-advance team, hyped me up to the football coaches.

"Oh, my kid is a star," he told them. "Wait until you see him play!"

Who was more disappointed—the coaches or me or my dad—I can't say, but when I arrived, none of us was excited. In Kansas, I was the man, but in a region where the SEC grows its own, I was a little guy, 135 pounds, half the size of most of my teammates. Dad had told the truth.

I had been the star quarterback in our small-town school in Kansas. But in my new hometown, the coaches saw me throw and put me fourth in the lineup of four for the quarterback position. They found special work for me and the other small kid on the team to do.

"You guys go run until we get tired," they told us. Basically: "Get out of here."

I wasn't benched. On the bench, I might have been in the way. I was never on the field and could barely even see it from where I stood. I hated every minute of it and couldn't quit fast enough.

"I'm giving up the football team," I told my father.

His response was firm. Adamant.

"You will not quit," he said. "You signed up for this, and you're going to finish it."

"But I'm not even going to play!" I argued. "It's just a complete waste of my time!"

"You will stay until the end of the year."

So I stayed, not because I wanted to but because I had no choice. I was angry, and I resented my father for making me stick it out. But consequently, hoping to be more competitive, I took up weightlifting. At least I could be respected in the weight room. I hoped.

And the rest? As clichéd as it sounds, it's history. Nearly everything that followed was a result of my staying on the football team in the tenth grade. From there, I went to Auburn University, studied accounting, audited banks, worked with my father, and assumed leadership of a company. I became a Taco Bell franchise operator, a husband, a father, an Ironman, a two-time Boston Marathon finisher, a Wendy's operator, and a guy responsible for more than a thousand paychecks.

I don't quit.

Until it's time—for something new.

Looking back, I see a timeline dotted with one challenge after another. Accountant to entrepreneur to CEO. Weightlifting to running to endurance sports. I remained in each endeavor until it was time to take it up a notch or until I felt the effort it required to progress was greater than the return.

In December 2020, we sold our northernmost Wendy's restaurants to tighten up the geography of our territory, bringing the total number of stores under our umbrella to twenty-eight. The next year, we built a new Taco Bell in LaGrange, bringing the total back up to twenty-nine.

In December 2021, we sold all eighteen of our Taco Bell restaurants to a family-owned business with a father and two sons at the helm, and I retired. I love knowing that our stores continue to be part of a family enterprise.

For two and a half more years, Georgia-Texas operated the remaining ten Wendy's restaurants in Georgia. Mike ran the company. The EOS operating system remained the guiding force for meetings, decisions, goals, and culture.

In 2022, Charles retired, and he and Carla moved to Mexico.

In August 2024, we sold those stores to the son of a tremendously successful Wendy's operator. Again, I loved knowing that our teams were becoming part of another family-based company. And the guy was about the same age I was when I went to work with my father. That felt all kinds of right, too. Abigail brought everything she learned with us to the table to help the new owner succeed, which made me happy for everyone.

When the dust settled on selling both brands, I held the real estate under twenty-five restaurants—seventeen Taco Bells and eight Wendy's. If I had not been maniacal about the strategy of owning the property under our stores, I would have walked away with a third of what I have today. This is my legacy, the ultra-race I am thankful to say I finished.

At the time of this writing, we still own a single Einstein's restaurant in Newnan. The manager there has been with us for fifteen years. She's worked hard to make the store profitable, and if the franchise approves the deal, we plan to give the restaurant to her before our lease expires. Mike is facilitating that process.

Other than working with our Einstein store, Mike doesn't know what he will do with the rest of his life. Play some golf, for sure, he says. There's still time for a second career. I look forward to seeing how he deploys the laser focus he has for numbers, data, and analysis.

Through seventeen years of ups and downs in business, my relationship with Mike has never faltered. Of all the outcomes I'm happy about, this is near the top. We kept our promise to each other: friendship above all else. Mike is a gem of a partner and an even better friend.

Except for my father's death, I can't think of anything in my life that was more unexpected than Naveen telling me it was time to go. I can't think of a decision I have ever made that was harder. I can't say that I have never had fairytale dreams of what we might have accomplished.

I can say that I'm not done.

For now, I spend my time enjoying my family, traveling, reading, cycling, skiing, playing guitar, and, as much as possible, avoiding the question, "What do you do?" I've learned not to say, "I'm retired." After hearing so often that fifty-one is "too young to retire," I wonder, *Who made that stupid rule?*

For thirty-three years, I lived in the shadow of my father's dream. Today, I am pondering dreams of my own.

What's next? I can't say.

Yet.

Georgia–Texas Enterprises Senior Leadership Team May 2021

EPILOGUE

"Carpe diem."

— HORACE

I MAY NOT BE THE ONLY GUY who ever signed up for a triathlon the day before the event, but my son, James, is almost certainly the only ten-year-old who can say that.

Around midday on Friday, July 15, 2022, James and I were riding our bikes along Jetties Beach on the north shores of Nantucket. One of the most popular beaches on the island, Jetties hosts many large events every year. The Boston Pops play there, and the 4th of July fireworks burst over its shores. That afternoon, we saw a sign for the 14th annual Nantucket Triathlon, which was taking place the next day.

"Hey, James, what do you think about doing a triathlon?" I asked.

"Will you do it with me?" he responded.

"Heck yeah!"

I hadn't trained—my last triathlon was in 2011, eleven years before—but I had been super active all year, skiing with Grant, cycling with James, and hiking with both all summer. I didn't care about how long it took us to do it, just that we might have a chance to do this together.

We parked our bikes and located a busy volunteer.

"Hey, me and my son want to do the triathlon tomorrow," I said. "Where can we sign up?"

She looked at James.

"How old are you?" she asked.

"I'm ten."

"I'm sorry, you can't participate," she said. "You have to be thirteen years or older to do it."

She wasn't mean. She was just giving us the rules. But James and I had been riding bikes together for months.

"Hey, he can do the distance," I told her. "I'm his dad. I know he can do it."

"Well, the race director will be here at 3:30," she said. "You can come back and ask him. He might be able to make an exception. I don't know."

"All right," I said.

So we rode around town and came back at 3:30 and found the director.

"We didn't even know this triathlon existed," I told him. "We just noticed the sign a few hours ago. We want to do it together."

I explained that we didn't care about being competitive; we just wanted to do a father-son race.

"Would y'all want to relay or do the whole thing?" he asked.

"We'll both go the whole distance," I said.

He looked at James.

"Can you swim a quarter of a mile?"

"Well, I'm on the swim team," he replied.

"How much do you swim on the swim team?"

"I don't know. I swim two hours three or four times a week."

"So you can swim a quarter of a mile?"

"Easy."

"All right. You know the bike portion is thirteen miles," he said. "Can you do that?"

"My dad and I just rode up the top of a mountain in Glacier National Park," he answered. "It was twenty miles."

"Well, it sounds like you can ride thirteen miles," the director said with a chuckle. "Can you run 3.1 miles?"

"We hiked four and five hours a day a couple of times a week in Glacier," he said.

"It sounds like you can do the distance," the director said.

"I know he can do the distance," I said.

So the director, who co-founded the race in 2009 with a buddy from his college days, made an exception for James. The next morning, we were up at five. I made him a little bit of breakfast, and we rode our bikes to 4 Bathing Beach Road, where we were two of 448 people assembling for the race that would begin at six thirty. People were tripping out over James. Even for his age, he was a small kid.

"You're doing the triathlon?" they'd ask him, amazed.

I laid out our strategy for the swim—the human washing machine— to James shortly before the race began. We started with the men's novice group in the last wave.

"All right now, on the swim, just stay with me, at my side or just a little behind me," I told James. "Just follow me."

Halfway into the swim, I couldn't hear because of the cap and all the noise around us. I stopped to make sure James was with me, but I couldn't see him.

Shit. Where is he?

I had thought he was right on my heels. I looked up, and he was fifty yards ahead.

I caught up to him, and when we got out of the water, he said, "Dad, I thought you were a fast swimmer! You are horrible at swimming! What's wrong with you?"

"Hey, let's go," I said, laughing. "Get on the bike!"

My goal was to finish the bike course in an hour. James was a little slower on the bike, so it took a little longer. Twelve and a half miles an hour was our pace. Not too bad.

When we got to the run, I told him, "Look, all we want to do is just keep moving. You do not want to walk."

"All right, I got it," he said.

James hadn't worn socks that morning. A blister developed on his heel, so he took his shoes off during the run. I told him that running without his shoes was a bad idea, but if that's what he had to do, then try to run on the grass.

"You'll tear your feet up on the road," I said, carrying his shoes.

Soon, he was struggling.

"Dad, I can't do this anymore. I want to walk."

"Okay, let's slow down for a little bit. We'll just walk for a while."

We started walking, and he reached for my hand. It seemed instinctive. I think he just needed me to be there for him. He held it while we chatted about the birds and dogs and people and stuff.

I had never been in the back of the race before. It was a humbling experience. Everyone was working hard. Most were beginners or not very athletic, but they were out there. They were doing it.

It was my turn to repay all of the people who had encouraged me over the years.

"Great job, man!" I would say.

"You're doing good, looking strong!"

"Thank you for that," I heard.

After a while, I asked James if he was ready to run again.

"I don't know if I can," he said.

"You look great," I told him. "You're doing awesome. Let's try to pick up the pace."

So we did. Other runners were giving it back to James.

"Man, you're crushing it," they told him.

A photographer started snapping pictures of the barefoot kid running a triathlon, which gave James a boost of energy.

"All right, all right," he said. "I got this!"

We crossed the finish line in two hours and five minutes, with James three seconds ahead of me. There was no age group for ten-year-olds, but the race director gave James special recognition during the awards presentation.

"Dad, Nantucket might be my favorite island in the whole world," James said after the race. "And Bill (the race director) is probably one of my greatest friends ever. I love that guy!"

He wore his medals for the rest of the day. A week later, he still hadn't washed his race number off his arm.

Heads up.

Seize the day.

ACKNOWLEDGMENTS

MANY PEOPLE DESERVE CREDIT for bringing this book to life. I am truly humbled and grateful to share this story with you, but I could not have done it alone.

I want to thank Connie Jones for introducing me to Joyce Beverly over five years ago. From the very first day we met in my office, Joyce deeply believed in this. Joyce, your talent, dedication, and insightful contributions have been invaluable throughout this journey. From the initial interviews to the final edits, your ability to capture my vision and voice has transformed my ideas into a cohesive narrative I am happy to share with the world. Also, a huge amount of gratitude to your husband, Cal Beverly, for listening, reading, and cheering from the sidelines.

Thanks to my family, Andrea, Grant, and James, for all your help and support as I worked on this book. Andrea, thank you for being the first to read the story and give me positive feedback. Grant, I am grateful to you for taking the time out of your hectic school schedule to read the early drafts and join calls with me and Joyce to discuss everything, including *The War on Colons. (>13 in Part 1!)* It means so much! James, thank you for all your questions and for being a BIG part of this story.

Thanks to Victoria Wolf for the creative genius deployed in the design of the cover and pages of this book and to Jennifer Jas for exceptional proofreading. Also, thank you to Christine Holzmann for photo editing.

Thanks to my mom, Jane Augustine, for believing in and supporting me as I embarked on the hero's journey. You gave me the strength and courage to stay in the fight and never give up.

Thanks to everyone at Georgia-Texas Enterprises, Inc. for allowing me to grow and evolve and continually push everyone out of their comfort zone. I especially want to thank my brother (from another mother), my business partner, and my best friend, Mike Bender. We created something special together and never let the business get in the way of our respect and love for one another.

A big thank you to Naveen Goyal at Auspex Capital for believing in Georgia-Texas and helping us achieve the impossible.

I am also grateful for my friendship and relationship with Brian Wooldridge, who has had my back more times than I can count since the day my dad died.

A special thanks to Scott Curson, Ben Green, Bobby Burgess, and Emil Brolik for seeing something and believing in me early on in my life. I can't say enough about how much I appreciate my senior leadership team: Charles Kuehl, Mark Grabowski, John Piotrowski, Shawn Medick, Collin Hilley, and Abigail Bishop. And back in the day, I don't know what we would have done without Carla Graham, Linda Limback, Lynn Bartley, and Rynda Mason.

Thanks to all my friends *(and Joyce's friends)* who read early versions of this work and offered wisdom. Most importantly, Nick Davis, I appreciate your honest feedback and generosity towards me and my family. I'm forever thankful for your thoughts and friendship.

Finally, to everyone going through hardship and difficult times in their own lives: this book is for you. Commit to doing one thing to propel you forward one day at a time, and you will get better.

Do not settle!

VIPS

The OG Team—Charles and Mom

Best Friend and Partner Ever—Mike Bender

ABOUT THE AUTHORS

DOUG AUGUSTINE is a former operator of Taco Bell, Burger King, Wendy's, and Einstein Bros. Bagels restaurants. He is also an endurance athlete, a guitarist, a proud graduate of Auburn University *(War Eagle!)*, and an evangelist for incremental progress.

Doug is at home in Newnan, Georgia; Auburn, Alabama; Whitefish, Montana; and traveling the world with his wife and sons.

www.dougaugustine.com

JOYCE BEVERLY followed a 40-year career in community journalism with an encore vocation helping people tell their stories. *When Pigs Fly* is her first collaboration as co-author of a memoir.

www.mystoryographer.com